Legacies of Empire

GU00394365

The nation state is a fairly recent historical phenomenon. Human history over the past two to four millennia has been dominated by empires, and the legacies of these empires continue to shape the contemporary world in ways that are not always recognized or fully understood.

Much research and writing about European colonial empires has focused on relationships between them and their colonies. This book examines the phenomenon of empire from a different perspective. It explores the imprint that imperial institutions, organizational principles, practices and logics have left on the modern world. It shows that many features of the contemporary world – modern armies, multiculturalism, globalized finance, modern city states, the United Nations – have been profoundly shaped by past empires. It also applies insights about the impact of past empires to contemporary politics and considers the long-term institutional legacies of the 'American empire'.

SANDRA HALPERIN is Professor of International Relations and Co-director of the Centre for Global and Transnational Politics in the Department of Politics and International Relations at Royal Holloway, University of London. She is the author of three cross-regional and trans-historical comparative studies: *In the Mirror of the Third World: Capitalist Development in Modern Europe* (1997), *War and Social Change in Modern Europe: The Great Transformation Revisited* (2004) and *Re-Envisioning Global Development: A 'Horizontal' Perspective* (2013). She is also the author of articles on globalization, development theory, historical sociology, nationalism, ethnic conflict, Islam and democracy in the Middle East.

RONEN PALAN is Professor of International Political Economy at City University London. He has published many articles and books on the subject of the offshore economy and theories of international political economy.

Legacies of Empire

Imperial Roots of the Contemporary Global Order

Edited by

SANDRA HALPERIN

and

RONEN PALAN

CAMBRIDGE
UNIVERSITY PRESS

CAMBRIDGE
UNIVERSITY PRESS

University Printing House, Cambridge CB2 8BS, United Kingdom

Cambridge University Press is part of the University of Cambridge.

It furthers the University's mission by disseminating knowledge in the pursuit of education, learning and research at the highest international levels of excellence.

www.cambridge.org
Information on this title: www.cambridge.org/9781107521612

First published 2015

Printed in the United Kingdom by Clays, St Ives plc

A catalogue record for this publication is available from the British Library

ISBN 978-1-107-10946-9 Hardback
ISBN 978-1-107-52161-2 Paperback

Contents

Figures

Tables

Contributors

Tarak Barkawi is Reader in International Relations in the Department of International Relations, London School of Economics and Political Science.

Alexander Cooley is Tow Professor of Political Science in the Department of Political Science at Barnard College, Columbia University.

Benjamin de Carvalho is a senior research fellow at the Norwegian Institute of International Affairs.

Sandra Halperin is Professor of International Relations in the Department of Politics and International Relations, Royal Holloway, University of London.

Ronnie D. Lipschutz is Professor of Politics in the Department of Politics, University of California, Santa Cruz.

Craig N. Murphy is Professor of Global Governance at the McCormack School of Policy and Global Studies, University of Massachusetts, Boston.

Iver B. Neumann is Montague Burton Professor of International Relations in the Department of International Relations, London School of Economics and Politics, and an Associate of the Norwegian Institute of International Affairs.

Ronen Palan is Professor of International Political Economy in the Department of International Politics, City University of London.

Herman Mark Schwartz is Professor of Politics in the Department of Politics, University of Virginia.

Einar Wigen is Lecturer in Turkish History in the Department of Culture Studies and Oriental Languages, University of Oslo.

Acknowledgments

This volume is a product of a collaborative research project sponsored by the Leverhulme Foundation, the International Studies Association and the British Academy.

The origins of the project are the result of a Leverhulme Foundation Research Grant Project entitled *Global Development: The Role of Trans-National Elites in Afro-Eurasia*. This project involved research by Sandra Halperin and two colleagues (Yasmin Khan and Stephanie Ortmann) on the Middle East and North Africa, South Asia, and Russia and Central Asia. Its aim was to make visible a *horizontal* or transnational set of connections, relations and processes that much historiography and social science tends to obscure. We pursued this aim by studying transitions from empire to independent states in the post-Ottoman Middle East (MENA), post-colonial India and post-Soviet Russia and Central Asia, and explored through comparative-historical study how these moments were shaped by, and worked to extend and reproduce, trans-national networks. Our hypothesis was that if these networks survived the transitions from empire to 'national independence' in MENA, South Asia and Russia and Central Asia, we should find evidence that trans-local/cross-regional networks played a larger role and exerted much more cultural and economic influence in these transitions than traditional periodization and nationalist narratives usually convey. Our plan of work involved much discussion and comparison of our individual findings and the securing of additional funds to support workshops and other activities that would enable us to present our findings and receive feedback from a broader community of scholars.

This is where Ronen Palan entered the picture, bringing with him the notion of 'legacies of empire' to characterize a salient dimension of our work. The term had resonance and, with it, we succeeded in piquing the curiosity of a group of scholars from the UK, Europe and the USA who were intrigued by the notion that the sorts of things they have been exploring within their own areas of expertise might better be understood as linked to the institutional inheritances and impacts of empires. We were also able to secure grants to support two workshops. The first was a Workshop Grant from the International Studies Association that enabled us to hold a day-long workshop, entitled *Legacies of Empire*, at the International Studies Association 53rd Annual Convention, 1–4 April, 2012, in San Diego, California. The second was a British Academy Small Grants Scheme award that enabled us to follow up with a second workshop in June 2012 at Royal Holloway University of London's central London base in Bedford Square. We wish to thank all the participants who attended these workshops: Tarak Barkawi, Alexander Cooley, Marcus Daeschel, Yasmin Khan, Ronnie Lipschutz, Craig Murphy, Iver Neumann, Stefanie Ortmann, Herman Schwartz and Einar Wigen. Though not all were able to contribute their papers to this volume, all participated in the discussions that inspired it, to many of the ideas included in its introduction and conclusions and to the overall conception, which we hope will be the basis for an ongoing programme of research.

We would like to acknowledge that Chapter 7 is based on material previously published in pages 37–40 of Murphy, Craig, Evolution of the UN development system, in Browne, Stephen and Weiss, Thomas G., Eds. *Post-2015 UN Development: Making Change Happen*. London: Routledge, pp. 35–54 and would like to thank Routledge for granting us permission to use this material.

We would like to thank our two anonymous referees, whose insightful comments proved extremely useful in developing this book. Last but not least, we would like to thank John Haslam and the production team at Cambridge University Press for all their help and support in bringing this volume to publication.

1 | Introduction

Legacies of empire

SANDRA HALPERIN AND RONEN PALAN

'Empires and civilizations come and go', or so it is generally assumed. But what actually happens when imperial powers decline? Do the institutions and logics of empire entirely disappear? A great deal of historical and archaeological evidence suggests that they do not, that they leave their mark on international structures and processes and on the institutions, cultures, politics and legal systems of the peoples who inhabit the territories of their former cores and peripheries. But if empires never entirely disappear, why does it matter? What implications are there for how we understand the contemporary, supposedly 'post-imperial', system of national states?

Much has been written about the European colonial empires, largely focusing on relations between imperial powers and their colonies, and the impact of these relations on both. This book examines the phenomenon of empire from a somewhat different perspective. It explores the imprint that empires – their institutions, organisational principles and logics – have left on the modern world. Students of international relations are accustomed to thinking of the contemporary world as post-imperial, as divided among discrete political entities founded on national communities, each jealously guarding its sovereignty and power against the dangers of an anarchic world; facing each other, in Thomas Hobbes' colourful metaphor, 'in the state and posture of gladiators ... their weapons pointing, and their eyes fixed on one another' (Hobbes 1951: 79). Yet, the reality is very different. While the contemporary world is conventionally seen as characterized by national states and, as some of the globalist literature suggests, increasingly post-national, it is our conviction that there is much to be gained by viewing the contemporary world through the lens of empire.

It is often assumed, wrongly, that empire is a form of political organization that existed in the past and that was eventually superseded or displaced by national states. Empire has not only been the norm throughout most of the past five or six millennia – but as recent discussions of the USA, the Soviet Union and even the European Union (Zielonka 2006) and rising powers such as China or India suggest – imperial power and politics also remain very much a part of the contemporary landscape. In many important respects *world history is imperial history*. Robert Gilpin says that '[t]he nature of international relations has not changed over the millennia … One must suspect that if somehow Thucydides were placed in our midst, he would … have little trouble in understanding the power struggle of our age' (1981: 211). Yet the world with which Thucydides was familiar was a world of empires, not of nation states.

Why, then, do we call the field of study concerned with cross-border relationships 'inter-national' relations? The concept of international relations reflects a certain perspective on the world that emerged at a specific time and within a specific social context. It made its appearance during the French Revolution and has been associated ever since with the theories and debates that accompanied the rise of European nationalism (Fédou 1971; Mairet 1997). The term implies that international politics are concerned with relationships among organic social groupings that are genuine political 'actors' in their own right. It was during the time of the French Revolution and its aftermath that a young philosopher destined for greatness declared: '[t]he universal which manifests itself in the State and is known in it – the form under which everything that is, is subsumed – is that which constitutes the culture of a nation' (Hegel 1975: 53). And those nations that failed to constitute themselves as states, he warned his fellow 'Germans' (most of whom did not know they were Germans), would fall by history's wayside.

Certainly the nationalist project promoted by the Fronde movement in France and by early nationalists such as Hegel or Fichte proved tremendously successful. Yet, as Daniel Chernilo points out, the nation state is at best 'an unfinished project that paradoxically presents itself as an already established form of socio-political organization' (2006: 16). It appears to us that the notion of an international system or society of states, or of a 'world capitalist system' politically divided into nation states, glosses over the mosaic of practices, institutions, and social structures that remain as legacies of past empires and civilizations. It might be argued, in fact, that we can only really understand the national project by considering it in the light of the diverse institutional habitat in which it has flourished.

In this book we explore how our understanding of the 'international system' changes when we trace the extent to which the cultural, political, military and economic legacies of empires remain embedded in, and constitutive of, contemporary political life. Our concern, therefore, is with continuities, with the durability and persistence of imperial organization and logics, and with the military, political and socio-economic continuities and pathways that remain during the times and in the places that are characterized as 'post-imperial'. What we are concerned to explore is whether seeing the current order as, in some part, constituted by legacies of empire illuminates dimensions and dynamics of the contemporary world that are obscured by national historiography and perspectives.

In exploring the world through the analytic lens of imperial legacies our intention is not simply to substitute 'empire' for 'state' as the central focus of inquiry in the study of international relations, but to pose intrinsic conceptual and empirical problems for the whole of the nationalist theoretical edifice. By bringing into clearer focus striated spaces, historical nuance and a world in which legacies of the past are pragmatically reconfigured and rebranded, the imperial lens challenges the tendency of International Relations perspectives to treat political units as homogeneous and human action and thought as universal and unhistorical.

This book shows that empires have left their imprint on the contemporary world in a variety of ways that we often fail to appreciate. Its aim is to enrich our understanding of the historical origins of the complex mosaic of institutions, practices, habits of thought and organization that make up the modern world; to develop a more subtle and nuanced understanding of the complex ecology of the international system, and an appreciation of the richly diverse elements that make it up. We hope that exploring the multiple dimensions of empires past will also enable us to gain insight into how the current American imperium will shape the future world.

The study of empire and its impacts

Empire is the focus of widespread public interest and academic debate. Interest in empire has been linked to questions concerning the conceptualization of contemporary structures and processes and the origins and nature of globalization. However, the lion's share of research and writing on the subject has focused on the legacies of empire in former imperial states and colonies and the lessons that past empires might hold for the USA.

Legacies are elements of the present that are shaped by the past. The legacies of European empires and imperial expansion include contemporary conflicts (e.g. in Palestine, Iraq, Kashmir, Burma, Sudan and Nigeria), patterns of migration, art, legal systems and patterns and conditions of nation- and state-building. There is a large literature focusing on the persistence of British imperial legacies, both in Britain itself as, for instance, with respect to post-imperial citizenship and national identities in the United Kingdom (e.g. Goulbourne 2009), and in successor states and former colonies (e.g. Kwarteng 2011; Midgeley and Piachaud 2011; Centeno and Enriquez 2010; Darwin 2009; Moore and Thomas 2007; Reynolds 2006; Calhoun, Cooper and Moore 2006).

Broader and more pervasive impacts of European empire are the focus of a body of research and writing called Dependency Theory. Andre Gunder Frank articulated its main tenet: that colonialism created fundamental and interrelated structural distortions in the economies of Third World countries and that these were continuing to thwart development.[1] A key structural distortion and difference between 'Western' and contemporary Third World development is the coexistence of an advanced or modern sector with a backward or traditional sector (Sunkel 1973; Cardoso and Falleto 1973; Amin 1976; Frank 1972; Dos Santos 1970). 'Dependency' describes a situation in which development is oriented to a restricted, limited elite-oriented type of market and society (Cardoso 1973), in which capital cannot find its essential dynamic component (Cardoso and Falletto 1979). The foreign-oriented 'corporate' sector encompasses all capital-intensive enterprise, whether in industry or agriculture, as well as utilities, transport and the civil service, but there is no investment beyond the enclave:

---

[1] Dependency writings in the 1970s delineated a variety of alternative paths possible for capitalist development in the periphery, including the 'semi-peripheral', 'dependent', 'associated-dependent' and 'unequal' paths. See, e.g. Evans 1979; Wallerstein 1974; Amin 1976; Cardoso 1973; Cardoso and Faletto 1979. Cardoso and Falletto (1979) also delineated different forms of dependency. The theorization of these various types of peripheral development continued to undergo refinement in the 1980s and 1990s (see, e.g. Hettne 1990; Kay 1989; Larrain 1989; Becker 1987).

profits are either reinvested there or exported, and improvements in technology do not diffuse outward to agriculture or to cottage industry. Thus, the economy as a whole is characterized by a lack of internal structural integration: the coexistence of an advanced or modern sector with a backward or traditional sector, the concomitant coexistence of pre-capitalist and capitalist relations of production, and dependency on outside capital, labour and markets.

In the 1970s and 1980s two perspectives on the colonial experience emerged: post-colonial theory and subaltern studies. Post-colonial theory investigates how Western knowledge systems are related to the exercise of Western power: how knowledge of colonized people has served the interests of colonizers, and how 'Western' canonical traditions and universalisms, as well as the colonial relationship itself, repress, exclude, marginalize and objectify the 'other'.[2] It focuses, in particular, on the legacies of nineteenth-century British and French colonial rule for its subject people as, for instance, the difficulties faced by former colonial peoples in developing national identity. The subaltern studies project emerged from within this general perspective beginning in the 1980s.[3] Its key concern was to recover history from 'the bottom up': to bring to light and assert the value of alternative experiences and ways of knowing and, in this way, illuminate the history, agency and autonomy of the common people. According to the subaltern studies perspective, elite-centred colonialist (Liberal), nationalist and Marxist narratives are incapable of representing the history of the masses in the Third World. They are forms of Western teleology, ideologies of modernity and progress, meta-narratives of

---

[2] Edward Said's book, *Orientalism* (1977) is considered by many to be the founding work of post-colonial theory. Said argued that 'the Orient' was a construct of 'the West' that shaped the real and imagined existences of those subjected to the fantasy, and that, in turn, this 'othering' process used the Orient to create, define and solidify the 'West'. The result, as Said notes in *Culture and Imperialism* (1993) is that, while former imperial powers may have physically left the lands they had ruled for decades and centuries, they still dominate them ideologically, culturally and intellectually.

[3] The 1988 *Selected Subaltern Studies* reader edited by Ranajit Guha and Gayatri Spivak, with a foreword by Edward Said, defined the theoretical and methodological contributions of the project. The original subaltern studies collective of scholars were South-Asian historians working primarily within a Gramscian tradition. The term 'subaltern' is taken from the writings of Antonio Gramsci (1881–1937), whose perspective on the political and cultural basis of hegemony has had an important impact, in particular, on Marxist thinking.

the advance of capitalism and the triumph of the nation state, that reproduce knowledges and practices grounded in European history, and that seek either to endorse or to universalize Europe's historical experience.[4]

While the literature on European empires tends to emphasize economic and cultural impacts on successor states and former colonies, the literature that focuses on contemporary empire tends to emphasize International Relations perspectives and concerns and, in particular, states and their strategic interactions. This is evident in the large literature on empire and the Cold War, much of which focuses on the 'neo-colonial' policies of powerful countries as a key element of that period.

The term 'neo-colonialism' was originally applied to European policies that were seen as schemes to maintain control of African and other dependencies.[5] Neo-colonialism came to be seen, more generally, as involving a coordinated effort by former colonial powers and other developed countries to block growth in developing countries and retain them as sources of cheap raw materials and cheap labour. This effort was seen as closely associated with the Cold War and, in particular, with the US policy known as the Truman Doctrine. Under this policy, the US government offered large amounts of money to any government prepared to accept US protection from Communism. This enabled the USA to extend its sphere of influence and, in some cases, to place foreign governments under its control. The USA and other developed countries have also ensured the subordination of developing countries by interfering in conflicts and in other ways helping to install regimes willing to act for the benefit of foreign companies and against their own country's interests.

However, neo-colonial governance is seen as generally operating through indirect forms of control and, in particular, by means of the economic, financial and trade policies of trans-national corporations

---

[4] See, e.g. Gupta 1998; Prakash 1996; Chakrabarty 2000, 1992; and, for an overview, Young 2001.

[5] The event that marked the beginning of this usage was the European summit in Paris in 1957, where six European heads of government agreed to include their overseas territories within the European Common Market under trade arrangements that were seen by some national leaders and groups as representing a new form of economic domination over French-occupied Africa and the colonial territories of Italy, Belgium and the Netherlands.

and global and multilateral institutions. It operates through the investments of multinational corporations that, while enriching a few in underdeveloped countries, keep those countries as a whole in a situation of dependency and cultivate them as reservoirs of cheap labour and raw materials. It operates also through international financial institutions such as the International Monetary Fund (IMF) and the World Bank, which make loans (as well as other forms of economic aid) conditional on the recipient nations taking steps favourable to the financial cartels represented by these institutions, but that are detrimental to their own economies. Thus, while many people see these corporations and institutions as part of an essentially new global order and a new form of global governance, the notion of neo-colonialism directs our attention to what, in this system and constellation of power, represents continuity between the present and recent past.

Much attention has been devoted to the nature and impact of American empire since the end of the Cold War and to investigating the politics behind US imperial ambitions, either in the form of interest groups or in the geo-political dilemmas of the post-Cold War world (e.g. Lutz 2009; Lazreg 2008; Hardt and Negri 2004; Lal 2004; Ferguson 2004, 2000; Johnson 2004; Mann 2003; Chomsky 2003; Harvey 2003; Bacevich 2003, 2002; Calhoun, Cooper and Moore 2005; Barber 2003; Todd 2003). Unlike a formal empire, in which emperors have claimed absolute sovereignty, not only over their inhabitants, but also sometimes over the rest of the planet or even the entire solar system, the USA is seen as pursuing practices associated with what has been described as 'informal empire'.[6] Here, the empire does not claim to be an empire, at all: the title is bestowed upon it by its rivals or enemies. With the end of the Cold War, interest became focused on the causes, processes and consequences of US imperial decline. A resurgence of interest in this subject was prompted by Paul Kennedy's *The Rise and Fall of the Great Powers*, published in 1987. Kennedy argued that imperial great powers inevitably tend to extend themselves beyond their means, and that the United States is following the same pattern.

---

[6] Comparative studies have endeavoured to distinguish between different types of empires and imperial practice. See e.g. Parsons 2010; Steinmetz 2005; Eisenstadt 1963.

Empires and nation states

As we have seen, much of the literature that explores the impacts of
European empires on their successor states and former colonies is concerned with understanding problems of national development and
national identity as legacies of former empires or imperial domination.
While this literature has brought to light many aspects of the imperial
enterprise that had previously been insufficiently understood and appre-
ciated, it also tends, by defining a sharp distinction between empire and
nation state, to obfuscate key dimensions of the contemporary political
order. Though it has been pre-eminently concerned to 'liberate "history"
from the meta-narrative of the nation-state' (Chakrabarty 1992: 19),
much of the scholarship associated with the subaltern studies project has
tended to assume and reinforce the nation as a concept and as a boundary. This is also true of post-colonial studies. We would argue that
analyses of imperial legacies generally work within a national frame.
By assuming that empires have been entirely supplanted or displaced by
nation states, they obscure the extent to which imperial institutions and
practices shape supposedly post-imperial times and places.

Empires and nations are typically defined in opposition to each other
by reference to a number of analytic distinctions. In contrast to the
imaginary proto-socialist collectives depicted in ideologies of the nation
state, each pursuing a collective, 'national interest', empires are hierarchical structures, and those who use the term 'empire' to describe contemporary political formations such as the USA, the Soviet Union or even the
European Union, emphasize the existence of hierarchy and the role of
power within them.

Unlike nation states, empires have a geographically, politically, economically and culturally identifiable core and periphery, and, with one
or two important exceptions, the core consists of a large city in control
of a vast peripheral hinterland. In contrast to empires, the nation state
exists in a world of like units, each of which is considered formally
equal to the others (sovereign), and each of which is predominantly
concerned with security because of the absence of a central governing
authority within the overarching system. The security problems faced
by nation states are external. It is assumed that inside the boundaries of
properly run nation states things are reasonably stable; if there is a
problem, it is caused by external factors and agents. In contrast, the
histories of empires are about the great logistical, cultural, political and

economic difficulties in sustaining the great imperial venture. Empires decay or implode; their problems are as much internal as external. Indeed, very often, external dangers are used to mobilize against the more real and present 'internal' dangers.

However, if we view the world through the lens of empire, rather than from within the national frame, a different story emerges, one that is less narrow and one-dimensional, less national and uniform, and more varied and complex, than the one that conventional international relations scholarship often presents. From this angle of vision it is less easy to distinguish the social, economic and institutional characteristics of national and imperial states, and the world of nation states from that of empires.

In *Nations and Nationalism* (1990), Eric Hobsbawm showed that, between 1830 and 1878, when intellectuals and state personnel in Europe were concerned with defining the principle of nationalism, the theoretical discourse of those engaged in debate and discussion about nations held that:

1. nations had to be of a sufficient size to be economically viable – thus, the principle of nationality applied only to nationalities of a certain size;
2. the process of building nations was inevitably a process of expansion – national movements were expected to be movements of unification or expansion; consequently
3. nation states would be nationally heterogeneous.

There were only three criteria that allowed a people, in practice, to be firmly classed as a nation: the historic association with either an existing state or one having a lengthy and recent past; the existence of a long-established cultural elite; and a proven capacity for conquest. The history of the Age of Nationalism in Europe is consistent with this discourse and practice.

Although the term 'imperialism' came to be used exclusively to mean the direct or indirect domination of overseas colonial territories by modern industrial states,[7] the process of building states in Europe and empires abroad was essentially identical. Underlining the similarity

---

[7] The original meaning of 'imperialism' referred to the personal sovereignty of a powerful ruler over numerous territories, either in Europe or overseas. See Koebner and Schmidt 1965.

between this process and the colonial situation, a number of scholars have referred to this dimension of the state-building process in Europe as 'internal colonialism'.[8] Like colonialism, it involved reshaping the social and economic institutions of the conquered areas to the needs of the centre. A militarily powerful 'core' imposed physical control over culturally distinct groups. These groups are discriminated against on the basis of their language, religion or other cultural forms. Often, they are treated as objects of exploitation, 'as a natural resource to be plundered', and with the brutality that states treat conquered foreign countries (Gouldner 1977–78: 41). The economy of the peripheral area was forced into complementary development to the core and generally relied on a single primary export. Juridical and political measures similar to those applied in overseas colonies were imposed in order to maintain the economic dependence of these areas. Members of the core monopolized commerce, trade and credit while in the peripheral area there was a relative lack of services and lower standard of living.

Movements to form 'nation states' in Europe during the nineteenth century were thoroughly bound up with imperialism. In fact, their *stated* aim was not to form 'nation states', but to resurrect or create empires.

At the end of the eighteenth century, Napoleon fused French nationalism with the Roman imperial idea and, as the alleged heir of Charlemagne, united France, Western Germany, Italy and the Low Countries in a new empire. At the peak of its power (1810), France directly governed all Germany left of the Rhine, Belgium, the Netherlands and North Germany eastwards to Lübeck, as well as Savoy, Piedmont, Liguria and Italy west of the Apennines down to the borders of Naples, and the Illyrian provinces from Carinthia down to and including Dalmatia. German nationalists put forth claims to territory regardless of whether the population directly concerned really desired to change its sovereignty.[9]

---

[8] Numerous scholars have underlined the similarity between processes of nation building and the colonial situation, including Antonio Gramsci (1957: 430), Fernand Braudel (1984: 42, 328–52), Eugen Weber (1976: 490–93), Maurice Dobb (1947: 194, 206–7, 209), Michael Hechter (1975: 30–33), Alvin Gouldner (1977–78) and Oscar Jaszi (1929: 185–212).

[9] The annexation by Germany of French Alsace-Lorraine in 1871 against the will of the population, was justified by Heinrich Treitschke, as follows:

We Germans . . . know better than these unfortunates themselves what is good for the people of Alsace, who have remained under the misleading influence of the French connection outside the sympathies of new Germany. We shall restore them to their true selves against their will. Quoted in Macartney 1934: 100.

This served as a template for subsequent 'nationalist' movements in Europe. Many in the Pan-German movement demanded 'union' of the Swiss, the Dutch and even the Scandinavians with Germany in a great racial Nordic brotherhood.[10] Italian nationalism became bound up with a mission to 'complete the *Risorgimento*' (unification movement) through expansion into contiguous and overseas territories. This was a theme of Giuseppe Mazzini, a leader of the *Risorgimento*, no less than it was of Mussolini. Mussolini shared Mazzini's hope for a 'Third Rome' which would exercise world leadership as the Rome of the Caesars and the Rome of the Popes had done (Kohn 1955: 81). The champion of Russian pan-Slavism, Nikolai Danilevsky argued that Russia must create and lead a Slav federation (in order to destroy 'the rotting west' for the benefit of all mankind) consisting of Russia (with Galicia, the Ukrainian parts of Bukovina and Hungary, and the Carpatho-Ukraine added), Trieste, Gorizia, Istria, the major part of Carinthia, Czechoslovakia, Romania, Hungary, Bulgaria, Greece and Constantinople.[11] Polish nationalists sought and won from the Peace Conference following World War I a resurrection of the supra-national seventeenth-century Polish commonwealth. Hungarian nationalism, as embodied in Lajos Kossuth's programme of March 3, 1848, envisaged not a Magyar nation state, but incorporation of Croatia-Slavonia, Transylvania and the co-called Military Frontier in the Kingdom of Hungary. When Balkan nationalisms came to the fore in the early nineteenth century, none of the Balkan nationalist movements, or their Great Power sponsors, was interested in dividing the Ottoman Empire according to the principles of nationality. The ideological cornerstone of Greek national politics until recent times was the *Megali* idea, based on the notion of the resurrection of the glory and power of the Byzantine Empire (Petropulos 1968: 455–57). The *Megali* idea culminated on August 4, 1936, when General Johannes Metaxas established a Fascist regime, inaugurating the 'Third Hellenic Civilization', with the Spartan salute as its symbol (Daphnas 1955).

During the nineteenth century, nationalists were not concerned with forming 'nation states', but with resurrecting or creating empires.

---

[10] The classical work on the Pan-German League is Wertheimer 1924.
[11] From *Russia and Europe* (1871) a collection of Danilevsky's articles; cited in Kohn 1946: 200. Similar plans were proposed by Rostislav Fedeeyev in his *Opinion on the Eastern Question* (1871).

Nationalists and nationalist writers (Fichte, Treitschke, Mazzini, Garibaldi, D'Annunzio, Kossuth, Obradovich, Danilevsky and others) did not call for political independence of national communities within national frontiers: they demanded the resurrection of the historical empires of Byzantium and Rome, of Charlemagne, Caesar, Dushan and Simeon. Even where there was no imperial past to recall, nationalist writers and leaders called for the widest possible extension of national boundaries, regardless of ethnic considerations and in fundamental opposition to the national idea: the Great Germany Crusade; the Italian fascist crusade to recreate a Roman empire; the Russian Pan-Slav movement and, within the pan-Slav movement, a Greater Croatia movement; Greater Macedonia, Greater Serbia, Greater Bulgaria. Still others are the pan-Celtic movement, to unite the Gaels, Welsh and Bretons, which was formed in the late nineteenth century; the Polish nationalist crusade to resurrect the supranational Polish Commonwealth; and the Lithuanian ambition to resurrect the Kingdom of Lithuania.

Processes of 'nation building' as they originally unfolded in Europe bore all the political, economic, cultural and military features of imperialism and colonialism. The process involved territorial expansion from political centres or 'cores', and the absorption of areas with distinctly different traditions and political institutions. Western European states were formed by groups who conquered and colonized territories and subjugated, massacred, expelled or forcibly assimilated their native populations. Where territories contained ethnically heterogeneous populations, claims were often based on 'historical rights' going back to medieval or even ancient times. Additional claims often enlarged the original territory on the basis of 'strategic' or economic considerations. These territories frequently contained either the most ethnically heterogeneous or the most homogeneously foreign population of the territories claimed by the state. Once statehood was achieved, the ruling nation in the new multi-national entity often finished the work, usually already well under way, of expelling, exterminating or forcibly assimilating ethnic minorities and other portions of the population with separate territorial claims or with the potential power to challenge the rule of the dominant group. Later, elite-led 'national' movements, with funds and military assistance provided by existing states, organized crusades to acquire territories for which they had created and advanced cultural or other claims. In sum: nationalism, in its essence, its origins and its methods, was similar to colonialism and imperialism, and its impact on large populations within Europe was similar to the impact of colonialism on Third World populations.

Some might argue, however, that cultural factors are, nonetheless, at the root of nationalist drives and aims. But in most cases, so-called 'national' cultures had no existence prior to the desire to form states and to foment nationalist movements, but were deliberately created for political purposes. National movements in Europe in the nineteenth century began with philological revivals whose political function was to prove the possession of a language fit for literature and, consequently, the right to national sovereignty. The purely cultural national movement was almost everywhere accompanied by a political ambition. Of the nationalist movements of the nineteenth century all, except perhaps the Belgian, were preceded and accompanied by the construction of a 'national' culture. In the nineteenth century, new states created in Europe (Italy, Germany, Greece, though perhaps not Belgium), as well as nationalist movements that arose within the Ottoman, Hapsburg, and Russian Empires (Romanian, Croatian, Slovenian, Serbian, Hungarian, Czechoslovakian, Bulgarian, Finnish, Polish and Albanian) and within existing 'nation states' (Welsh, Scottish, Catalan, Basque, Jurassic, Alsatian, Breton, Corsican Guadeloupan, South Tyrolean, Frisian and Greenlandish) all created 'national' cultures with materials that were either new or long dead, or some combination of the two.

Institutional legacies

There is an important, ongoing methodological debate in the social sciences about the utility of synchronic 'variable-oriented' versus diachronic or historically sensitive case-oriented methodologies of investigation.[12] Both serve useful purposes, as Charles Ragin (2000) argues, but there is a gulf between them that is difficult to bridge. An assessment of the historical legacies of empires, both as a concept and as a set of practices, and their impact on the contemporary world, inevitably draws on the latter.

---

[12] Much has been written on the topic. For an excellent summary of recent debates see Collins 1974, Redding 2005 and Tilly 2001.

While variable-oriented studies are undoubtedly 'powerful vehicles of generalisation', their homogenising assumptions 'structure how social scientists view populations, cases, and causes and thus constrain the dialogue between ideas and evidence in ways that limit discovery' (Ragin 2000: 5). Their tendency to dissolve cases into single variables blocks 'their ability to test the kind of configurational ideas which are part and parcel of sociological theory' (Agevall 2005: 9).[13]

Case-oriented studies, in contrast, 'are good at capturing complexity and diversity' because they tend to adopt what might be described as the 'heterogeneity principle': the assumption that the apparent unity of political order belies incredible diversity.[14] Historically oriented case studies, Karen Orren and Stephen Skowronek observe, reveal the extent to which 'it becomes less meaningful to talk about a political universe that is ordered than about the multiple orders that compose it and their relations with one another' (Orren and Skowronek 2004:15). Variable-oriented approaches tend to view the state in systemic terms, and even when they disaggregate the state and focus on its constituent parts – groups, classes, ethnicities, regions and so on – each of the disaggregated factors is treated as a part of some rational whole. In contrast, case-oriented approaches tend to view states as patchworks of institutional logics and rationalities, 'existing at a specific time', and 'representing nothing more than imperfect and pragmatic solutions to reconciling past conflicts' (Van der Ven 1993: 142). They consist of '[i]nstitutions, both individually and collectively, [and] juxtapose different logics of political order, each with their own temporal underpinnings' (Orren and Skowronek 1994: 320). This is an important point: while case-oriented approaches disaggregate the political process itself into its different historical constituents, variable-oriented approaches assume that the political process is animated necessarily by one pervasive political rationale.

There are practical reasons for the juxtaposition of logics and temporalities in the makeup of modern states: historically, states proved themselves highly adept at picking up ideas and institutions 'simply because [they] find them functioning' (Ellul 1965: 243). The successful journey of the state as an organizational model was, in Braudel's

---

[13]   See also King 1989 and Büthe 2002 for analysis of the limitations of variable-oriented modelling techniques and historical analysis.

[14]   See Palan 2012 for a discussion of the heterogeneity principle.

colourful language, a typical journey of war and conquest: the state 'shaped itself around preexisting political structures, inserting itself among them, forcing upon them whenever it could, its authority, its currency, taxation, justice and language of command. This was a process of both infiltration and superimposition, of conquest and accommodation' (Braudel 1981: 520). The modern law is an amalgam of Roman, Greek, Germanic and biblical norms and practices, as well as the 'common' law of the Anglo-Saxon people. The commercial laws that were introduced, or 'nationalized', were drawn from the practices of the law merchants of the Hanseatic League, the *lex mercatoria*. Techniques of administration and centralization of the absolutist state were more probably diffused from the East, perhaps from China and Persia through Byzantium to its neighbouring and highly successful Kingdom of the Two Sicilies, and from there to Europe at large. To this assemblage of techniques and technologies Foucault added his highly original theory of the diffusion of power technologies from the prison, the clinic and the army.

This book contributes an additional dimension to the study of 'empire', understood as an assemblage of institutions and techniques of power and organisation. We ask: have empires gone completely, or have they infiltrated the modern state system in ways that may not be readily apparent? And, if so, how are they present in those institutional juxtapositions we call 'states'? Contributors to this volume have, with the aid of historical analysis, disentangled the spatial construct we call 'the state' and shown how it is able to contain within it different political rationalities. Following this overall logic, some of our contributors have suggested that the 'international system' might best be treated, as well, as a patchwork of institutional arrangements and rationalities that possess, perhaps, only a minimal degree of coherency among them.

What this book explores, therefore, is the impact that empires – many of which are assumed to have disappeared without a trace – continue to have on the modern world. It has four aims. The first is to enrich our understanding of the historical origins of the complex and delicate mosaic of institutions, practices, habits of thought and organizations that make up the modern world. Its second aim is to develop a more subtle and nuanced understanding of the complex ecology of the international system, and an appreciation of the richly diverse elements that make it up. Third, the book aims to discover whether such an historically nuanced understanding of the nature and characteristics of the international system may shed light on contemporary processes and developments. Finally, it aims to discover whether the legacies of past empires might tell us anything about the likely impact of the American empire in future years.

Legacies of empire

What, then, are the broad legacies of empires in the modern world? This book does not present a comprehensive inventory of legacies of empire in the contemporary world, nor does it offer a theoretical perspective on them. Rather, the book illustrates how legacies of empire operate today and how they might shape the future. The individual chapters show how scholars, with different disciplinary orientations and research interests, confront legacies of empire in their exploration of the contemporary political world. They demonstrate the durability of institutions and practices over time: for instance, certain practices that are characterized as 'corrupt' in the area of former Mongol Empires that include post-Soviet entities which may, in fact, represent the survival of elements of Mongol political rule in that area. They show that the governance structure of the United Nations can be understood as representing a continuation of the imperial civil services as, for instance, with respect to the themes and organization of 'development'; and that the British Empire left its imprint in an integrated London-based set of finance centres that encompasses British dependencies such as the Cayman Islands, Bermuda and the old imperial outposts of Singapore and Hong Kong. Many old city states around the world that were revived or reproduced by the Spanish in the Americas, the Portuguese in India and East Africa, and by the British in other areas of the world are masquerading today as nation states. Colonial armies were transformed into armies of the new states and continued to function chiefly as instruments of 'internal security' tied to external powers. Together, these present a challenge to the conventional opposition between 'nation' and 'empire', and to the notion that nation states have supplanted or displaced imperial logics and practices.

Our starting point is to investigate structures of constituted power of peoples and territories. The imperial legacies discussed in this volume and their role in shaping contemporary regional and global structures and processes suggest that the international sphere is far more heterogeneous than is often assumed. Thinking of international relations from an imperial perspective takes us naturally and seamlessly beyond the formality of the rule of law, to the practice of power, and to practice per se. An imperial perspective is always inherently an historical perspective: it is largely about what people do, not about what they are supposed to do or believe in. Rather than exploring the legacies of empires with respect to the international system or international society of states, we are interested in exploring how a mosaic of practices, institutions, social structures and other leftovers of empires and civilizations long gone continue to endure and shape contemporary political structures and processes. To what extent are Byzantine, Ottoman, Mogul, British, Soviet, or other imperial legacies part of this contemporary mosaic? To what extent, and in what ways, are they still shaping political structures and processes in ways that we fail to recognize?

The book is divided into three thematic parts.

Part I addresses the issue of the continuing salience of empires that appear to have dissolved, but that are playing an important, if typically unrecognized, role in the modern world. Tarak Barkawi challenges assumptions that International Relations makes about the sovereign territorial and isomorphic configuration of the nation state and its national armed forces. He shows that national armed forces have emerged, in part, amid a world of flows based upon the political–military dimensions of imperialism and the co-constitution of core and periphery. 'Foreign forces' – those recruited from beyond the boundaries of the polity – have played a key role in the making of the modern world, shaping civil–military relations in the West and enabling intervention and expansion outside it.

Today's global financial centres are another legacy of empire. Ronen Palan shows that, as the British Empire disintegrated rapidly in the 1950s and 1960s, one of its key institutions, the City of London, was in danger of losing its position as the world's premier financial centre as well. Palan tells the story of a project that was described by one commentator at the time as 'the second British Empire': the seizure by City individuals and institutions of a few remaining imperial possessions (islands in the English Channel and in the Caribbean) and small colonial outposts (such as Hong Kong and Singapore), and the re-emergence of these at the centre of an integrated global financial centre specializing in complex financial instruments.

What is often seen as 'new' might best be understood as the re-surfacing reproduction, re-creation of pre-existing systemic or institutional logics, including those associated with imperial relations of power. With the breakup of Yugoslavia linkages were re-established that suggested a re-surfacing of the economic logic of the Austro-Hungarian Empire; the Black Sea Pact might reasonably call to mind the domain of Ottoman political economy. Sandra Halperin highlights three features of the nineteenth-century imperial order that recently have become more salient. She argues that what today are described as 'global city-regions' (Brenner 2004, 1998) and global cities (Sassen 1994, 2007) were constituent elements of the nineteenth-century imperial system; that they represent a re-surfacing of its systemic and institutional logics; and that what is often characterized as a new trans-national capitalist class can be seen as a reassertion of the horizontal solidarities of nineteenth-century imperialism. The trans-local sources of power and stability that these solidarities produced continue to transect the boundaries of states and to shape relations and developmental outcomes across, between and within them.

Part II explores how certain legacies of past empires continue to shape a distinct political rationale and behaviour that the dominant political discourse today characterizes as anomalous or corrupt. This can be seen, for instance, in the post-colonial effects that remain from the Eurasian steppe tradition. While this tradition had its origins in the Turko-Mongolic empires, its form also came to owe much to the Persian bureaucracy. Iver B. Neumann and Einar Wigen point out the important ways in which this tradition differs from the European tradition, but they also trace the hybridization of the steppe and the European traditions. This hybridization can be seen in the cases of Turkey and Russia, and is even more in evidence today in states such as Afghanistan.

Ben de Carvalho tells the fascinating story of the system of donatary captaincies, which had its roots in the Roman imperial tradition and was adopted by Portuguese colonisers in Africa and then in Brazil, leaving an imprint on the contemporary Brazilian state. He concludes his study by observing that 'Rather than understanding empires as distinct from the international system of states, any inquiry seeking to understand long-term development must take as a point of departure how different systems and modes of political organization intersect, coexist and influence each other.'

The impact of past empires can also be seen on contemporary international organizations and on the 'global architecture of governance'.

Craig N. Murphy argues that the organizational routines and original staff of the United Nations system – and, particularly, the UN *development* system (its operations in the less-industrialized world) – 'were, to a significant degree, legacies of late nineteenth-century inter-imperial cooperation'. They 'came from the wartime institutions that managed the economies of the Allies' colonies from North Africa to India as part of the war effort and form men and women who had administered the later, more progressive stages of Roosevelt's Good Neighbor policy in Latin America'. After World War II, decolonization 'eventually made "the UN system" and "the UN *development* system" all but equivalent'.

Part III is intended as a thought experiment. We ask in the light of the preceding two parts, what will be the likely impacts of the American empire on the world, say, fifty years from now? Commentators often refer to US overseas military bases as an 'empire', yet they rarely specify what such imperial dynamics entail, nor differentiate among different forms of these allegedly imperial arrangements. Alexander Cooley examines the evolution of US and other post-imperial basing relationships and how they shape nation building and democratization in the host countries.

Multiculturalism is often seen as a legacy of empire. Herman Schwartz explains how the timing of land development and industrialization produce varying degrees of heterogeneity. He argues that the British and American empires both largely developed through the exploitation of land cleared of its indigenous population, or within export processing zones to which labour migrated. While the exploitation of newly emptied lands allowed capital to operate freely as pure disembodied capital, it also created a need for labour to complement that capital. In a classic contradiction, a relatively homogeneous and pure capital pulled ethnically, religiously and racially disparate populations into these empty spaces. The modern politics of multiculturalism has a material base in the expansion of empire into newly homogenized space. One conclusion is that the US empire is likely to produce not homogenization or 'Westernization' but multiculturalism.

Ronnie D. Lipschutz argues that the legacy of US empire is, following Foucault, an increasingly dense system of bureaucratized global governmentality and discipline which normalizes and valorizes a 'steel web' of militaristic beliefs and practices. The global intensification of surveillance and discipline following 9/11 is a logical apotheosis of the gradual militarization of American and global life through the bureaucratization associated with globalization and the pacification of many, if not all, of state individual militaries. The war on internal terrorist threats has brought more and more people into the ambit of capitalism, while the centrifugal ideologization (Malesevic 2010) of the 'sovereign consumer' in a 'dangerous world' has served to limit the potential of collective solidarity and mobilization even as it socializes individuals into 'world war infinity'.

References

Adas, Michael (1998) 'Imperialism and Colonialism in Comparative Perspective'. *The International History Review*, 20(1), 371–88.

Agevall, Ola (2005) 'Thinking about Configurations: Max Weber and Modern Social Science'. *Ethics & Politics*, 2, 1–20.

Amin, S. (1976) *Unequal Development: An Essay on the Social Formation of Peripheral Capitalism*. New York and London: Monthly Review Press.

Bacevich, Andrew J. (ed.) (2003) *The Imperial Tense: Prospects and Problems of American Empire*. Chicago: Ivan R. Dee.

Barber, Benjamin (2003) *Fear's Empire: War, Terrorism and Democracy*. New York: W. W. Norton.

Becker, D. (1987) *Postimperialism: International Capitalism and Development in the Late Twentieth Century*. Boulder: Lynne Rienner.

Braudel, F. (1981) *Civilization and Capitalism, 15th–18th Century, Vol. I: The Structure of Everyday Life*. Trans. S. Reynolds. New York: Harper and Row.

(1984) *Civilization and Capitalism, 15th–18th Century, Vol. III: The Wheels of Commerce*. Trans. S. Reynolds. New York: Harper and Row.

Brenner, Neil (1998) 'Global Cities, Glocal States: Global City Formation and State Territorial Restructuring in Contemporary Europe'. *Review of International Political Economy*, 5(1), 1–37.

(2004) *New State Spaces: Urban Governance and the Rescaling of Statehood*. London: Oxford University Press.

Büthe, T. (2002) 'Taking Temporality Seriously: Modeling History and the Use of Narratives as Evidence'. *American Political Science Review*, 96(3), 481–93.

Calhoun, Craig, Frederick Cooper and Kevin W. Moore (eds.) (2006) *Lessons of Empire: Imperial Histories and American Power*. New York: The New Press.

Cardoso, F. H. (1973) 'Associated-Dependent Development: Theoretical and Practical Implications'. In A. Stepan (ed.) *Authoritarian Brazil: Origins, Policies, and Future*. New Haven: Yale University Press, 142–78.

Cardoso, F. H. and E. Faletto (1979) *Dependency and Development in Latin America*. Berkeley: University of California Press.

Centeno, Miguel Angel and Elaine Enriquez (2010) 'Legacies of Empire?' *Theory and Society*, 39(3–4), 343–60.

Chakrabarty, D. (1992) 'Postcoloniality and the Artifice of History: Who Speaks for "Indian" Pasts?' *Representations*, 37 (Winter), 1–26.

(2000) *Provincializing Europe: Postcolonial Thought and Historical Difference*. Princeton: Princeton University Press.

Chernilo, Daniel (2006) 'Social Theory's Methodological Nationalism: Myth and Reality'. *European Journal of Social Theory*, 9(1), 5–22.

Chomsky, Noam (2003) *Hegemony or Survival: America's Quest for Global Dominance*. New York: Metropolitan Books.

Collins, R. (1974) 'Reassessments of Sociological History: The Empirical Validity of the Conflict'. *Theory and Society*, 1(2), 147–78.

Daphnas, G. (1955) *Greece Between the Wars, 1923–1940*. Athenai: Ikaros.

Darwin, John (2009) *The Empire Project: The Rise and Fall of the British World-System, 1830–1970*. Cambridge: Cambridge University Press.

Dobb, M. (1963)[1947] *Studies in the Development of Capitalism*, revised edn. New York: International Publishers.

Dos Santos, Theotonio (1970) 'The Structure of Dependence'. *American Economic Review*, 60, 235–46.

Eisenstadt, S. N. (1963) *The Political Systems of Empires*. London: Free Press of Glencoe.

Ellul, J. (1965) *The Technological Society*. London: Jonathan Cape.

Evans, P. (1979) *Dependent Development*. Princeton: Princeton University Press.

Fédou, René (1971) *L'état au Moyen Âge*. Paris: PUF.

Ferguson, Niall (2002) *Empire: The Rise and Demise of the British World Order and the Lessons of Global Power*. New York: Basic Books.

(2004) *Colossus: The Rise and Fall of the American Empire*. London: Allen Lane.

Frank, A. (1972) 'The Development of Underdevelopment'. In J. Cockcroft, A. Frank and D. Johnson (eds.) *Dependence and Underdevelopment: Latin America's Political Economy*. New York: Doubleday Anchor Books, 3–17.

Gilpin, Robert (1981) *War and Change in World Politics*. Cambridge: Cambridge University Press.

Goulbourne, Harry (2009) *Ethnicity and Nationalism in Post-Imperial Britain*. Cambridge: Cambridge University Press.

Gouldner, A. W. (1977–78) 'Stalinism: A Study of Internal Colonialism'. *Telos*, 34: 5–48.

Guha, Ranajit and Gayatri Chakravorty Spivak (eds.) *Selected Subaltern Studies*. New York: Oxford University Press,

Gupta, A. (1998) *Postcolonial Developments: Agriculture in the Making of Modern India*. Durham, NC: Duke University Press.

Hardt, M. and A. Negri (2004) *Multitude: War and Democracy in the Age of Empire*. New York: Penguin Press.

Harvey, David (2003) *The New Imperialism*. Oxford: Oxford University Press.

Hechter, M. (1975) *Internal Colonialism: The Celtic Fringe in British National Development, 1536–1966*. Berkeley: University of California Press.

Hegel, Georg (1975) *Lectures on the Philosophy of World History: Introduction*. Trans. H. B. Nisbet. Cambridge: Cambridge University Press.

Hettne, B. (1990) *Development Theory and the Three Worlds*. Harlow: Longman.

Hobbes, Thomas (1951) *Leviathan*, ed. C. B. Macpherson. Harmondsworth: Penguin.

Hobsbawm, Eric (1990) *Nations and Nationalism since 1780: Programme, Myth, Reality*. Cambridge: Cambridge University Press.

Jászi, Oscar (1969) *Revolution and Counter-Revolution in Hungary*. New York: H. Fertig.

Johnson, Chalmers (2004) *The Sorrows of Empire: Militarism, Secrecy and the End of the Republic*. New York: Metropolitan Books.

Kay, C. (1989) *Latin American Theories of Development and Underdevelopment*. London: Routledge.

Kennedy, Paul (1987) *The Rise and Fall of the Great Powers: Economic Change and Military Conflict From 1500 to 2000*. New York: Random House.

King, G. (1989) 'Event Count Models for International Relations: Generalizations and Applications'. *International Studies Quarterly*, 33(2), 123–47.

Koebner, Richard and Helmut Dan Schmidt (1965) *Imperialism. The Story and Significance of a Political Word, 1840–1960*. Cambridge: Cambridge University Press.

Kohn, H. (1955) *Nationalism: Its Meaning and History*. Princeton: Princeton University Press.

Kwarteng, Kwasi (2011) *Ghosts of Empire: Britain's Legacies in the Modern World*. London: Bloomsbury Publishing.

Lal, Deepak (2004) *In Praise of Empires: Globalization and Order*. Basingstoke: Palgrave.

Larrain, J. (1989) *Theories of Development*. Cambridge: Polity Press.

Lazreg, Marnia (2008) *Torture and the Twilight of Empire: From Algiers to Baghdad*. Princeton: Princeton University Press.

Lutz, Catherine (2009) *The Bases of Empire: The Global Struggle Against U.S. Military Posts*. New York: New York University Press.

Macartney, C. A. (1934) *National States and National Minorities*. London: Oxford University Press.

Mairet, Gérard (1997) *Le Principe de Souveraineté: Histoires et Fondements du Pouvoir Moderne*. Paris: Gallimard.

Malesevic, Sinisa (2010) *The Sociology of War and Violence*. Cambridge: Cambridge University Press.

Mann, Michael (2003) *Incoherent Empire*. London: Verso.

Midgeley, James and Piachaud, David (eds.) (2011) *Colonialism and Welfare, Social Policy and the British Imperial Legacy*. Cheltenham: Edward Elgar Publishing.

Murphy, Craig N. (1994) *Industrial Organization and Industrial Change: Global Governance Since 1950*. Cambridge: Polity Press.

(2006) *The United Nations Development Programme: A Better Way?* Cambridge: Cambridge University Press.

Orren, K. and Skowronek, S. (2004) *The Search for American Political Approaches and Interpretations*. Boulder: Westview Press.

(1994) 'Beyond the Iconography of Order: Notes for a New Institutionalism'. In L. C. Dodd and C. C. Jilson (eds.) *The Dynamics of American Politics, Approaches and Interpretations*. Boulder: Westview Press, 311–30.

Palan, R. (2012) 'New Trends in Global Political Economy'. In R. Palan (ed.) *Global Political Economy: Contemporary Theories*. 2nd edn. London: Routledge, 1–12.

Parsons, Timothy H. (2010) *The Rule of Empires: Those Who Built Them, Those Who Endured Them, and Why They Always Fall*. Oxford: Oxford University Press.

Petropulos, A. (1968) *Politics and Statecraft in the Kingdom of Greece*. Princeton: Princeton University Press.

Prakash, G. (1996) *After Colonialism: Imperial Histories and Postcolonial Displacements*. Princeton: Princeton University Press.

Ragin, C. (2000) *Redesigning Social Inquiry: Fuzzy Sets and Beyond*. Chicago: Chicago University Press.

Redding, G. (2005) 'The Thick Description and Comparison of Societal Systems of Capitalism'. *Journal of International Business Studies*, 36, 123–55.

Reynolds, S. (2006) 'Empires: A Problem of Comparative History'. *Historical Research*, 79, 204, 151–63.

Said, Edward (1977) *Orientalism*. London: Penguin.

Sassen, Saskia (2007) *A Sociology of Globalization*. London. W. W. Norton. (1994) *Cities in a World Economy*. Thousand Oaks: Pine Forge Press.

Steinmetz, George (2005) 'Return to Empire: The New US Imperialism in Comparative Historical Perspective'. *Sociological Theory*, 23(4), 339–67.

Sunkel, O. (1973) 'Transnational Capitalism and National Disintegration in Latin America'. *Social and Economic Studies*, 22, 132–76.

Tilly, C. (2001) 'Mechanisms in Political Processes'. *Annual Review of Political Science*, 4, 21–41.

Todd, E. (2003) *After the Empire: The Breakdown of the American Order*. New York: Columbia University Press.

Van de Ven, A. H. (1993) 'The Institutional Theory of John R. Commons: A Review and Commentary'. *The Academy of Management Review*, 18(1), 139–52.

Wallerstein, I. (1974) *The Modern World System*. New York: Academic Press.

Weber, E. (1976) *Peasants into Frenchmen: The Modernization of Rural France, 1870–1914*. Stanford: Stanford University Press.

Wertheimer, M. S. (1924) *The Pan-German League, 1890–1914*. New York: Columbia University Press.

Young, R. (2001) *Postcolonialism: An Historical Introduction*. Oxford: Blackwell.

Zielonka, Jan (2006) *Europe as Empire: The Nature of the Enlarged European Union*. Oxford: Oxford University Press.

PART I

Incomplete transitions
from empires to nation states

2 | Political military legacies of empire in world politics

TARAK BARKAWI

This book examines the legacies of empire in world politics. It is about the imprint that the old imperial organization of world politics has left on the contemporary 'international' world. What erstwhile logics, institutions and organizational principles continue to work their effects? How, half a century on from decolonization, does the formal imperial world still shape relations between peoples and places? How might it still limit political possibilities around the globe?

In the social sciences and humanities, empire and imperialism usually appear under the signs of political economy and culture. When we think empire, we think of economic exploitation and Orientalism or, more mundanely, Indian restaurants on British high streets. What we do not think of are political military relations. An exception is the renewed interest in American empire that followed the invasions of Afghanistan and Iraq.[1] This did not produce thoroughgoing, systematic inquiry into imperial security dynamics, especially as a path to understanding more general features of world politics. Broadly speaking, with insightful exceptions to the contrary, the political military dimensions of empire and imperialism have not received concerted scholarly attention, or been seen as important topics outside of more or less arcane sub-fields.[2]

This is striking when it is recalled just how frequently and violently people have resisted imperialism around the world. It is downright surprising when the historical consequences of that resistance are tallied. Armed resistance to foreign influence and rule has shaped everything from the Melian Dialogue to the People's Republic of China. Imperial powers were under few delusions, and took considerable

This chapter draws on Barkawi 2011 and 2010a.
[1] See e.g. Cox 2005; Gregory 2004.
[2] See Barkawi 2010a for discussion and citations.

precautions (see, e.g. Hevia 2012; Kiernan 1998). Notably, empires often organized their security internationally. Carve-ups like the Scramble for Africa were diplomatically managed, while the great powers ensured that international law regarded irregulars as illegitimate combatants (Kinsella 2011).

This chapter focuses on a very significant, if veiled, legacy of empire concerning the organization of armed force in world politics. Putatively speaking, in the international world, armed force is organized in Westphalian terms, with each sovereign nation state fielding its 'own' armed forces. But a world in which the armed forces of nearly every state have a similar institutional structure is a product of empire. The imperial powers exported their military systems, raising local forces to secure and expand imperial rule. In fact, most of the armed forces in the world began their institutional histories in a colonial context or under other forms of imperial tutelage. The Kenyan army, and several others in East Africa, was formed out of the King's African Rifles. The Nigerian army, and several others in West Africa, started life as the Royal West African Frontier Force. The story is similar in much of former French Africa and in the successor states to the British Raj in South Asia and elsewhere. Other armies have mixed or informal imperial parentage. The South Korean army and national police began life in Japanese imperial service and then developed into national armed forces in the late 1940s under US occupation. Latin and Central American armies and other security forces have been trained, advised and supported by the USA for over a century. Armies may appear to be the principal national – even nationalist – institution, but their histories are usually imperial.

What is the significance of the imperial origins of armed forces? It is often observed that in the decades after 1945 the number of international wars declined while civil wars rose (Holsti 1996). Armed forces were being used primarily *inside* sovereign states, for purposes of 'internal security'. Foreign powers – often former imperial patrons – provided 'advice and support' to one side or another in many of these 'civil' wars (see, e.g. Kolko 1988). Much like in the imperial world, local armed forces were organized by great powers for regional and global projects of order making. The military legacy of empire left in place a global coercive infrastructure for purposes of power projection, along with the modalities – shared colonial military histories, advice and support – to make use of it.

Rejigged for new times, an imperial military order functioned beneath the sovereign veil of the national–international world. It is this order that made it possible in the Cold War to fight in Indochina using primarily 'Asian boys',[3] or to put down popular challenges in the Third World without dispatching First World expeditionary forces. The continuing significance of these kinds of military relations is evident in the importance placed on training Iraqi and Afghan forces in order to secure governments set up by foreign powers.

The discussion below begins by contrasting the Westphalian image of the international organization of armed force with that of an imperial order. It then turns, in the second section, to the globalization of the regular military institution under imperial auspices. How did states constitute armed force from foreign populations on a global scale? The third section covers the transition from colonial armies to the advice and support of client forces. A conclusion addresses some implications for inquiry into world politics.

The sovereign veil

In the discipline of International Relations (IR), the central problematic is that of a system of sovereign states competing with one another in the absence of higher authority. How states manage or resolve the ever-present possibility of war among 'like units' under 'no common power' is amenable to realist, liberal and constructivist analyses, and as such is the site of defining debates in security studies and IR (Waltz 1979; Wendt 1999). The 'units' are formally alike, in that they are sovereign entities, even if they differ in their relative power and capabilities. The 'international' is separated sharply from the 'domestic', with the former the site of collective action problems and strategic interaction, and the latter a realm of order provided by the sovereign state's 'monopoly on violence'. There are many exceptions to this broad characterization,

---

[3] '[W]e are not about to send American boys 9 or 10,000 miles away from home to do what Asian boys ought to be doing for themselves.' Lyndon B. Johnson, Remarks in Memorial Hall, University of Akron, 21 October 1964, available online at www.presidency.ucsb.edu/ws/?pid=26635, accessed 30 September 2014. Even at the height of the US deployment to South Vietnam, US-supported South Vietnamese forces outnumbered US forces by two to one, and suffered many times the number of dead.

but it is difficult to overestimate the power of a nation state ontology of world politics, not only for IR but also for the social sciences and humanities in general.

Underpinning this world of units is a set of assumptions about the organization of armed force, signalled by the invocation of Max Weber's definition of the state involving an administrative staff that successfully upholds the claim to the monopoly on the legitimate use of force in a given territorial area (Weber 1978: 54). The monopoly of violence is conceived as the essence of the state–force–territory relation and the basis of sovereign power. The rule of the state over population and territory is backed up by coercive bureaucracies. This control over force makes the state a 'social-territorial totality', or a 'bordered power container' (Giddens 1985: 120; Halliday 1994: 78–79). The state becomes a national community of fate, unifying government, people and territory. Control of one's 'own' armed forces is essential. As John Herz put it in his seminal article on the territorial state, 'The decisive criterion . . . is actual control of one's "estates" by one's military power, which excludes any other power from within and without' (1957: 479). These assumptions about the organization of armed force form the hard core of the sovereign and territorial state. The problem of security concerns how such 'like' states protect their interests from one another in an ultimately anarchic international system.

This Westphalian image of sovereign units squared off against one another is significant well beyond IR. The concept of the nation state organizes much of the social sciences and humanities and is central to any idea of political modernity. In a nation state, state, army and society come in an isomorphic, sovereign territorial package. Army–society relations are 'civil–military' relations. From the time of the 'French and American revolutions, participation in armed conflict has been an integral aspect of the normative definition of citizenship' (Janowitz 1976: 190). Those areas of inquiry explicitly concerned with armed forces and war, such as IR or military history and sociology, focus attention nearly entirely on the armies and wars of Western nation states (Black 2004). Debates over the move to citizen armies, for example, focus on the timing and nature of military reforms in the major European states (Avant 2000; Percy 2007; Posen 1993). Greek and Roman ideas about the virtues of citizen soldiers inform political and democratic theory (Hanson 1989; Levi 1997; Machiavelli 1998). In these and other ways, assumptions about the political military undergird basic conceptions of politics and society. They make the study of 'national' societies, polities and economies the normal situation (Chatterjee 1986).

The problems begin with the evident Eurocentrism of the package of assumptions that form the nation state. Consider the sociology of state formation. It is about the transition from the late medieval to the early modern order in Europe, yet is taken to provide universal ideas about what a state and a state system is (see, e.g. Sassen 2006). It is not that such inquiry is wrong or misguided so much that it is *provincial* (Chakrabarty 2000). The Eurocentric co-location of state, armed forces and national society is inadequate for understanding the organization of force in *world* politics, either in the contemporary era or in that of formal empire. It lacks purchase not only on the histories of others, but on the ways in which Western and non-Western histories have been intertwined.

In imperial context, the political military takes different forms. Foreign powers raise armed forces from local societies. Armed forces are not necessarily 'national'. The coercive powers of states have international and transnational dimensions. The modalities vary historically, but practices such as raising colonial armies, the advice and support of the armed forces of subordinate states, and covert or deniable uses of foreign military manpower were widespread and profoundly consequential for the fates of many peoples and places (Kiernan 1998; Lumpe 2002; McClintock 1992; Spector 1985). There were territorial monopolies on force, but they were often held in whole or in part by foreign powers. The formal sovereign world veils imperial practices and relations in the past and in the present.

The 'foreign forces' involved in imperial security relations were normally used to exert power over colonized populations and the Third World or Global South. But their significance is not limited to subordinate states and societies in world politics. They have direct implications for the character of civil–military relations in core states and for the kinds of imperial and foreign policies they can sustain. From the early modern period onwards, the processes of European expansion that interconnected the world – making possible the capitalist world system – relied on the availability of armed force. This was because imperial intervention and rule continually encountered and generated armed resistance. The primary military burden fell not on the populations of core states but on those being subjugated. Foreign forces enabled the histories of imperialism and core–periphery relations that continue to shape the modern world.

The institutional histories and the political pathways through which foreign forces were constituted and used are rooted in eras of European expansion and dominance. They comprise the political military legacies of empire. At their core is a disciplinary technology, the army, used to raise forces around the world.

The globalization of the army

The worldwide circulation of people, goods and ideas has a much longer history than is generally realized (Hopkins 2002). Such circulation has always required what we euphemistically call 'security', that is, armed force, to protect it. So, too, does contesting or restricting it. Armed forces are both part of global circulation, and necessary for it. From the sixteenth century, European soldiers and their military practices went abroad with European explorers, missionaries and traders. They secured the factories, mines, trading entrepôts, plantations and colonies established by European sovereigns and their chartered companies. They guarded lines of communications with homelands and markets, and with sources of free and slave labour.

White troops were expensive and died from disease at alarming rates. From early on two ways to augment Western military power with locally recruited forces were developed. One was to ally with local powers and their armed forces – native allies – such as Hernán Cortés used in his conquest of the Aztec Empire or the British and the French in North America. A second was to directly recruit, train and officer local troops in regular style. When European powers were relatively weak, and their outposts amounted to tiny footholds on the edges of continents, allegiances with local powers were the most obvious route to security. Modern arms and other forms of military assistance could be used to increase the armed power of the indigenous rulers who allied with the Europeans. The deft management of such alliances over time could considerably strengthen the European position and set the stage for decisive wars of conquest.

As the Europeans gained strength, and especially as they became settled rulers of much of the world outside Europe, they turned to the direct organization of indigenous military forces along Western lines. What began as locally hired armed guards turned into regiments of native infantry, such as those of the East India Company. These were used to fight other European powers and to defeat indigenous rulers. As the Europeans established various forms of long-term colonial rule, they created military, police and intelligence bureaucracies and trained indigenous personnel to staff them. In this manner, considerable military power was generated in the non-European world for Western purposes, especially by the British in India and the French in West and North Africa. The Russians raised considerable forces from their empire, and on a lesser scale so too did the Dutch and the USA. These forces could be used for wars of imperial conquest and in great power war. Everywhere there were European colonies, there were local native soldiers and police (see Killingray and Omissi 1999 for an overview). In providing security for empire, they were part and parcel of the globalization of Western forms of military organization.

How could the army be globalized? In what sense is it Western? It is a mistake to think that military discipline has a distinctly Western or Greco-Roman heritage. Disciplined Indian infantry opposed Alexander the Great's incursions into the Punjab, and drill and organized warfare are found in ancient China as well. 'As African and Asian archers had released arrows on command for thousands of years, the non-Western world did not have to wait to be told that firearms could be used in the same manner' (Cooper 2005: 537). What makes the army 'globalizable' is that it is a cosmopolitan form of discipline. Disciplined soldiers can be raised from any population. Military organization can have varied relations with ethnicity and nationality. Many modern and effective imperial armed forces, such as those of British India, were multi-ethnic. There is nothing essentially Western about being a soldier. But it is largely the Westerners who in modern times went around the world raising armies and other security forces. It is therefore with Western states that the militaries of many new states share institutional histories and links. But regardless of direct imperial parentage the institutional similarity of militaries around the world created by empire facilitates dense patterns of international interchange.

France and Britain created substantial military establishments in their largest and most enduring colonial possessions. In 1863, the British fielded an Indian Army of 135,000 alongside 62,000 British army troops stationed in India (Menezes 1999: 189). During World War I, France deployed over 200,000 West and North African soldiers on the Western Front (Clayton 1988: 98). Britain sent over 500,000 Indian soldiers abroad to fight in France, the Middle East and Africa in 1914–18 (Perry 1988: 96). The world wars and the growing struggle against anti-colonial movements prompted modernization of colonial armed forces and security bureaucracies. Nascent modern naval and air forces were created, as in the formation of the Royal Indian Air Force and the Royal Indian Navy in the early 1930s. The French sought to counter their demographic imbalance with Germany by expanding their North and West African forces, while the British Indian Army reached a strength of over two million during the Second World War. As opposition to colonialism became a form of mass politics in the early decades of the twentieth century, colonial security bureaucracies increased in size and widened the scope of their operations in response to both armed and unarmed resistance. In Indochina in 1953, the French fielded nearly 74,000 European troops, over 47,000 West and North African troops, 53,000 Indochinese in French colonial service and 150,000 more in the army of the French-sponsored Vietnamese state as well as 13,000 each in its Laotian and Cambodian counterparts (Clayton 1988: 160).

The significance of colonial armed forces was not limited to providing security in the colonies and conquering new territories. The commitment of resources, military and otherwise, was always an obstacle for metropolitan advocates of empire, and often at the centre of political debates over imperialism.[4] With the extension of the franchise and the emergence of a literate mass public from the second half of the nineteenth century, political military events in the extra-European world played an increasingly important role in electoral politics and the rise and fall of governments, from William Gladstone to William McKinley.

That the Western forces used in imperial adventures consisted almost entirely of professionals and volunteers testifies to the political sensitivities involved. The French evolved a colonial marine service for such expeditions, while the Foreign Legion always accounted for a heavy proportion of their white troops on imperial service. The British army remained a professional force until World War I. When the enlistments of US volunteers serving in the Philippines ran out in 1901, the USA

---

[4] See, e.g. Cain and Hopkins 2002: 281; Ferguson 2004: 170–71; Kanya-Forstner 1969.

stepped up formation of a paramilitary Philippine Constabulary reaching some 7,000 in number by 1904. This was in addition to the Philippine Scouts, a force of similar size integrated into the US army. Together, along with local police, they carried on counter-guerrilla operations for years after the war was formally over, without need to call upon more 'citizen soldiers' from the USA (Jose 1992: 18; Linn 1999: 118–19; 2000: 204, 215–16).

The overall contribution of colonial and other foreign forces was not only in their military significance, but in the more or less delicate political dispensations they enabled in Western civil–military relations. This made possible empire on the cheap, from a Western perspective, the only kind of empire Western publics were reliably willing to stomach. Among their other advantages, colonial troops were less costly to maintain and less likely to die of disease.

This broad survey of the constitution and use of foreign forces gives some idea of the nature and character of imperial security relations; of the use of military discipline to turn the colonized into guardians of the colonial order; and of how foreign forces made possible the era of European empire and the globalized world it created. But what were the legacies left behind by colonial armies? What old imperial practices were adapted for use in a sovereign state system that went global in the decades after 1945?

From colonial to client armies, from officers to advisors

In regular colonial military forces, Europeans served as commissioned officers, generally with the assistance of a class of indigenous sub-officers. Nationalist movements demanded the 'nationalization' of the officer corps. Expansion and casualties in the world wars added further pressures to commission indigenous officers, who appeared in increasing numbers as the colonial era came to an end. The officers who rose to command the Indian and Pakistani armies in the decades after independence began their careers in the British Indian Army.

The sovereign independence of the new states meant that Europeans generally could no longer serve as commissioned officers. With some exceptions, Western officers now transitioned into an advisory role in many of their contacts with foreign armed forces. Missions of 'advice and support' became a significant way in which Western soldiers participated in international military relations after 1945 (Stoker 2008). Such missions echoed the early period of European expansion, of military assistance to native allies, in which the Europeans could not exercise direct control but had to rely more on persuasion and bargaining with local elites, while respecting their independence.

After 1945, both the scale and political salience of wars and revolts in the Third World increased dramatically. The mass politics of anti-colonial resistance led to significant fighting in Asia and Africa in a Cold War context. The advent of nuclear weapons further shunted superpower conflict into the Third World. Wars fought there by proxy on at least one side were less likely to lead to nuclear confrontation, and offered the superpower blocs opportunities for strategic advantage (Aron 1968). At the same time, these conflicts generated political crises in the West, leading to regime change in France and Portugal. The Vietnam War toppled a US president and split the country for more than a generation, determining the fates of presidential candidates as late as 2004.

The military and political demand for indigenous forces remained, yet the colonial framework that produced their most powerful expression in the regular colonial armies was disappearing. It is at this juncture that the characteristic modality for the constitution of foreign forces in a sovereign state system came into its own: the 'advice and support' of the armies of formally independent but subordinate states. It is an example of what Andrew Scott has referred to as 'techniques of informal penetration' that blossomed after World War II and gave powerful governments 'direct access to the people and processes of another society' (1982: xi).

Both the superpowers developed extensive programmes for foreign military training, advising and the supply, sale and maintenance of weapons, equipment and munitions (Johnson 2004: 131–40; Neuman 1986). In other cases, the ex-imperial powers maintained links to former colonial militaries, which had become the national armed forces of the new states and were now avenues for various kinds of influence (Luckham 1971; Martin 1995). Elsewhere, the USA took charge of the transition from colonial to sovereign army. The USA based the South Korean army as well as the national police on Koreans who had served the Japanese (Cumings 1981: 169, 172–76). In the last stages of their presence in Indochina, the French created a Vietnamese state and formed a Vietnamese National Army. After the Geneva Accords in 1954, this

became the Army of the Republic of (South) Vietnam (ARVN), and the
USA took over the role of patron.

Well before Nixon expanded Vietnamization, the ARVN and other
South Vietnamese forces supplied the majority of the troops and suffered the majority of casualties. ARVN strength hovered at around
700,000 between 1964 and 1968, and rose to a million between 1969
and 1975, suffering around 250,000 KIA during the war; numbers that
do not include the numerous paramilitary forces raised by Saigon
(Brigham 2006: x). The USA clothed, trained, supplied and armed the
ARVN, as well as advising it down to the company level in combat. The
ARVN played a primary role in projecting US power in Indochina,
defending the Saigon regime as well as invading Cambodia and Laos
and carrying the war largely on its own for the final three years. The
ARVN was only one of many Third World militaries drawn into US
policies concerned with the defence of the Free World from much of its
own population. An informal empire was maintained primarily with
locally raised forces in the face of indigenous revolt. The ARVN and its
ilk were new model iterations of the British Indian Army.

The US was constrained in using its national armed forces, partly
because of limited resources and, especially following the war in
Indochina, because of popular disenchantment. It sought to raise, train
and advise foreign forces for purposes of countering what was seen as
informal Soviet aggression, just as today it trains foreign armies to fight
'terrorists'. Successive US presidents in the Cold War conceived of the
various programmes for advice and support as a means of utilizing
foreign manpower for their own purposes. As President Eisenhower
put it, 'The United States could not maintain old-fashioned forces all
around the world', so it sought 'to develop within the various areas and
regions of the free world indigenous forces for the maintenance of order,
the safeguarding of frontiers, and the provision of the bulk of the ground
capability'. After the trauma of the Korean War, for Eisenhower, 'the
kernel of the whole thing' was to have indigenous forces bear the brunt of
any future fighting (quoted in Gaddis 1982: 153). After Vietnam, the
Nixon Doctrine was similarly concerned with limiting the role of US
national forces. The USA would 'look to the nation directly threatened to
assume primary responsibility of providing manpower for its defense'.[5]

---

[5] From a clarification of the Nixon Doctrine provided by the White House and
quoted in Gaddis 1982, 298.

The underlying idea behind such foreign forces was to bolster the military power of a client unable to constitute sufficient force from its own internal resources. This is an international form of the constitution of force, for patron and client. In a sovereign state system, deniable or disguised modalities of this kind become more important. This is because a national principle underlies the system in the post-1945 world. Peoples ostensibly determine their own conditions of rule. This was the concession the architects of the United Nations made to anti-imperial politics among the peoples and leaders of the new states (Mazower 2009). In formal terms, force had to be made to look as if it arose from within the political community concerned. The USA claimed it was helping free peoples defend their countries from a minority influenced (and assisted) by international communism. The Soviets were caught in the same politics, representing their policies as fraternal assistance. This type of intervention was not limited to sovereign clients. A rebel group representing the 'true' desires of the people could also be supported or more or less invented, as in the case of the Nicaraguan Contras. Even when it was relatively obvious to one or another audience that denials of foreign support were false, both superpowers often maintained an official front of non-involvement in order to appear to respect the principle of non-intervention and relevant treaty commitments.

The private sector offered another sphere in which foreign forces could be cobbled together for imperial purposes. This had the advantage of distancing the sponsoring power from intervention. As with other kinds of foreign raised forces, there were antecedents from the era of European empire. After the Opium War of 1839–42, Western powers sought to prop up the newly pliable Qing dynasty in the face of a series of domestic revolts inspired in significant measure by foreign influence on the decaying imperial regime. They supported 'private' mercenary armies led by Western soldiers and recruited from third country nationals, such as Frederick Townsend Ward's Ever Victorious Army which recruited Filipinos and played a role in defeating the Taiping rebellion (Carr 1992).

The post-1945 world has seen a considerable expansion in the use of private forces as an avenue for states to draw upon foreign sources of military manpower (Abrahamsen and Williams 2011; Singer 2003). The CIA's covert action arm, for example, involved a mix of public and private and of national and foreign, much like the armed forces of the old imperial chartered companies. In the early Cold War, the CIA's proprietary airline, Civil Air Transport (CAT), was comprised of CIA officers, USAF personnel on secondment and a variety of foreign pilots privately hired but with anti-communist credentials, such as Nationalist Chinese, or Poles and Czechoslovaks who had flown for the Royal Air Force in the Second World War and were effectively stateless. The Chinese flew strike missions for the CIA in Guatemala, while the Poles were active in Albania and Indonesia. The CIA force that invaded Guatemala in 1954 was ostensibly an indigenous revolt but was composed of North and Latin American mercenaries trained and directed by CIA officers (Leary 2002; Prados 1996). These practices continued to be adapted to conflicts with an imperial character. The wars in Iraq and Afghanistan saw extensive use of third-country nationals and private military companies (Chatterjee 2009).

The old imperial powers could also mix their institutional legacies with private modalities in maintaining influence after the end of empire. In assisting the Sultan of Oman's Armed Forces (SAF) from the late 1950s, the British and their client even drew on feudal legacies as well. A British officer was seconded to command the SAF along with British officers and NCOs who volunteered to serve in the SAF. Other British officers were hired privately directly into the SAF and known as contract officers, many having been recently discharged from the Indian Army (which continued to employ British officers for some years after 1947). Due to feudal rights, the Sultan could recruit soldiers from Baluchistan. Baluchis made up around 67 per cent of the SAF in 1961 as the Dhofar rebellion got underway. Indians were hired as dentists, doctors and other specialists, and as navy officers. The air force had all 'white faces'. The relative lack of Omani nationals in the SAF was politicized by the Dhofar rebels. The British and the Sultan created an 'Omanization' plan in response. Along with efforts to recruit more Arabs, this had the Sultan proclaiming in one speech in 1972 that 'everyone knows the air force is an Omani air force, and that the navy is an Omani navy, and that our Omani army is the only force which protects the land of our nation', all of which was true formally speaking, if not in terms of actual personnel.[6]

---

[6] Gardiner 2006; author's interview with Major-General John Graham (ret.), former commander of the SAF, 26 September 2004; 'Addresses given by HM Sultan Qaboos', 3/3 Graham Papers, Oman Archive, The Middle East Centre, St. Antony's College Oxford; 'Report on Tenure of Command of SAF by Col. Smiley from April 1958 to March 1961', 1/1 Smiley Papers, Oman Archive.

Like the British Indian Army in its heyday, the SAF was a multinational, multi-ethnic force set up to secure a territory against some portion of its own population and to forcibly interconnect it to the world economy.

Conclusion: an imperial turn?

In a variety of sites in modern times, security relations took imperial form. Armed forces, societies and polities are by no means always in isomorphic relations, even in a sovereign state system. The guardians of the ship of state often hail from foreign shores and serve foreign interests. Powers of state structure these processes but not always in ways suggested by Eurocentric frames of inquiry. The constitution and use of force has regularly involved personnel recruited from outside national and sovereign borders, and from among colonized and subordinate populations, for purposes of securing and extending influence and rule in peripheral lands. This is not a world of formally alike units in anarchic relations, but one of hierarchies, cores and peripheries in respect of the organization of armed force as well as of economy and culture. Foreign and clandestine forces had a particular utility for the various combinations of political and economic interests behind Western expansion and intervention in the modern era, providing 'untraceable troops' that could evade democratic accountability and regulation (Lens 1987: 105). These personnel and forces also formed reserves and fire brigades for great power war. Organized as regulars and long service professionals, their military qualities were often significant as were their numbers.

That said, scale in terms of the size of forces involved in war, or their casualties or military qualities, also can be subject to Eurocentric distortion. However lacking in comparison to first-rate metropolitan forces, colonial and client state regulars and security services mounted credible and enduring opposition to indigenous powers and local revolt. The historic consequences and the numbers of people affected by imperial conflict and organized violence between the strong and the weak are immense, even though the wars themselves are often 'small' and do not usually command the same scholarly attention as big ones. However tiny a war the Dhofar rebellion was, it determined the fate of Oman for decades. In relations between the strong and the weak relatively small armed forces can determine the fates of substantial populations.

To identify these imperial relations between states, societies and armed forces is not to suggest that Eurocentric inquiry is somehow fundamentally invalidated, or that citizen armies are not also a reality. It is to question the purview of such inquiry, its reach to unfamiliar places, and its pretensions to universality. Many of the forces and events described above have been invisible or misconstrued in inquiry shaped by nation-state ontologies of the organization of violence. The politics of foreign forces contradict thinking framed by nation states, republics and citizens. These forces derive their various utilities from the fact that they come from outside the nation or citizenry; they are used to evade democratic limits at home and impose rule on others abroad. It might be more accurate to say that the politics of foreign forces *underpin* those of the nation state, and of imperial republics. These forces enabled the political bargains behind imperial expansion and intervention, and have made historically possible, among other things, the different imperial liberalisms of Britain and the USA.

Foreign forces, and the broader imperial contexts in which they were located, played a constitutive role in Western politics and society. They were consequential not only for peripheral peoples and their histories, but for those of the core as well. Eurocentric inquiry is not fully adequate for understanding European realities. The imperial and the peripheral are in part constitutive of the metropolitan. Here, armed force is not only being conceived as an instrument deployed by state actors in the service of their interests, as in strategic thought and IR. Rather, the organization of violence is seen as socially productive, as generative of certain political orders, at home, abroad and internationally. The critique of Westphalian security relations prompts a rethinking of force as constitutive of world politics, not simply as an instrument of power.

War and the organization of armed force are richly creative and generative sets of social processes and interactions, they *make possible* particular social and political worlds while destroying others. The consequences of major wars and Western armed forces for industrialization, capitalism, state capacity, science and technology are well-trodden themes in historical sociology. This chapter draws attention to the ways in which imperial and neo-imperial relations of organized violence have structured relations between the powerful and the weak in world politics, making possible particular political, social and economic arrangements in and between the Global North and South, during and after the era of formal empire.

In recent decades, the notion of an imperial turn has shaped the work of historians, sociologists and anthropologists. The basic idea is that of the co-constitution of core and periphery, in cultural and social as well as political-economic terms (Cooper and Stoler 1997). Much of this work is written in a cultural register, and has led to an extensive multidisciplinary conversation. Implicit in this work is a rich conception of the international as a 'thick' social space of interaction and co-constitution. In this respect, the imperial turn points the way to a social science of international relations of far broader purview than that found in IR. At the same time, to read much of the work that travels under the label of the imperial turn is to enter a world in which domination and exploitation occur seemingly entirely in the realm of culture and political economy. It is as if no native powers ever had to be militarily subdued, or any rebels lined up and shot.

In IR, 'small wars' have prompted questions about how and why the 'weak' prove so formidable in places such as Vietnam and Algeria, winning wars against major powers. More recently there is extensive interest in counterinsurgencies arising from US involvement in Iraq and Afghanistan. These projects remain in the realm of force as an instrument, inquiring about the conditions under which it is successful or not. The imperial turn, and the political military legacies it draws attention to, opens up a much broader research agenda focused on the significant and consequential role foreign forces and 'small wars' have come to play in metropolitan politics, society and culture and in the making of world orders. The imperial turn suggests strongly that there is much to be gained by reconnecting IR and the study of the international more generally with the histories and legacies of empires and of their armies and other foreign forces discussed in this chapter. Doing so would revive and deepen the insights of those realists who have long argued for the decisive role of the political military in shaping human affairs.

References

Abrahamsen, Rita and Michael C. Williams (2011) *Security Beyond the State: Private Security in International Politics*. Cambridge: Cambridge University Press.

Aron, Raymond (1968) *On War*. New York: W. W. Norton.

Avant, Deborah (2000) 'From Mercenary to Citizen Armies'. *International Organization*, 54(1), 41–72.

Barkawi, Tarak (2010a) 'Empire and Order in International Relations and Security Studies'. In Robert A. Denemark (ed.) *The International Studies Encyclopedia*, Vol. III. Chichester: Wiley-Blackwell, 1360–79.

(2010b) 'State and Armed Force in International Context'. In Alex Colas and Bryan Mabee (eds.) *Mercenaries, Pirates, Bandits and Empires: Private Violence in Historical Context*. London: Hurst, 33–53.

(2011) '"Defence Diplomacy" in North/South Relations'. *International Journal*, 66(3), 597–612.

Barkawi, Tarak and Mark Laffey (2006) 'The Postcolonial Moment in Security Studies'. *Review of International Studies*, 32(4), 329–52.

Black, Jeremy (2004) *Rethinking Military History*. London: Routledge.

Brigham, Robert (2006) *ARVN*. Lawrence: University Press of Kansas.

Cain, P. J. and A. G. Hopkins (2002) *British Imperialism 1688–2000*. London: Longman.

Carr, Caleb (1992) *The Devil Soldier*. New York: Random House.

Chakrabarty, Dipesh (2000) *Provincializing Europe: Postcolonial Thought and Historical Difference*. Princeton: Princeton University Press.

Clayton, Anthony (1988) *France, Soldiers and Africa*. London: Brassey's.

Cooper, Frederick and Ann Laura Stoler (eds.) (1997) *Tensions of Empire*. Berkeley: University of California Press.

Cooper, Randolf (2005) 'Culture, Combat and Colonialism in Eighteenth- and Nineteenth-Century India'. *International History Review*, 27(3), 534–49.

Chatterjee, Partha (1986) *Nationalist Thought and the Colonial World: A Derivative Discourse*. London: Zed Books.

Chatterjee, Pratap (2009) *Haliburton's Army*. New York: Nation Books.

Cox, Michael (2005) 'Empire by Denial'. *International Affairs*, 81(1), 15–30.

Cumings, Bruce (1981) *The Origins of the Korean War*. Princeton: Princeton University Press.

Ferguson, Niall (2004) *Empire*. London: Penguin.

Gaddis, John Lewis (1982) *Strategies of Containment*. Oxford: Oxford University Press.

Gardiner, Ian (2006) *In the Service of the Sultan: A First Hand Account of the Dhofar Insurgency*. Barnsley: Pen and Sword.

Giddens, Anthony (1985) *The Nation-State and Violence*. Cambridge: Polity.

Gregory, Derek (2004) *The Colonial Present*. Oxford: Blackwell.

Halliday, Fred (1994) *Rethinking International Relations*. Vancouver: University of British Columbia Press.

Hanson, Victor Davis (1989) *The Western Way of War*. New York: Oxford University Press.

Herz, John (1957) 'Rise and Demise of the Territorial State'. *World Politics*, 9(4), 473–93.

Hevia, James (2012) *The Imperial Security State*. Cambridge: Cambridge University Press.

Holsti, Kalevi (1996) *The State, War, and the State of War*. Cambridge: Cambridge University Press.

Hopkins, A. G. (ed.) (2002) *Globalization in World History*. London: Pimlico.

Janowitz, Morris (1976) 'Military Institutions and Citizenship in Western Societies'. *Armed Forces and Society*, 2(2), 185–204.

Johnson, Chalmers (2004) *The Sorrows of Empire*. London: Verso.

Jose, Ricardo Trota (1992) *The Philippine Army, 1935–1942*. Quezon City: Ateneo de Manila University Press.

Kanya-Forstner, A. S. (1969) *The Conquest of the Western Sudan*. London: Cambridge University Press.

Kiernan, V. G. (1998) *Colonial Empires and Armies 1815–1960*. Stroud: Sutton.

Killingray, David and David Omissi (eds.) (1999) *Guardians of Empire*. Manchester: Manchester University Press.

Kinsella, Helen (2011) *The Image before the Weapon: A Critical History of the Distinction between Combatant and Civilian*. Ithaca: Cornell University Press.

Kolko, Gabriel (1988) *Confronting the Third World: United States Foreign Policy 1945–1980*. New York: Pantheon Books.

Leary, William M. (2002) *Perilous Missions: Civil Air Transport and CIA Covert Operations in Asia*. Washington, DC: Smithsonian Institution Press.

Lens, Sidney (1987) *Permanent War*. New York: Shocken Books.

Levi, Margaret (1997) *Consent, Dissent, and Patriotism*. Cambridge: Cambridge University Press.

Linn, Brian McAllister (1999) 'Cerberus' Dilemma'. In David Killingray and David Omissi (eds.) *Guardians of Empire*. Manchester: Manchester University Press.

(2000) *The Philippine War 1899–1902*. Lawrence: University Press of Kansas.

Luckham, Robin (1971) *The Nigerian Military*. Cambridge: Cambridge University Press.

Lumpe, Lora (2002) 'US Foreign Military Training: Global Reach, Global Power, and Oversight Issues'. Albuquerque: Interhemispheric Resource Center and the Institute for Policy Studies.

Machiavelli, Niccolo (1998) *The Discourses*. London: Penguin.

Martin, Guy (1995) 'Continuity and Change in Franco-African Relations'. *Journal of Modern African Studies*, 33(1), 1–20.

Mazower, Mark (2009) *No Enchanted Palace: The End of Empire and the Ideological Origins of the United Nations*. Princeton: Princeton University Press.

McClintock, Michael (1992) *Instruments of Statecraft*. New York: Pantheon Books.

Menezes, S. L. (1999) *Fidelity and Honour: The Indian Army from the Seventeenth to the Twenty-first Century*. New Delhi: Oxford University Press.

Neuman, Stephanie (1986) *Military Assistance in Recent Wars*. New York: Praeger.

Percy, Sarah (2007) *Mercenaries*. Oxford: Oxford University Press.

Perry, F. W. (1988) *The Commonwealth Armies: Manpower and Organisation in Two World Wars*. Manchester: Manchester University Press.

Posen, Barry (1993) 'Nationalism, the Mass Army, and Military Power'. *International Security*, 18(2), 80–124.

Prados, John (1996) *Presidents' Secret Wars: CIA and Pentagon Covert Operations from World War II through the Persian Gulf*. Chicago: Elephant.

Sassen, Saskia (2006) *Territory, Authority, Rights: From Medieval to Global Assemblages*. Princeton: Princeton University Press.

Scott, Andrew (1982) *The Revolution in Statecraft*. Durham: Duke University Press.

Singer, P. W. (2003) *Corporate Warriors*. Ithaca: Cornell University Press.

Spector, Ronald (1985) *Advice and Support*. New York: Free Press.

Stoker, Donald (ed.) (2008) *Military Advising and Assistance*. Abingdon: Routledge.

Waltz, Kenneth (1979) *Theory of International Politics*. New York: McGraw-Hill.

Weber, Max (1978) *Economy and Society*. Berkeley: University of California Press.

Wendt, Alexander (1999) *Social Theory of International Politics*. Cambridge: Cambridge University Press.

3 | The second British Empire and the re-emergence of global finance

RONEN PALAN

The British Empire was a remarkable empire for many good reasons. First, it belonged to that very rare club of empires, which included as far as I can tell only two (the Spanish 'empire') over which the sun never set. Indeed, at its peak, the British Empire was the largest formal empire the world had ever known. True to size, the British Empire extended its power and influence in the nineteenth century over a very large tract of lands mostly in Latin and Central America which was formally sovereign but colloquially known as the 'informal empire'. Second, considering its size and wealth, the rapid and generally speaking orderly collapse of the British Empire after World War II was even more remarkable. By the 1980s, the largest empire the world has ever seen shrank down to contain just remnants and debris, including the United Kingdom, three adjacent Crown territories – Jersey, Guernsey and the Isle of Man – and fifteen dependent territories – since 2002 called 'overseas territories'– which include some small Caribbean islands, the Falkland Islands and Gibraltar. Collectively these overseas territories encompass a population of approximately 260,000 people and a land area of 1.7 million square kilometres, the vast majority of which constitutes the British Antarctic Territory.

A third remarkable fact about the British Empire is that while it disappeared completely from most contemporary maps of the world, it remains very much alive in one crucial map: the map of contemporary international finance. Indeed, the contemporary map of international financial markets is configured principally around two poles. One pole has a distinct British Imperial flavour. It consists, first and foremost, of the City of London and includes, in addition, the British Crown dependencies of Jersey, Guernsey and the Isle of Man, as well as British overseas territories of which the most significant are the Cayman Islands, Bermuda, British Virgin Islands, Turks and Caicos and Gibraltar, and recently independent British colonies and protectorates such as Hong Kong, Singapore, the Bahamas, Cyprus, Bahrain and Dubai.[1] This British imperial pole accounted for 39.9 per cent of all outstanding international loans and 37.3 per cent of all outstanding international deposits by March 2009 (see Table 3.2). The other pole consists of a string of mid-sized European states known uniquely for their welfare provisions as well as for serving as tax havens. This pole includes the Benelux countries – Belgium, Netherlands and Luxembourg – Ireland, Switzerland and Austria. This pole accounted for 17.3 per cent of all outstanding international loans by March 2009 and 19.4 per cent of all outstanding international deposits by March 2009.[2] Combined, the two poles account for approximately 57 per cent of all international banking assets and liabilities by March 2009. The USA, in contrast, during the same period accounted for 12.4 per cent and 12.9 per cent of all outstanding international loans and deposits respectively, and Japan for 4.5 per cent and 3.8 per cent.[3]

The unusual geo-political configuration of the international financial market has so far attracted little scholarly attention, for reasons that are difficult to fathom.[4] This is despite the fact that the Cayman Islands,

[1] This pole includes in addition Bermuda, which is the largest captive insurance centre in the world, but contains a relatively small banking centre, and the more numerous, but less significant in terms of impact, former British colonies in the Pacific. For discussion of Bermuda's financial centre see Crombie, 2008. On Pacific offshore centres and their relationship to the UK see Sharman and Mistry 2008.

[2] A survey of the eleven best known and most authoritative lists of tax havens of the world found that Switzerland is considered as a tax haven by nine of them, Luxembourg and Ireland by eight, the Netherlands by two, Belgium by one and Austria was considered a tax haven until it repealed its stringent bank secrecy law in 2001 under enormous pressure from the European Union. Nevertheless, Austria is included in this list because its financial centre grew primarily during the years it served as a tax haven. Switzerland and Liechtenstein share a customs union as well as strong political links. Observers tend to treat the two countries as a linked financial centre; see Kuentzler 2007 for discussion.

[3] The figures are for all international loans and deposits, which are the figures used commonly for ranking international financial centres. See discussion in following section. Aggregate figures for loans and deposits in financial centres, which include domestic and international loans and deposits, show a very different picture. According to the McKinsey report the leading centres in terms of aggregate bank deposits in 2008 were the emerging economies with US$ 14.3 trillion, followed by the Eurozone with US$ 13.1 trillion and the USA $12.5 trillion and Japan US$ 11.5 trillion. The McKinsey report does not even devote a separate entry for the UK which is classified as one among 'other mature economies'. See Roxborough *et al.* 2009.

[4] The literature on international financial centres typically considers only the UK, USA, Japan, Switzerland, Germany, France and sometimes the Cayman Islands

for instance, ranks consistently among the largest international financial centres since the Bank of International Settlements (BIS) began to produce locational statistics on international lending and deposit taking in 1982, and ever since, the small islands of Jersey and Guernsey have never been too far behind. One possible explanation for the lacunae is that the BIS tends to treat British Crown dependencies as well as British overseas territories as independent jurisdictions separate from the UK, which they are not, and hence underplays the British link.[5]

In this chapter I discuss the exceptional case of the emergence of this 'second' British financial empire out of the ashes of the first. I begin with a broad discussion of the development of financial centres, followed by an explanation of how the legacy of the British Empire survived in modern finance.

among the leading financial centres. See, for instance, Goetz 2007 and Yeandle *et al.* 2005. For an historical analysis of the emergence of the British imperial network of financial centres see Palan 2009.

[5] The relationship between the British state and its various dependencies is complex, fluid and appears to have evolved on the basis of tacit understandings between the two sides. Yet, none of them possess anything approaching full sovereignty. Indeed, reports in the British press suggest that the UK may have to bail out a number of these tax havens. Jersey, Guernsey and the Isle of Man are Crown dependencies. They are possessions of the British Crown and, strictly speaking, are not part of the UK or the EU. Executive power in the three Crown Dependencies is exercised by the representatives of the British Crown, and hence primarily through the British Home Office. The relationship between the islands and the British state has evolved over time and the islands today possess greater autonomy – although that trend may have gone into reverse during the current financial crisis. Le Hérissier 1998 describes the relationship between the British state and the Channel Islands as pragmatic, with the UK exercising prudence. In financial matters, however, the British Treasury exercises far greater control over the islands than is normally admitted. For discussion see also Mitchell and Sikka 2002; Hampton and Christensen 1999. In addition, the UK retains responsibilities for fourteen overseas territories, 11 of which are permanently populated and remain under British sovereignty. The territories are not constitutionally part of the UK, but the UK government maintains responsibilities towards them, and the Foreign and Commonwealth Office is the department mainly responsible for dealing with them. Among these Overseas Territories, the Cayman Islands, Bermuda and British Virgin Islands have emerged as very significant OFCs, while Turks, Caicos and Gibraltar are medium-sized centres and Anguilla, Montserrat and Pitcairn Islands possess insignificant offshore financial centres. See NAO 2007 for detail. During and after the G-20 meeting in London, April 2008, the UK government has acknowledged its responsibilities for regulation of these OFCs.

Theories of international financial centres

Over the past three decades the concept of the international finance centre has been going in and out of fashion, but still remains highly contested. Predictably, conceptual debates in this area have tended to spill over into empirical arguments about the measurement and ranking of financial centres and vice versa. One popular methodology of ranking financial centres is based on the headquarters count formula. The theory is that banks and other financial institutions are likely to locate their headquarters near where the action is, and hence, headquarter location is indicative of the importance of a financial centre (Gehrig 2000; Choi, Park and Tschoegl 1996). The headquarter formula was particularly popular before the Bank of International Settlements introduced locational data in the second quarter of 1982. The data first alerted observers to the importance of offshore financial centres, in particular the Cayman Islands, and has been used ever since as the principal source of data for measuring and ranking international financial centres.

Table 3.1 is based on BIS locational statistics as of March 2009. In addition to the unassailable position of London, the table shows that the Cayman Islands, which were in fifth position in 2006, were ranked fourth by 2009. The table also shows the importance of other tax havens such as Jersey, Guernsey and the Bahamas as international financial centres.

Table 3.2 regroups Table 3.1 on a thematic basis. The exercise reveals a number of interesting trends that are obscured by the conventional method of ranking financial centres. The most obvious among them is the role played by the UK's financial centre in international finance. The UK consists of the famous Square Mile (the City of London), Canary Wharf, Mayfair and the Home Counties, as well as subsidiary financial centres located in the British Isles, such as Edinburgh and Manchester (Yeandle *et al.* 2005). UK figures exclude British overseas territories which, according to all available reports, are still closely linked to the City of London. If we add jurisdictions that are under British control, then the British state accounts for 31 per cent of all outstanding international loans and 29.6 per cent of deposits in March 2009. With the addition of former colonies such as Singapore, Hong Kong and the Bahamas, the share of British imperial jurisdictions rises to 39.9 per cent and 37.3 per cent respectively.

Table 3.1 *Top 20 international financial centres, 2010*

	Reporting countries	External loans (amount outstanding)	% share of total	Considered tax haven
1	UK	4,417.2	20.5	X
2	US	3,274.2	15.2	X
3	Germany	2,965.9	13.8	X
4	Cayman Islands	1,554.7	7.2	Y
5	France	1,434.4	6.6	X
6	Japan	867.5	4.0	X
7	Netherlands	825.2	3.8	Y
8	Switzerland	780.8	3.6	Y
9	Singapore	702.2	3.2	Y
10	Luxembourg	567.3	2.6	Y
11	Belgium	514.2	2.4	Y
12	Hong Kong SAR	497.0	2.3	Y
13	Ireland	464.3	2.2	Y
14	Bahamas	467.3	2.2	Y
15	Canada	386.2	1.8	X
16	Austria	311.8	1.5	X
17	Spain	309.3	1.5	X
18	Jersey	287.4	1.3	Y
19	Italy	239.4	1.1	X
20	Sweden	224.8	1.0	X
	All countries	21,497.0		

X = not considered tax haven
Y = considered a tax haven
External loans of banks in all currencies vis-à-vis all sectors
In individual reporting countries, in billions of US dollars, March 2010

Table 3.2 contains a significant amount of double counting. I submit, however, it offers a more accurate and honest depiction of the character of the international financial market than Table 3.1. Table 3.2 reveals the overwhelming significance of what I call the Second British Empire in shaping international financial activities. It also reveals, more generally, that the international financial market – the market that is

Table 3.2 *Aggregative list of top international financial centres, 2010*

IFCs networks	External loans (amounts outstanding)	Share of total (%)
British Empire + European tax havens[1]	11,354.0	52.8
British Empire[2]	8,203.0	38.1
UK, Crown dependencies and overseas territories[3]	6,476.0	30.1
US	3,274.2	15.2
European havens[4]	3,151.0	14.6
All countries	21,497.0	

External loans of banks in all currencies vis-à-vis all sectors
[1] City of London, Jersey, Guernsey, Isle of Man, Cayman Islands, Bermuda, British Virgin Islands, Hong Kong, Bahamas, Bahrain, Cyprus, Benelux countries, Ireland and Switzerland
[2] City of London, Jersey, Guernsey, Isle of Man, Cayman Islands, Bermuda, British Virgin Islands, Hong Kong, Jersey, Bahamas, Bahrain and Cyprus
[3] City of London, Jersey, Guernsey, Isle of Man, Cayman Islands, Bermuda, British Virgin Islands
[4] Benelux countries, Ireland and Switzerland

supposed to be the most advanced, sophisticated and modern – exhibits a preference for small and often somewhat anachronistic polities including the British Empire and its remnants, city states, or European dukedoms and monarchies. Existing theories provide little explanation for this. Why is that?

The modern study of international financial centres may legitimately be considered to have originated with the publication of Charles Kindleberger's seminal study, *The Formation of Financial Centers* (1974). Kindleberger represents large financial centres as a variant of the Marshallian district theory. According to the theory, large financial centres such as London or Amsterdam, and in the twentieth century, New York and Tokyo, develop organically around the major trading centres. In time, the agglomeration of know-how and skills presents centres with an unassailable competitive advantage. Nonetheless, in increasingly internationalized financial markets, other centres can develop if their governments are prepared to offer alternative methods of cost reduction, including liberalized regimes of regulation and taxation. Kindleberger explains, therefore, the development and the geographical spread of international financial centres in terms of a trade-off between two competing tendencies: market efficiencies and scale economies, on the one hand, and geographical and informational and discriminatory business practices on the other.

By the early 1980s, Y. S. Park observed the growth of new types of financial centres developing in conjunction with the traditional centres. Park identified four types of international financial centres which he described as: (i) 'primary centres', such as London or New York; (ii) 'booking centres', such as the Bahamas or the Cayman Islands, specializing as 'registration havens' for Euromarket transactions (Park 1982); (iii) 'funding centres', such as Singapore or Panama, that tend to channel Euromarket funds into regional financial centres; and (iv) 'collection centres', such as Bahrain that are engaged primarily in channelling regional funds into the Euromarket.

A less elegant, if somewhat more popular theory suggests that OFCs are still primarily 'booking centres', and serve merely as conduits for transactions that are conceived and organized elsewhere.[6] This may explain why the literature on international financial centres has opted, by and large, to ignore the OFC phenomenon, on the grounds that they represent little in terms of genuine banking or capital market activity.

---

[6] Thirty years on, there is still a debate whether leading OFCs such as the Cayman Islands, or Jersey have developed genuine financial centres or remain largely booking centres. Many OFCs maintain that they have matured into fully functioning financial centres, yet available data does not lend support to their claims. The Cayman Islands' assets and liabilities are roughly one third of the UK financial centre's (Table 3.1). Yet while the Corporation of the City of London reports 338,000 people working directly in the Square Mile, the UK's National Audit Office reports that only 5,400 people work in the Cayman OFC. The disparity between the two figures suggests that either the Cayman Islands is exceedingly efficient, or it is still largely a booking centre with relatively little 'real' banking activity; see NAO 2007. The US General Accounting Office's study into the activities of the largest legal firm on the Cayman Islands, Maples and Calder was made famous by Barack Obama's remark: 'You've got a building in the Cayman Islands that supposedly houses 12,000 corporations. That's either the biggest building or the biggest tax scam on record.' Obama may have given an underestimate. GAO reports that 'the sole occupant of Ugland House is Maples and Calder, a law firm and company-services provider that serves as registered office for 18,857 entities it created as of March 2008' (GAO 2008, 2). GAO concluded that at least 96 per cent of these were effectively of the 'brass plate' type of virtual entities. In the Netherlands, one building in Amsterdam serves as registered office for 18,857 entities as of March 2008. See also Lewis and Davis 1987.

The view is mirrored by a considerable and growing literature on tax havens, which on the whole, has ignored their role and function in the financial system.

Until recently, theories of international financial centres were predicated on the assumption that financial centres are in competition with each other. But from the late 1950s, the focus of banking shifted from retail to wholesale activity (Lewis and Davis 1987), and subsequently from intermediation to risk trading, so the relationship between financial centres became more complex and competition was supplemented by cooperation. A study commissioned by the Bank of England has demonstrated that many OFCs were oriented in their business model to serve London and New York's banking community (Dixon 2001). Similarly, a BIS study acknowledges the increasingly cooperative nature of modern international finance, arguing that the large international financial centres serve nowadays as global hubs of financial activities.

None of the above offers an explanation for the geo-political character of the international financial system as shown in Table 3.2. Aggregative measures and the use of techniques such as regression analysis or even more sophisticated statistical techniques in the economist toolkit so far provide, at best, a fuzzy picture. Nevertheless, the consensus appears to be that the traditional model of financial centres as agglomerations of banking and financial activities serving the needs of an economy has been supplanted by a model of financial centres serving one another. Since such behaviour does not conform to an idealized notion of the efficiency and utility of financial markets, an explanation for such behaviour must be sought elsewhere, in externalities such as regulatory competition or geographical location, which is where political economic theories come into the picture.

An alternative theory for the rise of the British pole in the international financial markets is based on a different interpretation of the techniques of construction of geo-political alliances that stresses not universal economic logic, but rather the parochial technique of institutional constructions that are often driven by opportunistic cost/benefit analysis. According to this perspective, actors encounter the world largely as a set of opportunities, penalties and rewards. They seek to take advantage of opportunities that open to them, and yet avoid penalties in doing so. A bloated financial centre in the City of London, that was traditionally politically powerful, was left behind by a rapidly collapsing trading empire. The City contained many competing financial institutions, including banks, insurance companies, accounting and legal companies, left stranded without the geo-political umbrella that the British Empire offered them. They were desperately searching for new business opportunities, and when one of those opportunities was discovered – almost by mistake in 1957 with the emergence of the Euromarkets – then like a pack of hyenas, they all poured into the new markets. They soon learned that as British law was applicable in the remnants of the Empire in the Caribbean (and indeed the Pacific islands, although these islands never developed into significant tax havens) they could introduce Euromarket operations in these localized communities. City financiers developed these remnants into a second British Empire, not because of a sense of patriotism or even having some grand strategic perspective. Rather, they developed these territories as financial–colonial outposts for two related reasons. First, although the City of London was largely unregulated, it was still taxed, and heavily so; Crown and overseas territories offered great opportunities for avoiding British tax while taking advantage of the British lack of regulation (known euphemistically as 'self-regulation'). Second, as befitting financial actors that evolved in an empire where the sun never set, the remnants of the Empire in the Caribbean, Asia and the Pacific offered logistical advantages in terms of sharing time zones with other crucial trading centres in the USA and Asia. Thus, the City of London could become, through the British colonial outposts, a 24-hour integrated financial centre present everywhere in the world.

The rise of the Euromarket

These opportunistic sets of considerations are borne out by the history of the modern international financial system. It appears that the significant spark, or the historical institutional disturbance, that began the process of differentiation among financial centres took place in the late 1950s in London, in what Philip Cogan described as 'probably the single most important development in the international financial markets since the Second World War', namely, the Euromarket (Cogan 2002: 102).

Despite its importance, a great deal of confusion surrounds the Euromarket, or as it used to be called, the Euro-dollar market. Some very distinguished economists believe that the Euromarket is any wholesale financial market, or an inter-bank market, trading in non-resident denominated currencies and assets. According to this view, the Euromarket evolved as a system trading in US dollars in European markets and took off on the European continent in the mid 1950s (Schenk 1998; Bryant 1983). In time, the Euromarket has come to denote any market trading in non-resident 'hard' currencies, such as pounds sterling, the yen, the Swiss franc, the Deutsche Mark and the euro.

There is a different theory, however, suggesting that the Euromarket is a very specific type of market that emerged in late 1957 in London, ironically, for reasons that are directly linked to the collapsing empire (Burn 2005). Faced with mounting speculation against the pound after the Suez crisis, the British government imposed strict restrictions on the use of sterling in trade credits with non-residents. But many City banks, primarily commercial banks, which had evolved over more than a century as specialists in international lending particularly to British imperial outposts and the so-called British informal empire in Latin America, saw their core business disappear overnight. They responded by using US dollars in their international dealings, arguing to a receptive Bank of England (whose deputy, John Bolton, was a banker who only a few years before had headed one of the successful commercial banks specializing in central American trade) that such transactions had no bearing on UK balance of payment issues. At this point, the precise policy and legal steps that gave rise to the Euromarket become somewhat vague. It appears that the Bank of England decided without consulting the Treasury that it would not intervene in transactions between non-residents and in a foreign currency, at that time the US dollar but subsequently other currencies entered the same pool. These sorts of transactions were interpreted then in the context of the English common law to imply that the Bank accounted for certain types of financial transactions between non-resident parties undertaken in foreign currency as if they did not take place in the UK. As these transactions were taking place in London, they could not be regulated by any other regulatory authority and ended therefore in a regulatory vacuum, which is called the Euromarket, or the offshore financial market (Burn 2005; Altman 1969; Hanzawa 1991).

The Euromarket was therefore an opportunistic development that emerged to sort out a specific problem that City banks were facing. Because it was not a planned policy outcome, it remained small and practically unknown for about three or four years. However, by the early 1960s, US banks, hemmed in by series of New Deal financial legislations, discovered the opportunities that London offered them to escape their own financial regulations, and began to set up branches in London specializing in Euromarket operations. It soon became clear that the market could be employed not only to circumvent the Treasury's decision of 1956, but also, crucially, to circumvent the very strict capital control regulations that were imposed under the Bretton Woods regime. In addition, American banks flocked to the market where they could avoid Regulation Q, which was introduced in the 1930s. Regulation Q placed an interest rate ceiling on time deposits in US banks.[7] It kept bank interest rates on time deposits very low, a situation that met with little objection from the banks for a long time, but as the world economy began to flourish in the late 1950s, American banks found themselves at a disadvantage.

By the early 1960s, the flow of money to the Euromarket became a veritable flood. Then crucially, in 1963 the Kennedy administration proposed a tax that achieved exactly the opposite of what it intended. It introduced the Interest Equalization Tax, a 15 per cent tax on interest received from investments in foreign bonds, in order to make investment in such bonds unattractive to US investors. The tax was supposed to stem the flow of capital out of the United States. In practice, American corporations refused to repatriate capital, to avoid paying the interest equalization tax, and in the process fuelled the growth of the Euromarket.

The Euromarket and the Channel Islands

London was able to reduce one crucial fixed cost dimension of trading in incorporeal assets, namely, regulation. London seized, in effect, the initiative in the development of the international financial markets, to which other states had to respond. That the initiative lay with London, or rather with London-based actors, can be seen very clearly in

---

[7] Regulation Q prohibits member banks from paying interest on demand deposits. See Electronic Code of Federal Regulations (e-CFR). The National Recovery Administration, which was set up under the New Deal, sought to fix prices in industry in order to eliminate 'ruinous' competition, and Regulation Q attempted to do the same thing in the banking sector.

subsequent developments. Contrary to popular perception, the US Treasury initially objected to the rise of the unregulated market in London and put forward proposals for a new regulatory framework (Kapstein 1994). Failing that, and with the active encouragement of the New York banking community, particularly Citibank and Chase, the US Treasury came to the conclusion that rather than fight the onset of an unregulated market, the USA stood to gain by encouraging a domestic variant of the offshore market. A swift volte-face took place, culminating in the establishment on 3 December 1981 of the New York offshore market, the New York International Banking Facilities (IBF), which is a more restricted type of London offshore. The IBFs were set up as a defensive measure representing 'an attempt by U.S. government regulators to "internalize" the Euromarkets into the U.S. banking system. Japan then followed suit in 1986 by establishing its own IBF, the Japanese Offshore Market (JOM)' (Moffett and Stonehill 1989, 93; see also Hanzawa 1991).

London's however, was by then already in the lead. The success of London was built around two pillars of strength: concentration of professionals with the necessary technical know-how, and the rise of the Euromarket in the early 1960s. Combined, these two pillars propelled the City of London into the position of the world's premier international financial centre. London had, however, some disadvantages. First and foremost among them was that while the market was largely unregulated or 'offshore', banks were subject to corporate taxation. Furthermore, British banks and corporations, as opposed to foreign banks, were paradoxically at a disadvantage vis-à-vis foreign institutions because they could not pose as non-residents for taxation purposes, whereas American banks could take advantage of transfer pricing to ensure low taxation. In addition, as the market grew in size, the cost of conducting business in London became an issue as well.

For all or any of these reasons, and since London had in effect emerged as a large and flourishing OFC, or a conduit through which bankers – increasingly of American, Japanese and German origins – had learned to register financial transactions to avoid various regulations, the idea of using other, closely related jurisdictions sharing British law and regulations but with the added advantage of low taxation seemed logical. At this juncture it appears that the expansion of the Euromarket throughout the globe followed three time-honoured institutional precepts:

1. The process was driven from the centre, by London's and New York's financial, legal and accounting firms searching for alternative low-tax locations to 'book' transactions in order to obtain tax savings.
2. In their quest for alternative locations, these financial operators appear to have followed a clear geographical path, beginning from those islands nearest to the UK mainland, namely, the Channel Islands, soon followed by the British-held Caribbean jurisdictions, then Asia and lastly British-held Pacific islands. The process took about ten years to complete.
3. In expanding operations internationally, London institutions appear to have sought the path of least resistance, selecting British imperial polities that broadly resembled the City of London's unique political structure. As a result, the Euromarket developed in typically quasi-feudal polities such as the Channel Islands, and other small British dependencies. This resulted in a network of British-dominated financial centres with close links between them.

Institutional affinities and the development of the Euromarket

The remaining bits of empire offered other advantages, including institutional affinities. The City of London is a unique political entity, described invariably as quasi-feudal or quasi-democratic. It is noteworthy that the City shares many attributes with other remnants of the British Empire, such as the Channel Islands, the Caribbean British possessions, Hong Kong (until 1997) or British Pacific Islands. The City of London describes itself rather modestly as the oldest local authority in England. It is a local authority within the Square Mile, and is responsible for services such as housing, refuse collection, education, social services, environmental and health but also much, much more. The Corporation of London, in fact, oversees its own police force, and also runs two of London's best loved parks, Epping Forest and Hampstead Heath, which are not within the Square Mile. Most importantly, the voting structure in the City is dominated by what is called non-residential business vote. The City of London Corporation was not reformed, like other UK municipalities, by the Municipal Corporation Act of 1835. As a result, eligible voters in the borough are either residents who are 18 years old and citizens of the UK, the Commonwealth or the EU, or – and this is where the difference with other boroughs comes to light – are sole traders or partners in an unlimited partnership or appointees of qualifying bodies. Each body or organization, whether incorporated or unincorporated, with premises in the City may appoint a number of voters based on the number of workers it employs. As a result qualified voters can vote twice, while residents of the City can vote only once. Consequently, for all intents and purposes, the City of London is run more like a guild in the control of the financial and business interests resident in the Square Mile.

The City elects a Lord Mayor, who plays a significant diplomatic role negotiating both with the British state and overseas heads of state, and is supported by a committee of Aldermen, nearly all of whom are representatives of financial, legal and accounting firms located in the City. The Lord Mayor, the committee of Aldermen and the entire political structure of the City unashamedly are the representatives of corporate financial interests.

The spillover from London to other centres began in early 1960s and followed what appears to be a quest for institutional affinities in other centres. Hence the spillover began most naturally with British jurisdictions adjacent to the UK, sharing British law, and whose political and institutional organizations shared many of the unique political attributes of the City. The Island of Jersey was the first to develop as a Euromarket outpost, and is a typical case in point.

Jersey seemed an obvious starting point for the expansion of City Euromarket operations: it shared the UK common law, was protected under the UK's security umbrella and used the British pound. Labour and real estate costs were much lower than London's at the time, although the situation has changed dramatically since then, not least because of the success of Jersey as an offshore financial centre. Jersey was also known since the 1930s as a tax haven for UK tax exiles. Mark Hampton demonstrates very clearly that 'the emerging offshore centre [in Jersey] was driven by international financial capital, merchant banks, which set up in the island to service certain wealthy customers' (Hampton 2007: 4). London banks took the lead and began to set up subsidiaries in Jersey, Guernsey and the Isle of Man in the early 1960s. By 1964, the three big American banks – Citibank, Chase Manhattan and the Bank of America – arrived on the scene as well (Toniolo 2005: 454).

The Channel Islands proved attractive, in addition, not least due to their unique semi-feudal type of politics, more akin to the politics of the Corporation of London than to modern democracy. Austin Mitchell and Prem Sikka described Jersey as a 'town government writ large, with all its intimacies and inefficiencies' (Mitchell and Sikka, 1999: 40). The island became a possession of the British Crown in 1204, the last of the French possessions retained by the British Crown. Executive authority resides with the Lieutenant Governor, who acts as the Crown's representative on the island. In reality, the Lieutenant Governor consults with the States of Jersey and both executive and legislative powers lie primarily with the States of Jersey. In that sense, it is largely autonomous.

Second and third wave expansion of the Euromarket

We also know from various reports that, faced with the high infrastructural costs of a London base, some of the smaller American and Canadian banks 'realized that the British Caribbean jurisdictions offered cheaper and equally attractive regulatory environment – free of exchange controls, reserve requirements and interest rate ceilings, and in the same time zone as New York' (Hudson 1998: 541). The Caribbean booking centres were not subject, crucially, to the Act of 1948. They were developed by the North American banking community to serve as conduits for Euromarket transactions.

The OFCs in question were British-held territories. The early spillover into territories such as the Bahamas and the Cayman Islands, suggests Sylla, 'was, like the London Euromarket, not motivated by tax advantages, but because it was cheaper to set up branches in these locations' (2002: 53). Bhattacharya also makes an argument based on costs. In 1980 'the average annual wages for a bookkeeper in the Bahamas are a meager $6,000, and the annual fee for an offshore banking (Category "B") license in the Cayman Islands is only $6,098.7. The total cost of operating a branch in these islands is much lower than in the primary centers of Eurocurrency operation' (1980, 37).

Three Caribbean centres, the Cayman Islands, the Bahamas and Bermuda benefited in particular from the rapid expansion of the Euromarket, while Bermuda chose a somewhat separate developmental path as the world's premier captive insurance centre. By the late 1970s, the Caribbean basin accounted for one fifth of the gross size of total Eurocurrency operations. By the 1980s, US bank branches in the Caribbean comprised more than one-third of the assets of all US foreign bank branches in the American region. Yet both Panama and the Bahamas have declined since, while the Cayman Islands forged ahead. The reasons are very obviously the British link (Bhattacharya 1980, 37). The Bahamas opted for independence and was tainted by political scandal and began its decline.

The theory of social and political affinities may help explain the development of the Asian OFCs with strong British links as well. As the widening Indochina war in the mid-1960s increased foreign exchange expenditure in the region, a tightening of credit occurred in 1967 and 1968, contributing to rising interest rates in the Eurodollar market. Tapping existing dollar balances in the Asia-Pacific region became attractive for many banks. The Bank of America was the first to hit on the idea of setting up a specialized facility for Eurodollar operations in East Asia.

Initially the Bank of America approached the one jurisdiction that shared many of the characteristics described above, namely, Hong Kong. The Hong Kong colonial government, however, was not particularly forthcoming. It had placed restrictions on the financial sector as far back as the early 1950s.

Having failed to persuade the Hong Kong government, the Bank of America turned to the next available jurisdiction that shared many of the above characteristics. This time an ex-British colony, Singapore, proved far more accommodating. Singapore responded in 1968 by setting up facilities, called the Asian Currency Unit (ACU), that provided incentives for branches of international banks to relocate to Singapore. Singapore licensed the first branch of the Bank of America to set up a special international department to handle transactions for non-residents. As with all other Euromarket operations, the ACU created a separate set of accounts in which all transactions with non-residents are recorded. Although the ACU was not subject to exchange controls, banks were required to submit to the exchange control authority detailed monthly reports of their transactions. In that sense, the ACU is a more restricted type of an offshore financial centre.

The moratorium on the establishment of new banks in Hong Kong was lifted in 1978 and proved a great success. In February 1982, the interest withholding tax on foreign currency deposits was abolished. In

1989, all forms of tax on interest were abolished. With the government becoming more proactive, by 1995–96, Hong Kong had quickly become the second largest OFC in the Asia-Pacific region, and between the sixth and seventh largest IFC in the world (Jao 1979).

Conclusion

The 'second' British Empire emerged partly as an accident of history, and partly because of the traditional role of the City in the first empire. Once an unregulated financial market developed in London, it became clear that trading through the small remnants of the empire gave London a distinct advantage. The UK was never too keen on making political capital out of these developments, maintaining a relatively low profile in the international arena but always insisting on maintaining London's system of financial self-regulation.

Whether intentionally or not, the City of London went about dispersing its assets among closely linked offshore financial centres, largely in order to achieve what is nowadays euphemistically described as 'tax neutrality', but in the process it also diffused somewhat the perception of power accumulating in London. This has resulted in British-centred networks specializing in trading in incorporeal assets that together have quietly shaped and defined the international financial market. That the Euromarket proved to be the most significant development in international finance in the post-war period is well known and accepted among scholars on the two sides of the Atlantic, yet the link between these developments and theories of state structural power and hegemony are somehow missing. Many scholars still believe that the USA was the key agent driving the trend towards international financial deregulation, which is clearly not the case.

References

Albert, Michel (1993) *Capitalism Against Capitalism*. London: Whurr.

Altman, Oscar L. (1969) 'Eurodollars'. In Eric B. Chalmers (ed.) *Reading in the Euro-Dollar*. London: W. P. Griffith, 33–55.

Arrow, Kenneth J. (1962) 'The Economic Implications of Learning by Doing'. *Review of Economic Studies*, 29, 155–73.

Axelrod, Robert (1984) *The Evolution of Cooperation*. New York: Basic Books.

Baldacchino, Godfrey (2006) 'Managing the Hinterland Beyond: Two Ideal-Type Strategies of Economic Development for Small Island Territories'. *Asia Pacific Viewpoint*, 47(1), 45–60.

Bazzoli, Laure (2000) 'Institutional Economics and the Specificity of Social Evolution: About the Contribution of J.R. Commons'. In M. Perlman and F. Louca (eds.) *Is Economics an Evolutionary Science?* Cheltenham: Edward Elgar, 64–82.

Bhattacharya, Anindyak (1980) 'Offshore Banking in the Caribbean'. *Journal of International Business Studies*, 11(3), 37–46.

Bianchi, Patrizio and Sandrine Labory (2004) 'The Political Economy of Intangible Assets'. In Patrizio Bianchi and Sandrine Labory (eds.) *The Economic Importance of Intangible Assets*. London: Ashgate, 1–26.

Brinkman, Richard L. and June E. Brinkman (2006) 'Cultural Lag: In the Tradition of Veblenian Economics'. *Journal of Economic Issues*, 40(4), 1009–28.

Bryant, Ralph C. (1989) 'The Evolution of Singapore as a Financial Centre'. In Kernial Singh Sandhu and Paul Wheatley (eds.) *Management of Success: The Moulding of Modern Singapore*. Singapore: Institute of Southeast Asian Studies.

Burn, Gary (2005) *Re-Emergence of Global Finance*. London: Palgrave.

Choi, S. R, D. Park and A. Tschoegl (1996) 'Banks and the World's Major Banking Centers, 1990'. *Review of World Economics*, 132(4), 774–93

Cogan, Philip (2002) *The Money Machine: How the City Works*, 5th edition. London: Penguin.

Commons, John R. (1959)[1924] *The Legal Foundations of Capitalism*. Madison: The University of Wisconsin Press.

(1961) *Institutional Economics*. Madison: University of Wisconsin Press.

Crombie, Roger (2008) 'Bermuda in-Depth Series, Part I: Lighting and Fire' *Risk and Insurance*, 1 January. Available at: http://www.thefreelibrary. com/Lighting+a+fire%3A+at+60,+Bermuda+rightly+deserves+a+place+in+the...-a0174008411

Dharmapala, Dhammika A. and James R. Hines (2006) 'Which Countries Become Tax Havens?' *NBER Working Paper* No. W12802.

Dijk, Michael Van, Francis Weyzig and Richard Murphy (2006) *The Netherlands: A Tax Haven?* Amsterdam: Somo.

Dixon, Liz (2001) 'Financial Flows Via Offshore Financial Centers'. *Financial Stability Review*, 10: 104–15.

Dumenil, Gerard and David Levy (2004) *Capital Resurgent*. Cambridge, MA: Harvard University Press.

ECOFIN (1999) *Code of Conduct: Business Taxation Council of The European Union*. Available at: http://ec.europa.eu/taxation_customs/resources/documents/primarolo_en.pdf

Financial Stability Forum (FSF) (2000) *Report of the Working Group on Offshore Centers*. Available at: www.fsformum.org/Reports/RepOFC. pdf.

Foster, A. and M. Rosenzweig (1995) 'Learning by Doing and Learning from Others: Human Capital and Technical Change in Agriculture'. *Journal of Political Economy*, 103, 1176–209.

Gehrig, Thomas (2000) 'Cities and the Geography of Financial Centres'. In Jean-Marie Huriot and Jacques-François Thisse (eds.) *Economies of Cities: Theoretical Perspectives*. Cambridge: Cambridge University Press, 415–45.

Goetz, Von Peter (2007) 'International Banking Centres: A Network Perspective'. *BIS Quarterly Review*, December, 33–49.

Goodfriend, Marvin (1998) 'Eurodollar'. In Timothy Q. Cook and Robert K. Laroche (eds.) *Instruments of Money Market*, 7th edition. Richmond: Federal Reserve Bank of Richmond, Virginia.

Government Accounting Office (GAO) (2008) '*Cayman Islands: Business and Tax Advantages Attract U.S. Persons and Enforcement Challenges Exist*'. Report to the Chairman and Ranking Member, Committee on Finance, US Senate.

Gowa, Joanne (1995) *Allies, Adversaries and International Trade*. Princeton: Princeton University Press.

Gowan, Peter (1999) *The Global Gamble: Washington's Faustian Bid for World Dominance*. London, Verso.

Guex, Sébastien (1998) *L'argent de l'état: Parcours des finances publiques au xxe siècle*. Lausanne: Réalités sociales.

Hall, John and Oliver Whybrow (2008) 'Continuity and Continuousness: The Chain of Ideas Linking Peirce's Synechism to Veblen's Cumulative Causation'. *Journal of Economic Issues*, 42(2), 350–54

Hampton, Mark (2007) 'Offshore Finance Centers and Rapid Complex Constant Change'. Kent Business School, Working Paper No. 132.

(1996) *The Offshore Interface: Tax Havens in the Global Economy*. Basingstoke: Macmillan.

Hampton, M. P and John Christensen (1999) 'A Legislature for Hire: the Capture of the State in Jersey's Offshore Finance Centre'. In M. P. Hampton and J. P. Abbott (eds.), *Offshore Finance Centres and Tax Havens: the Rise of Global Capital*. London: Macmillan.

Hazawa, Masamitsu (1991) 'The Tokyo Offshore Market'. In Masamitsu Hazawa (ed.), *Japan's Financial Markets*. Tokyo: Foundation for Advanced Information and Research,

Harvey, David (2007) *A Brief History of Neoliberalism*. Oxford: Oxford University Press.

Heyvaert, Werner (2006) 'ECJ Ruling Extends Belgian Coordination Center Regime'. *Tax Notes International*, 10 July, 105.

Hudson, Alan C. (1998) 'Reshaping the Regulatory Landscape: Border Skirmishes around the Bahamas and Cayman Offshore Financial Centers'. *RIPE*, 5(3), 534–64.

IFSL (2007) *International Financial Markets in the UK*. Available at: www. IFSL.org.uk/research

Jao, Y. C. (1979) 'The Rise of Hong Kong as a Financial Center'. *Asian Survey*, 19(7), 674–94.

Jin, Jim Y., Juan Perote-Pena and Michael Troege (2004) 'Learning by Doing, Spillovers and Shakeouts'. *Journal of Evolutionary Economics*, 14, 85–98.

Johns, R. A. and C. M. Le Marchant (1993) *Finance Centres: British Isle Offshore Development Since 1979*. London: Pinter Publishers.

Kapstein, Ethan B. (1994) *Governing the Global Economy: International Finance and the State*. Cambridge, MA: Harvard University Press.

Kindleberger, Charles (1974) *The Formation of Financial Centres: A Study in Comparative Economic History*. Princeton: Princeton University Press.

Konings, Martin (2008) 'The Institutional Foundations of US Structural Power in International Finance: From the Re-Emergence of Global Finance to the Monetarist Turn'. *RIPE*, 15(1), 35–61.

Kuenzler, Roman (2007) 'Les paradis fiscaux'. MA thesis, University of Geneva.

Le Hérissier, Roy (1998) 'Jersey: Exercising Executive Power in a Non-Party System'. *Public Administration and Development*, 18, 169–84.

Lewis Mervyn, K. and Kevin T. Davis (1987) *Domestic and International Banking*. Cambridge, MA: MIT Press.

Lipietz, Alain (1987) *Mirages and Miracles: The Crisis of Global Fordism*. London: Verso.

Low, L. (1998) *The Political Economy of a City-State: Government-made Singapore*. New York: Oxford University Press.

Marshall, Don D. (1996) 'Understanding Late-Twentieth-Century Capitalism'. *Government and Opposition*, 31, 193–214.

Mitchel, Austin and Prem Sikka (2002) 'Jersey: Auditors' Liabilities versus People's Rights'. *Political Quarterly*, 70: 3–15.

Moffett, Michael H. and Arthur Stonehill (1989) 'International Banking Facilities Revisited'. *Journal of International Financial Management and Accounting*, 1(1), 88–103.

Murray, G and A. Pereira (1996) *Singapore: The Global City-State*. Basingstoke: Palgrave Macmillan.

Mutti, John and Harry Grubert (2006) 'New Development in the Effects of Taxes on Royalties and the Migration of Intangible Assets Abroad'. *NBER/CRIW Conference on International Service Flows*, Washington, DC, 28 April. Available at: www.nber.org/books_in_progress/criws06/mutti-grubert8-4-06.pdf

National Audit Office NAO (2007), 'Managing Risk in the Overseas Territories'. Report by the Comptroller and Auditor General, HC 4 Session 2007–2008, 16 November. London: The Stationery Office.

Naylor, R. T. (1987) *Hot Money and the Politics of Debt*. London: Unwin Hyman.

Orren, Karren and Stephen Skowronek (2004) *The Search for American Political Development*. New York: Cambridge University Press.

Panitch, L. and S. Gindin (2005) 'Finance and American Empire'. In L. Panitch and C. Leys (eds.) *Socialist Register 2005*, London: Merlin, 46–81.

Papke, Leslie E. (2000) 'One-Way Treaty with the World: The US Witholding Tax and the Netherland Antilles'. *International Tax and Public Finance*, 7: 295–313.

Park, Y. S. (1982) 'The Economics of Offshore Financial Centers'. *Columbia Journal of World Business*, 17(4), 31–36.

Peillon, V. and A. Montebourg (2001) 'La Cité de Londres, Gibraltar et les Dépendances de la Couronne: des centres offshore, sanctuaires de l'argent sale'. *Rapport d'information de l'Assemblée nationale*, no. 2311.52/2001.

Preinreich, Gabriel (1936) 'The Law of Goodwill'. *The Accounting Review*, 11(4), 21–35.

Ragin, Charles (2000) *Redesigning Social Inquiry: Fuzzy Sets and Beyond*. Chicago and London: Chicago University Press.

Reed, H. C. (1981) *The Preeminence of International Financial Centers*. New York: Praeger Publishers.

Regini, Marino (2000) 'Between Deregulation and Social Pacts: The Responses of European Economies to Globalization'. *Politics & Society*, 28(5), 5–35.

Regnier, P. (1991) *Singapore: City-State in South-East Asia*. Honolulu: University of Hawaii Press.

Roberts, R. and D. Kynaston (2002) *City State: A Contemporary History of the City of London and how Money Triumphed*. London: Profile.

Roxburgh, Charles, Susan Lund, Charles Atkins, Stanislas Belot, Wayne W. Hu and Moira S. Pierce (2009) *Global Capital Markets: Entering a New Era*. McKinsey Global Institute. McKinsey & Co.

Ruggie, J. G. (1982) 'International Regimes, Transactions and Change: Embedded Liberalism in the Postwar Economic Order'. *International Organization*, 36, 397–415.

Schanble, H. (1991) 'Agenda-Diffusion and Innovation: A Simulation Model'. *Journal of Evolutionary Economics*, 1, 65–85.

Schelling, T. C. (1978) *Micromotives and Macrobehaviour*. New York: W. W. Norton.

Schenk, Cathrine R. (1998) 'The Origins of the Eurodollar Market in London 1955–63'. *Explorations in Economic History*, 21, 1–19.

Seabrooke, Leonard (2001) *US Power in International Finance: The Victor of Dividends*. New York: Palgrave.

Sharman, Jason and Percy S. Mistry (2008) *Considering the Consequences: The Development Implications of Initiatives on Taxation, Anti-Money Laundering and Combating the Financing of Terrorism*. London: Commonwealth Secretariat.

Spruyt, Hendrik (1994) *The Sovereign State and Its Competitors: An Analysis of Systems Change*. Princeton: Princeton University Press.

Steward, Jim (2005) 'Fiscal Incentives, Corporate Structure and Financial Aspects of Treasury Management'. *Accounting Forum*, 29, 271–88.

Stiglitz, Joseph (2002) 'The Roaring Nineties'. *The Atlantic Monthly*. October. Available at: http://www.theatlantic.com/past/docs/issues/2002/10/stiglitz.htm

Strange, Susan (1988) *States and Markets: An Introduction to International Political Economy*. New York: Basil Blackwell.

Swank, Duane (2006) 'Tax Policy in an Era of Internationalization: Explaining the Spread of Neoliberalism'. *International Organization*, 60, 847–82.

Sylla, Richard (2002) 'United States Banks and Europe: Strategy and Attitudes'. In Stefano Battilossi and Youssef Cassis (eds.) *European Banks and the American Challenge: Competition and Cooperation in International Banking under Bretton Woods*. Oxford: Oxford University Press.

Tesfatsion, Leigh (2001) 'Introduction to the Special Issue of Agent-Based Computational Economics'. *Journal of Economic Dynamics & Control*, 25, 281–93.

Thelen, Kathrin (1999) 'Historical Institutionalism in Comparative Politics'. *Annual Review of Political Science*, 2, 369–404.

Toniolo, Gianni (2005) *Central Bank Cooperation at the Bank for International Settlements, 1930–1973*. Cambridge: Cambridge University Press.

Tschoegl, Adrian E. (1989) 'The Benefits and Costs of Hosting Financial Centres'. In Yoon S. Park and M. Essayyad (eds.) *International Banking and Financial Centres*. Amsterdam: Kluwer, 175–87.

Van de Ven, Andrew (1993) 'The Institutional Theory of John R. Commons: A Review and Commentary'. *The Academy of Management Review*, 18(1), 139–52.

Veblen, Thorstein (1961) 'On the Nature of Capital'. Reprinted in Thorstein Veblen, *The Place of Science in Modern Civilization and Other Essays*. New York: Russell & Russell.

Wade, Robert and Frank Veneroso (1998) 'The Asian Crisis: The High Debt Model Versus The Wall Street–Treasury–IMF Complex'. *New Left Review*, 228, 3–24.

Warner, Philip J. (2004) *Luxembourg in International Tax Planning*. IBFD publication

Weichenrieder, Alfons (1996) 'Fighting International Tax Avoidance: The Case of Germany'. *Fiscal Studies*, 171, 37–58.

Yeandle, Mark, Michael Mainelli and Adrian Berendt (2005) *The Competitive Position of London as a Global Financial Centre*. London: Corporation of London. Available at: www.cityoflondon.gov.uk/economicresearch

4 | Imperial city states, national states and post-national spatialities

SANDRA HALPERIN

Changes in the nature of space – specifically, the 'deterritorialization' of national states and the yielding of national spaces to sub- and cross-national structures and flows – have been the subject of much recent research and writing. Analyses of these 'post-national spatialities', as they are conceived to be, are focusing increasingly on new 'global cities' and 'city regions' and on the assertion these are developing as the key structures of an emerging post-national order.[1]

These analyses usually converge around a number of common assumptions. First, they tend to assume that the modern national state is the culmination of the unilinear development of a particular historical sequence of forms in which each form, including the national form, supplanted or displaced the logics and practices associated with previous ones. Second, and following from this, they assume that recent changes represent the beginning of a further move along that trajectory and transition to a new, historically unprecedented, form of state.

These assumptions form the basis of Saskia Sassen's influential analyses of 'global cities'. Sassen argues that today's global cities are different from the cities through which global trade was organized in the past because they were 'produced in a context where most territory is encased in a thick and highly formalized national framework marked by the exclusive authority of the national state' (2003: 5). She argues that these 'global cities' – these 'command points in the organization of the world economy' (1994: 4) – are deploying capabilities once associated with nation states for new purposes.

Sassen associates the 'national' with Keynesian policies aimed at strengthening the 'national' economy, increasing the 'national' consumption capacity and raising the educational level of 'national'

---

[1] See especially Sassen 2007, 1997 and 1994; Yeoh 1999; Taylor 2003; Pries 2001; Hoogvelt 1997; Hannerz 1996; Castells 1996; and Arrighi 1994. On 'global city-regions', see Brenner 2004, 1998.

workforces (2003: 8–9). Other scholars, as for example Neil Brenner, also associate fully realized national states with the adoption of Keynesian policies. Thus, Brenner associates the emergence of *post-*national structures, what he calls 'world cities', with the introduction in Western Europe of *post-*Keynesian spatial policies beginning in the early 1980s (Brenner 2004).

The assumption that national states were only fully consolidated during the Keynesian era is, in my view, correct. But here, the assumption of a unilinear developmental trajectory, from the pre-national through the national to the post-national, ceases to be convincing. Why should we assume that the world cities that emerged within recently consolidated and ultimately short-lived nation states are different from those that existed in the recent, *pre-*national past? In fact, most global cities are in the Third World where Keynesian policies were not adopted and the development of the 'national' has been partial. These world cities there are associated with *pre-*national spatialities. This suggests that the post-national structures and spatialities that are the focus of so much recent interest do not represent new structures and spatialities, but only ones that were briefly submerged as a result of Keynesian/national policies in First World countries and are now re-surfacing, is a proposition worth considering. Then there are previous world cities, like Singapore and Hong Kong, that are tremendously successful and seen as having 'a head start on other "global cities"' (Olds and Yeung 2004: 508). These world cities were neither incorporated within, nor did they become, national states. Instead, they became city states – a form of state supposedly that had been superseded by the national form. This suggests, again, that today's world cities are not new structures, but are only newly resurfacing in Western European and other First World countries.

The notion of change as unilinear leads to the assumption that forms of state are wholly and permanently displaced or destroyed by the emergence of new forms; that national states, the successor states of empires, city states and former colonies represent a wholly new form of state; and that post-national/post-Keynesian structures (global cities and city regions) represent the emergence of another new form. The assumption of unilinear change neglect leads us to consider whether a given change represents the *re-*emergence or renewed salience of *pre-existing* phenomena, rather than the emergence of something fundamentally new.

Figure 4.1 Changes in the nature of space: I

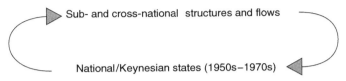

Figure 4.2 Changes in the nature of space: II

To sum up, the assumption of much recent research and writing is that post-Keynesian policies and 'national' spatialities are generating structures that are fundamentally new. Changes in the nature of space over time, according to this view, are represented in Figure 4.1.

This chapter explores the extent to which cultural, political, military and economic dimensions of *pre*-national structures are constitutive of the supposedly *post*-national structures currently emerging. The premise to be explored, in contrast to the scheme shown in Figure 4.1, is represented in Figure 4.2.

The following sections argue that pre-national forms of state were not displaced or supplanted by a new, national form. What we call the nation state was not the successor to imperial or city states but was itself a form of the European imperial city state that had driven the expansion of capitalism in previous centuries. Moreover, with the dismantling of Keynesian policies and national economies, these pre-national (pre-Keynesian) structures are resurfacing. In sum, the emergence of 'global cities' and city regions represents the resurgence of a durable, historically dominant and still existing form of state: the imperial city state form. The first section revisits the supposed differences between city states and national states. The following two sections offer a re-interpretation of the form of state that developed in Europe after the sixteenth century and remained dominant there until World War II. The final section argues that the emergence of national states appears to have constituted a brief post-World War II interregnum in some parts of the world, which may be coming to an end with the re-assertion of pre-national policies and spatialities. The 're-scaling' of nation states and growing prominence of 'global cities' and 'city regions' are heralding the end of the brief history of actually existing nation states and the re-deployment of the imperial city state model.

Nation states versus city states

The nation state is generally assumed to have superseded previous forms of state. Typically it is defined in opposition to city states and empires. This section will compare the nation state and the city state. The following section will focus on the extent to which the nature and development of what we call nation states has been until only very recently, and in very many respects, similar to the imperial state.

The national state is often contrasted with the city state on the grounds that, unlike the city state, it is a *territorial* state. But a city state is also a territorial state.[2] The territorial states that were consolidated in Europe during the nineteenth century bore all the features of city states: they consisted of a dominant area surrounded by a domain of influence, produced successful economies, established central banks that functioned as lenders of last resort and as 'instruments of power and international domination', and employed similar means of domination and surveillance (the fleet and the army, and violence) (Braudel 1982: 295). Like city states, they depended on imports of foodstuffs and raw materials and on long-distance trade and export production.[3]

City states had existed for millennia. They flourished all along the Silk Road and throughout Asia (as well as in Africa and the Americas). They have existed in the Americas, throughout Afro-Eurasia, and more or less continuously around the Mediterranean for at least 3,000 years. Phoenician city states (Byblos, Tyre, Sidon, Arados) in 1200 BCE expanded and intensified maritime trade and established a territorial division of labour in the Mediterranean littoral. This political form had therefore already become widespread throughout the

---

[2] The opposite of both is the non-territorial state as, for instance, the nomadic state or the feudal state (a patchwork of often disconnected small pieces of land). The idea of a 'territorial state' emerged to describe the 'Westphalian state' that, through the Treaties of Westphalia concluded in Europe in 1648, was held to represent a contrast to the feudal state (Hansen 2000: 9–10; see also Finer 1997: 6–7).

[3] Blockmans 1994: 226. City states were effective as geopolitical units at a time in which maritime trade had become the principal basis of economic life. Territorial states that were not based on cities were far less effective 'and even acted as an impediment to successful economic and scientific advance' (Parker 2004: 21).

Mediterranean when the Greeks established a political system based on the city state.

With the westward extension of Asian trade into Europe, city states were established in southern Europe to take advantage of opportunities to extend the Silk Road trade inland to the north and further west. In Europe, the city state form first emerged around the shores of the Adriatic, an area strategically located to take the products brought along the Silk Road to the barbarian north and west. It was on the swamps, islands and sandbanks at the head of the Adriatic Sea that the city state of Venice was established. By the eleventh century, Venice 'had become the largest and most prosperous city in Europe after Byzantium' (Parker 2004: 80).

During the ensuing centuries, different versions of the Venetian *polis* became 'familiar features of the European scene' (Parker 2004: 87). In the fifteenth and sixteenth centuries, along with the city states of Venice and Genoa, which were the leading trading powers of the Mediterranean Sea, Florence, Siena and Lucca emerged as large and important Italian city states. All five viewed themselves and their institutions as the heirs of the city states of ancient Rome and Greece. Each subjugated its own dependent territory or peripheral hinterland (*contado*), and larger cities such as Florence and Milan 'conquered and dominated *contadi* that included formerly independent cities and their hinterlands' (Tilly 1994: 17).

The Italian city state system expanded into a European state system with the emergence of city states to its north and west (see Lane 1973). The states that emerged on the Baltic Sea and Atlantic littorals were based on trade and manufacturing (in contrast to the largely rural Swiss city states) and were principally concerned to secure trade routes and control the growth of rural industry in order to profit from trade linking the Baltic Sea to the Mediterranean along the Atlantic coast. Important commercial cities emerged in the Netherlands and Belgium, western Germany, northern France and southern England. City states were established in the Netherlands, which was, like Venice, an area of swamps, deltas, sand bars and low-lying plains. Brugge (Bruges), which, like Venice, was near the mouth of a great river on a coast of sandbars and marshes, became closely linked with the Baltic trade and, in 1277, it established the first important maritime connection between northern Europe and the Mediterranean (Genoa) (Parker 2004: 163–64). In the fourteenth century, the cities of the Netherlands gained most of the freedoms enjoyed by sovereign city states. Amsterdam was, from the start, a sovereign city, and it 'can be seen as being essentially a city-state, of which the province was the rural part'.[4]

In the fifteenth century, the expansion of trade generated incentives to more securely weld cities to hinterlands and to larger, more militarily powerful territorial domains (Tilly 1994: 26). Maritime states along the Atlantic littoral loaded heavy cannon onto the ocean-going ships that had been developed to carry this trade and set out to muscle their way into the Asian commercial world. Having succeeded in this, and in securing vast new opportunities for the pursuit of profit through overseas trade, these states then sought to extend their control over larger territories so as to secure resources and labour needed for a massive expansion of production for export.

The military conquest of cities by rural-based rulers led to the consolidation of urban and rural areas into larger territorial states. However, in the process of integration of cities and urban hinterlands and, in some cases, absorption of cities into neighbouring land empires, cities remained dominant within the larger territorial units that formed around them.[5] While the new territorial political units operated 'chiefly as containers and deployers of coercive means, especially armed force' (Tilly 1994: 8), cities continued to control and channel capital flows. The de-industrialisation of rural areas and concentration of industry in urban areas made cities the focus, not only of industrial production, but of wealth accumulation, culture and power. Since labour was mobilized, not for 'national' markets, but for exports, cities became essentially 'glocul' in nature and increasingly powerful both in absolute terms and relative to rural areas. The form of state that this produced

---

[4] Parker 2004: 179. In the seventeenth century a series of commercial wars with
     England and territorial wars with France weakened the Dutch Republic; but what
     was in effect a grouping of city states 'in the guise of a territorial (nation) state,
     persisted into the twentieth century' (Parker 2004: 182).
[5] Centralizing monarchs laid claim to networks that had been developed by private
     and municipal organisations. In the early commercial cities, merchants had to
     undertake to provide security for roads, protection from tolls and arbitrary
     seizures, settlement of disputes between sellers and buyers, supervision of
     exchange values. 'What later became the fields of interstate diplomatic relations –
     royal coinage prerogatives and monarchical jurisdictions – were primarily shaped
     by merchants' networks at a time when no prince had the ability or the vision to
     meet these typically urban needs' (Blockmans 1994: 233). With the emergence of
     industrial production, states that were not based on cities – e.g. the Balkans,
     Poland – remained weak and were easily absorbed by other states.

far more closely resembled the imperial city states of the past 5000 years than the nationally integrated states of national cultural imaginaries and nation state ideology.[6] Thus, the formation of large territorial units resulted in a re-definition of the state, rather than the emergence of an essentially different state form.[7] By the eighteenth century Europe was 'organized as a series of regions, each containing a dominant city, a subordinate hierarchy of cities, and an agricultural hinterland from which the cities drew the major part of their subsistence' (Tilly 1983: 132). But while this became the basis for the consolidation of large territories states, these states adopted the social and political institutions and practices associated with city states. Like city states, they operated to expand and protect external trade; and, as city states typically do, they pursued this through overseas imperial expansion.

Nation states, or the development of modern imperial city states?

The notion of national territoriality emerged in the context of the expansion of cross-border commercial networks, the industrial production of exports and the development of new forms of exploitation.

---

[6] The first large empire in history, the Akkadian Empire (2270–2083 BCE), was a coalition of city states.

[7] Robert Brenner (2003) and Ellen Meiksins Wood (2002) have argued that the basis of the English state was qualitatively different from Renaissance city states. It was different, they argue, in two respects. The first was that in early modern England the landed elite no longer had to rely on the state to provide the non-economic coercion necessary to extract surplus value from the English peasantry but could rely, instead, on competitive economic rents. Second, domestic producers were becoming more dependent on the emergence of an integrated domestic market resulting from the development of linkages between capitalist agriculture and emerging industries, and so were less dependent upon their position within the overseas networks of commercial activity for their social reproduction. But, elites continued to rely on the state for extra-economic coercion to extract surplus value. There was no separation of economic (class) power from political (state) power but, rather a structure of power that fused both for extraction of surplus, locally and abroad (Halperin 2013, 2004). Moreover, the English state, like other European states we would characterise as 'national' territorial states, operated largely to promote external trade rather than an integrated 'national market'. The production of goods and services principally for the trans-local/global, rather than the local, economy worked to reproduce the city state form, rather than supplanting it by nationally integrated territorial states.

It was linked with the struggle for control of resources within increasingly differentiated realms – the burgeoning cities and de-industrializing hinterlands – that characterized the territories claimed by states. However, the territorial states that developed in Europe and that, throughout the nineteenth century, were developed and promoted by Europeans there and elsewhere, came to resemble far more closely imperial city states than the nationally integrated state form of national cultural imaginaries and nation state ideology.[8]

Nation states are thought to differ from empires because, while empires have a geographically, politically, economically and culturally identifiable core and periphery, usually consisting of a large city in control of vast peripheral hinterlands, nation states are said to use productive resources to generate and distribute wealth and material wellbeing throughout the whole territory of the state. However, the export-oriented economies of European states in the nineteenth century resembled those of imperial city states in the past; as with past imperial city states, they acquired larger territorial domains, not to develop 'national markets', but to increase production of goods for export.

Nation states are typically contrasted both with city states and empires because, unlike these forms of state, they are said to be bound by a common political and cultural identity.[9] But, 'very few countries are nation-states in the strict sense of the term; seldom is an independent political territory coterminous with the territory of a self-consciously united people' (Lewis and Wigen 1997: 8). Walker Connor, in a widely cited article, maintains that 'all but fourteen of today's states contain at least one significant minority and half of the fourteen exceptions are characterized by the so-called irredentist situation in which the dominant ethnic group extends beyond the state's borders' (Connor 1973: 1). The fourteen states are Austria, Denmark,

---

[8] Rome was the biggest imperial city state in history. Even with such giant cities as Alexandria and Antioch, its empire 'was merely one big hinterland of the capital city, Rome' (Schneider 1963: 133). The city absorbed surrounding territories in order to secure itself from the dangers which surrounded it, creating 'a large territorial state that gradually eliminated the independence of the other peoples who lived within it'. The process of expansion and consolidation that this involved 'was generated by the growth, and bound up with the fortunes, of one huge city' (Parker 2004: 63).

[9] According to a widely cited and influential definition, they are based on a principle of political legitimacy that holds that the political and national unit should be congruent (Gellner 1983).

West and East Germany, Iceland, Ireland, Japan, North and South Korea, Lesotho, Luxembourg, the Netherlands, Norway and Portugal. Connor maintains that, if one discards the states characterized by the irredentist situation (Austria, the Germanies, Ireland, the Koreas and Lesotho), the total number of people living in a state closely corresponding to the distribution of their ethnic group is less than four per cent – and, if we exclude the Japanese, less than one per cent.

In general, movements to form 'nation states' in Europe during the nineteenth century involved territorial expansion from urban political centres or 'cores', and the absorption of areas with distinctly different traditions and political institutions. These movements generally bore all the political, economic, cultural and military features of imperialism and colonialism and, in many cases, the resurrection or creation of empires was their stated aim.[10] Cities were at the centre of these processes and, in each 'national' domain, functioned as a seat of imperial power.

From the sixteenth century, London created and directed the establishment of England by establishing its provincial economies as satellites of the capital (Braudel 1984: 365). England then expanded into Ireland, Scotland and Wales, where Celtic populations were subjugated by military conquest and forcibly united with England in different ways (the British revenue collector was as alien to the inhabitants of Great Britain as the officials of large military/bureaucratic states such as the Romanov or the Habsburg Empires). The English exercised dominance over the commerce and trade of these lands, and all of them sank into the position of 'peripheral' countries (Hechter 1975: 147–50). The English appropriated three-quarters of the land of Ireland for their own advantage, and totally subjugated the country to the English market (Cullen 1968: chs 2–4; Hechter 1975: 84–95; Plumb 1950: 179). In the eighteenth century, London controlled all of England's production and distribution and handled at least four-fifths of its trade (Braudel 1984: 365–66). In 1914, London was as large as the next twelve cities combined and 'the centre of an imperium that was a city state, not unlike ancient Rome' (Schneider 1963: 229).

---

[10]   As Eric Hobsbawm (1990) has recounted, the Liberal discourse regarding nation states in Europe during the nineteenth century focused on optimum size and economic viability, rather than any cultural criterion.

The region around Paris (the Ile de France) created France through the sometimes violent subjugation and incorporation of numerous territories: Normandy (1204) and Occitania (1271) – in which there lived essentially a different people, with a different (Mediterranean) culture and a different language (*langue d'oc*); and, by 1500, Burgundy, Brittany (a region of Celtic culture) and Aquitaine. These areas were subordinated to the Ile de France for centuries.[11] Unequal exchange between Paris and the provinces ensured that Paris would continue 'to grow more handsome and more populous . . . at the expense of the rest of the country' (Braudel 1984: 328). Spain, like France, grew by absorbing kingdoms markedly dissimilar in cultural and legal traditions and institutions, either through dynastic marriage (Castile, Aragon) or annexation by force (Navarre, Granada). In the eighteenth century, Lisbon was the seat of imperial administration, tenuously linked to its rural hinterland, with the monarchy maintaining 'only symbolic ties' with 'Portugal' (Hespanha 1994: 194).

Although the term 'imperialism' came to be used exclusively to mean the direct or indirect domination of overseas colonial territories by modern industrial states, the process of building states in Europe and empires abroad was essentially similar.[12] Underlining this similarity, a number of scholars have referred to state-building processes in Europe as 'internal colonialism'.[13]

Like colonialism, state building in Europe involved reshaping the social and economic institutions of conquered areas to the needs of a militarily powerful 'core' that imposed physical control over culturally

---

[11] In the eighteenth century, Montesquieu observed that, 'In France there is only Paris – and a few outlying provinces Paris hasn't yet found time to gobble up' (quoted in de Tocqueville 1955: 72). 'It is no exaggeration to say that Paris *was* France', de Tocqueville wrote at the end of the century, with the metropolis attracting to itself 'all that was most vital in the nation' (72–73). 'Paris', wrote Turgot, 'swallow[s] up all the riches of the state' (cited in Braudel 1982: 328). The Marquis de Mirabeau observed that the provinces were in 'a state of dependence on the capital, their inhabitants treated as a sort of inferior species' (in de Tocqueville 1955: 72–73).

[12] The original meaning of 'imperialism' referred to the personal sovereignty of a powerful ruler over numerous territories, either in Europe or overseas. See Koebner and Schmidt 1965.

[13] Numerous scholars have underlined the similarity between processes of nation building and the colonial situation, including Antonio Gramsci (1957: 430), Fernand Braudel (1984: 42, 328–52), Eugen Weber (1976: 490–93), Maurice Dobb (1947: 194, 206–07, 209), Michael Hechter (1975: 30–33), Alvin Gouldner (1977–78) and Oscar Jaszi (1929: 185–212).

distinct groups that were discriminated against on the basis of their language, religion or other cultural attributes. Often, they were treated as objects of exploitation, 'as a natural resource to be plundered' (Gouldner 1977–78: 41), and with the brutality that states treat conquered foreign countries. The economy of the peripheral area was forced into complementary development to the core, and generally rested on a single primary export. Juridical and political measures similar to those applied in overseas colonies were imposed in order to maintain the economic dependence of these areas. Members of the core monopolized commerce, trade and credit, while in peripheral areas there was a relative lack of services and lower standard of living.

The creation of Germany was achieved under the direction of Prussia and through the military conquest, enforced cultural assimilation, and economic subordination of peoples living in territories annexed from Poland, Denmark and France. The creation of Italy was brought about by the conquest and annexation by Piedmont, a territory not even considered by most of its inhabitants to be part of Italy.[14] The south was treated as an area for quasi-colonial exploitation by the north,[15] and southerners were considered by many northerners to be a biologically inferior race of barbarians.[16] In the nineteenth century, the Italian peninsula still consisted of a 'system of small territorial states each dominated by the oligarchy of a single city' (Tilly 1994: 18).

---

[14] In fact, the Piedmontese traveller who went to Florence, Rome or Venice, used to say that he was going to Italy (Graf 1911: 5–6). Though some Italian provinces had allied with Piedmont as a means of gaining autonomy from other overlords (e.g. Sicily from Naples), they were annexed by Piedmont against their will (Smith 1971: 33).

[15] The north, Gramsci wrote, was an 'octopus', which enriched itself at the expense of the South, 'its economic increment in direct proportion to the impoverishment of the economy and the agriculture of the South' (1971: 71).

[16] This was a widespread current of thought. Alfredo Niceforo writes: 'Within the single womb of a political Italy two societies exist, wholly different in their level of civilization, in their social life, in their moral colour: northern Italy on the one hand, and southern Italy on the other; in a word, *two Italies*, quite distinct. While one of these two Italies, that of the north, can be seen to possess the physiognomy of a more diffuse, fresher, more modern civilization, the other Italy, that of the south, possesses a moral and social structure which recalls primitive, perhaps even barbarian times, with a social structure typical of inferior civilizations' (Niceforo 1890: 296–99).

World cities, city states and the nineteenth-century imperial order

The expansion of industrial production in the nineteenth century brought cities, urban commercial centres and export sectors across the world into closer interdependence, creating dynamic focal points of growth that developed through trans-local interaction and connection. As trading networks expanded, it was cities, not states that were incorporated into the system. The capabilities and functions that, according to Saskia Sassen and others, are associated with *today's* global cities were characteristic of the cities that formed the basis of the European-dominated imperial system of the nineteenth century.

Beginning in the fifteenth century, and using ocean-going ships that had been developed to carry goods from the Baltic Sea to the Mediterranean along Europe's Atlantic coast, fleets of Portuguese, Spanish, Dutch and British warrior merchants sought to gain control of Asia's trade. The Portuguese established a chain of forts and commercial outposts along the main sea route that ran between Southeast Asia and the Middle East along the Malabar coast, creating dozens of fortified trading enclaves from Sofala (in Mozambique) to Macao in Southern China.[17] Like Lisbon itself, these were port cities oriented to trade and the exploitation of their own subject territories: transit points in the export of agricultural products from their hinterlands. From these bases, Portuguese warrior merchants established a loose network of imperial authority over the sea lanes, taxing ships in transit in return for protection. In Indian Ocean ports, they forced rulers to pay tribute and to allow them to establish settlements and acquire local lands. In East Africa, they operated within the framework of the independent city states that existed along the coast (Mombasa, Gedi, Pate, Lamu, Malindi, Zanzibar and Kilwa).

Spanish, Dutch and English warrior merchants who swarmed out of Europe were also primarily interested in creating and maintaining enclaves, forts and trading posts. Spain recreated the old city states of pre-Colombian America in establishing the administrative divisions of 'New Spain' (Darwin 2007: 64). These large cities had sophisticated road and irrigation networks, and systems of slave labour and tribute

---

[17] These included Cochin (1503), Cannalore (1505), Goa (1510) and Malacca (1511).

(Colley 2008: 44). At the time of the Spanish conquest, Mayan city states existed in the Yucatan peninsula as did the three major city states that formed the Aztec empire: Taxco, Tiatelolco and Tenochtitlan – which at that time was larger than any city in Europe.[18] The Spanish established a network of urban centres, including Lima, Puebla, Mérida, Oaxaca, Santiago de los Caballeros de Guatemala, Cuzco, Quito, Trujillo, Cali, Bogotá, the first foundation of Buenos Aires and Potosi – which, in 1600, was one of the largest cities in the world. In 1580, there were 225 towns in the Spanish Indies: by 1759, perhaps 13 per cent of the population of Spanish America lived in cities with more than 20,000 inhabitants (Elliot 2006). Spanish settlers made use of the towns and had only very limited contact with the Amerindian populations of the interior (Colley 2008: 44).

Like that of previous imperial city states, the imperial expansion of states along Europe's Atlantic coast relied primarily on what William Thompson (1999) calls 'the Venetian model': the development of sea power to gain trading privileges rather than territorial possessions.[19] Venice built a commercial empire through establishing nodes, forts and trading posts to control other cities, many of which became city states.[20] This was the model of overseas commercial and imperial expansion that was adopted first by Lisbon and then by Amsterdam and London, all of which reproduced small-scale versions of what they themselves constituted: 'small enclaves oriented to long-distant trade' (Thompson 1999: 156).

The Dutch and British East India Companies were 'fashioned in the spirit of the Venetian state-galley system' (Cox 1959: 230). In Venice, large trading galleys (*galere da mercato*), constructed in the state-run shipyards of the Arsenal, were 'a combination of state enterprise' and 'a kind of consortium of export merchants' (Braudel 1984: 126). The Dutch envisioned securing commercial domination of trade in Asian waters by avoiding territorial control and establishing a network of bases. But violent local succession struggles and rivalries constantly

[18] The Spanish created Mexico City in Tenochtitlan in the first half of the sixteenth century.

[19] Though, as he notes, Venetians did not invent it.

[20] Among the most important of these were Zara, Spalato, Durazzo and Ragusa (later, Dubrovnik). Ragusa became, with Venice, one of the two principal city states in the Adriatic (Parker 2004: 87).

embroiled the Dutch in military conflict and shifted their strategy to one of establishing direct rule (Thompson 1999: 165). The British East India Company established trading posts in Madras (1639), Galle (1640), Bombay (1661) and Calcutta (1690). Two clusters of city states emerged within the ambit of the British Empire: Singapore and Hong Kong, in the Far East; Kuwait, Bahrain, Qatar and what became the United Arab Emirates, in the Middle East.

Cities in Europe and cities elsewhere formed a dynamic field of transnational production and exchange. With the expansion of trade around the world, cities expanded and large new ones emerged. Singapore (founded in 1819) grew up as a hub of Southeast Asian trade. After 1842, the port of Shanghai became the commercial outlet of China's Yangtze basin. Edo (Tokyo), by 1868, had become one of the largest cities in the world. Treaty ports were the sites of a 'disproportionately large part of the wealth and enterprise of China' (Hubbard 1935: 195). The commercial hub of the pampas, Buenos Aires' population grew from 300,000 in 1880 to 1.3 million in 1920 (Darwin 2007: 332). Cape Town rapidly expanded to serve as a commercial centre for the diamond and gold mined inland. Melbourne and Sydney emerged on the Australian coast. Ottoman port cities on the Eastern Mediterranean and the Black Sea, and also the great commercial cities of Constantinople and Cairo, experienced continuous population and commercial growth during the nineteenth century. Salonica, an industrial city that manufactured cloth, carpets, soap and faience, had silk-weaving and glass-blowing industries and, along with Smyrna, was an important source of cotton for Europe. Trabzon was a centre for exports that came through the Iranian transit trade and the coastal trade along the Black Sea, supplemented by the products of the East Anatolian hinterland (Kasaba, Çağlar and Tabak 1986: 130–31). Alexandria in the nineteenth century was one of the world's greatest entrepôts. By the end of the nineteenth century, the Pacific trade had led to the emergence of San Francisco, Los Angeles and Vancouver.

All these were developed to serve global trade and served as 'entry or exit points for the movement of goods, labour and capital . . . [as] nodal centres for the reception and transmission of culture, knowledge and information' (Tan 2007: 853). And all 'followed similar trajectories: rapid economic growth, physical transformation, and the emergence of an outward-looking, plural population linked to a dense network of maritime connections engendered by international trade'.[21] British exports promoted this urban 'development' by building banks, telegraphs and other public services, port and city infrastructures, urban dwellings, harbour improvements, docks, rail yards and railroads, customs houses, hotels, clubs and residences for the prosperous merchant class.

As European military power intensified and extended trading networks, it was cities, not states that were incorporated into the system.[22] Lisbon, Seville, Bahia, Havana, Mexico City, Amsterdam, Le Havre, London and New York linked together the Atlantic trade in the sixteenth century. Seville, Amsterdam, Acapulco, Manila, Edo (later renamed Tokyo), Guangdong and Beijing tied together circuits of silver in the seventeenth century. The British and Ottoman Empires were intertwined through Bombay, Karachi, Bushire, Basra, Port Said and Jidda. Port cities linking Europe and the Ottoman Empire included Corfu, Salonica, Smyrna (Izmir), Odessa, Alexandria, Beirut, Trabzon and Trieste in the Ottoman Empire; Amsterdam, London, Venice, Genoa, Nantes, Bordeaux, Lisbon, Cadiz, Seville, Rotterdam and Le Havre in Europe.

The interregnum and re-emergence of pre-Keynesian spatialities

As more and more countries pursued externally oriented expansion, opportunities for overseas expansion decreased, and an escalation of European rivalries ultimately culminated in two world wars. The wartime demand for labour and the need for its cooperation during the second of these world wars compelled a political accommodation of working-class movements; and the need for working-class cooperation in resuming the fight against socialism after the war sustained this accommodation.[23] The 'compromise' involved a shift that oriented

---

[21] Tan 2007: 852. Tan Tai-Yong is here describing Singapore and Calcutta; but the description applies to port cities everywhere.

[22] At the beginning of the nineteenth century the world was perhaps about 3 per cent urban; at its end some 15 per cent of the world's population was urban (Hay 1977: 74).

[23] The struggle against socialism had been interrupted when Germany's invasion of France and attack on Britain had forced the non-fascist capitalist countries to enter into a temporary alliance with the Soviet Union. But following the interruption of World War II, the struggle against the Soviet Union that had

Table 4.1 *Regional inequality in Europe before 1945*
(per capita income of region relative to national average)

Sweden (1930)	Stockholmstad	264.2	Gotlands	58.1
France (1864)	Paris Region	175.1	Brittany	62.1
Netherlands (1938)	North-Holland	141.2	Drenthe	50.0
Germany (1926)	Hamburg	154.8	East Prussia	69.5
Italy (1928)	Piedmont	155.6	Sicily	69.7

Source: Williamson 1965

investment and production towards the domestic market. For a time, and through welfare reforms and market and industry regulation, investment and production were made to serve the expansion and integration of national markets.[24]

Before World War II, every European state was marked by sharp regional inequalities: Italy's Mezzogiorno, Spain's Andalusia, France's western and southern regions, West Germany's agricultural peripheries and border zones, Belgium's Limburg coal-mining district, the Dutch north-eastern peripheries, Denmark's north-western regions and islands, more generally the Scandinavian North, western Ireland and much of Northern Ireland. Table 4.1 shows these regional inequalities in a few western European countries.

After World War II, governments introduced policies to alleviate these regional inequalities by spreading growth 'as evenly as possible across the entire surface of each national territory' (Brenner 2004: 51). For much of the modern era and nearly everywhere, the socio-economic, political and cultural interrelationships that bound cities across the world to each other had been denser than those that have bound together national territories. But regional industrial and

commenced with the Bolshevik revolution in 1917 was resumed, and it continued unabated until 1989.

[24] Those countries whose development, following World War II, was characterized by a relatively broad-based and inclusive development were those that: (1) never had an entrenched landed elite (Canada, New Zealand and Australia); (2) saw a significant decline in the power of landowners as a result of civil war (the United States); (3) experienced a breakdown of their traditional social structures and massive land reforms as a result of devastating wars (most of Europe); or (4) had a massive land reform imposed by external forces and experienced, as a consequence, the breakdown of their traditional class structures (Japan).

infrastructural policies introduced in Europe and a few other areas between the 1950s and 1970s were designed to 'rechannel employment and growth capacities into underdeveloped regions and rural peripheries throughout the national territory' (Brenner 2004: 135, 137). Government policies in Britain promoted the economic regeneration of its coal-mining regions of south Wales, northern England, west Cumberland and central Scotland (the Distribution of Industry Acts of 1945); in 1966, an Industrial Development Act broadened this initiative to areas 'encompassing 40 percent of British territory and 20 percent of the total population' (Brenner 2004: 141). Projects introduced in the Netherlands in the 1960s sought to disperse industry, population and employment from the western Randstad regions (Amsterdam, Utrecht, Rotterdam and the Hague) to the depressed peripheral regions of the north, east and south. French post-war regional policies were designed 'to decentralize industrial capacities and employment out of the dominant Paris region and into major provincial cities, towns, rural areas, and border zones' (Brenner 2004: 141). Italy's Southern Italy Development Agency was established in 1950 to promote agricultural modernization and industrial growth throughout the south. West Germany's Spatial Planning Law of 1965 promoted 'equal life conditions' across the entire national territory, targeting in particular, rural peripheries and eastern border areas.[25]

It was as a result of these polices, introduced in a few places in the immediate post-war decades, that there emerged a form of state – the nation state – based on the development of local, rather than external, markets. However, this was to be only a brief interregnum; by the late 1970s, policies associated with globalization, driven by the social logics that drove the global expansion of the nineteenth century, began fuelling the rise of cities within national territories and reproducing the political economy of city states. The structures that had developed over previous centuries never entirely disappeared, and after the brief interregnum of the 1950s and 1960s (characterized by Keynesian policies aimed at strengthening the 'national' economy and 'national' consumption capacity), key aspects of this system began to re-surface.

---

[25] See, e.g. Myrdal 1957; Hirschman 1958; Sabel 1994; Swyngedouw 1997; Martin and Sunley 1997; Martin 1989; Albrechts and Swyngedouw 1989; Clout 1981; Holland 1976.

In 1968, a series of uprisings and demonstrations throughout the world marked the beginning of the end of the post-World War II order. In the USA, the activities of anti-Cold War (Vietnam) and civil rights movements upset the balance of power on which the post-World War II Keynesian compromise in that country had depended, and this began a shift in policies that deregulated capital and began a broader process of dis-embedding the US economy. In the 1970s, governments in other First World countries introduced measures to eliminate restrictions on capital mobility and dismantle regulatory agencies and social welfare programmes.[26] These measures were characterized as a necessity demanded by the emergence of 'globalization'; but government policies were designed, not to adjust to new circumstances but to promote a return to the export-oriented growth and capital exports that had characterized the pre-world war international political economy.

The dismantling of nationally embedded economies and return to pre-war policies brought the brief post-World War II interregnum to an end, and with its end, pre-war structures and transnational spatialities began quickly to re-emerge. Productive resources became concentrated, once again, in cities and sub-state regions, and global trade and technology flows and capital movements were restored to their former prominence, along with the transnational flows, networks and organizations that have always characterized it. Post-Keynesian spatial policies introduced by Western European states in the 1980s actively intensified 'uneven geographical development by strengthening globally linked city-regions'.[27] Today, just forty of these 'city-regions', according to Parag Khanna, account for two thirds of the world economy and 90 per cent of its innovation (Khanna 2009). These developments are characterized as 'new', but have only re-emerged with the adoption by governments of initiatives to re-instate, deepen, or extend pre-war structures. Khanna points out the recent restructuring initiatives are likely to generate the rebirth of the 'mighty Hanseatic League'

---

[26] By the end of the 1980s, a drastic, 'shock therapy' version of these policies was introduced in 'second world' countries and quickly reinstated the dualistic and monopoly capitalist structures that had characterized their economies before the world wars.

[27] Brenner 2004: 16. On growing regional inequalities in western Europe, see, Keating 1998, 2001; Kloosterman 2001; Macleod 2001; Macleod and Jones 2001; Paasi 2003; Donaldson 2006.

(a 'constellation of well-armed North and Baltic Sea trading hubs in the late Middle Ages') as 'cities such as Hamburg and Dubai form commercial alliances and operate "free zones" across Africa like the ones Dubai Ports World is building. Add in sovereign wealth funds and private military contractors', he observes, 'and you have the agile geopolitical units of a neomedieval world.'[28]

The dismantling of national economies has also led to the re-emergence, in First World countries, of what scholars today are calling 'global cities'. 'Global cities' were characteristic of the nineteenth century: nodes of the global imperial order. The renewed salience of the nineteenth-century system's global cities under the impact of globalization represents a re-surfacing of that system's spatialities and institutional logics. As Peter Taylor points out, 'European cities as city states led the pace' to a modern era characterized by monopolistic, anti-market accumulation. Taylor argues that today's global cities facilitate monopolistic, anti-market accumulation, and that spatial networks and hierarchies capped by 'world cities' are the geographic counterpart of the increasing concentration of power and wealth in the hands of global monopolies (Taylor 2000).

That world cities linked to post-Keynesian spatial policies in First World countries are not newly emerging, but re-emerging, can be seen by their resemblance to structures found in Third World countries that never adopted the policies that produced broad-based, nationally embedded growth in the First World. With economic growth contained within urban-based export sectors, the centrality and overriding prominence of their cities never receded. Third World cities enjoy a high degree of autonomy, and in some cases play a major role in the world economy. In fact, most of today's 'global cities' are located in Third World states. Of the world's sixteen largest cities, each with more than ten million inhabitants, twelve are in the Third World (Mexico City, Mumbai and Sao Paulo are among the world's five largest) (Gugler 2004: 3). That these global cities did not emerge in 'a context where most territory is encased in a thick and highly formalized national framework marked by the exclusive authority of the national state' (Sassen 2003: 5), and that the global cities that Sassen and others

---

[28] Khanna 2009. In 1980, former Hanseatic League members established a 'new Hanse' in Zwolle, Netherlands. The new Hansa, now headquartered in Lübeck, Germany, fosters and develops business links, tourism and cultural exchange. www.hanse.org/en/the_hansa

associate with post-national states are also common to pre-national ones, suggest that these spatialities represent, not a further point along a unilinear trajectory, but the re-surfacing of pre-national phenomena.

Today's new global cities and regions are similar to Third World cities in a number of ways. According to Manuel Castells, Europe's global cities have 'a structural tendency to generate a polarized occupational structure' (1994: 29–30): at one pole is a cosmopolitan elite, 'living on a daily connection to the whole world (functionally, socially, culturally)'; at the other pole is 'the tribalism of local communities, retrenched in their spaces that they try to control as their last stand against the macro-forces that shape their lives out of their reach' (1994: 30). This dualism is reinforced wherever downgraded jobs are filled by immigrant workers, as in Western European societies, where a massive import of foreign workers had begun to form a new 'sub-proletariat' by the end of the 1960s. For the most part, these workers are found 'in the least attractive and worst paid manual jobs' (Castles 1984: 149). Unrepresented in the government and unorganized, they have been unable to bring effective pressure on either employers or governments for higher wages, shorter hours or better working conditions. Those from poorer lands, in particular, are often content with or resigned to poorer living conditions, creating, as David Landes observed, 'a situation reminiscent, in small, of the industrial slums of the early nineteenth century' (1969: 501). China's rapid urban development in recent years has been described in similar terms. Less than 0.5 per cent of Chinese households now own over 60 per cent of the nation's personal wealth, while 'the 150 million-odd migrant workers building China's gleaming cities and the millions more in antiquated rural factories live in Dickensian squalor' (Chanda 2007: 313). Today, cities all around the world – 'Los Angeles and Miami, Moscow and Madrid, Bogota and Kuala Lumpur' (Castells 1994: 19) – are fundamentally dualistic, characterized by 'elite enclaves in which offices, hotels, luxury housing, high-scale infrastructure, and up-scale shops and restaurants have displaced low-income residents' (Gugler 2004: 10).

Much research and writing argues that the scale and magnitude of global economic interaction has fundamentally transformed the state, that states are no longer the major 'containers' of economic and social relations, that a new form of state is emerging as a result of a 'reterritorialization' or 're-scaling' of the state so as to produce a type of state in which the national and urban converge (Brenner 2004). But, as Neil

Brenner notes, city states like Singapore and Hong Kong already have this national-urban scaling, and unconstrained 'by the tensions inherent in the national-versus-urban politics of non-city states', they are 'better able to mobilize strategic resources'. Moreover, 'because they are, from the start, intertwined in global networks, they enjoy 'a head start on other "global cities"'.[29] This suggests that, rather than producing a new form of state, current trends may just as likely be returning us to a previous form. In fact, Manuel Castells surmises that the revival of the city state could be 'the necessary complement to the expansion of a global economy' (1994: 30).

The city state of Singapore is a highly industrialized city state producing 18 per cent more manufacturing output per capita than the USA (Chang 2008: 215), and it has played a significant role in the evolution of modern Southeast Asia.[30] Other sovereign city states today include the UAE, Bahrain, Qatar, Kuwait, the Vatican, Monaco, Andorra, Lichtenstein, San Marino and Luxembourg. There are also autonomous cities within unitary states, including Hong Kong and Macau (in China), Ceuta and Melilla (Spanish, but located in North Africa). Cities are also component states of federations. Some have a high degree of autonomy and function as city states, e.g. Buenos Aires (formally known in English as the 'Autonomous City of Buenos Aires'), Canberra, Vienna, Brussels, Brazilia, Berlin, Hamburg, Bremen, Moscow, St. Petersburg, Geneva, Basel-Stadt; and the emirates of Abu-Dhabi, Dubai, Ajman, Sharjah, Ras al-Khaimah, Fujairah and Umm al-Qaiwain. Addis Ababa and Dire Dawa are chartered cities having the status of both a city and a state. There are also numerous federally administered cities: Delhi, which has been given partial statehood, and Chandigarh in India; Islamabad (Islamabad Capital Territory) in Pakistan; Kuala Lumpur, Putrajaya and Labuan, an offshore international financial centre, in Malaysia; Mexico City (the Mexican Federal District, Mexico); Abuja (Federal Capital Territory, Nigeria); Washington, DC (USA); and 'The City of London' – the 'financial district' that pays no tax, has its own courts, laws, flag, and is under the jurisdiction of a City of London Police Force that is separate from the territorial police force.

---

[29] Olds and Yeung 2004: 508. A number of scholars have highlighted the success of previous world cities that became city states after World War II, most notably Singapore, which became a highly industrialized city state after the war.

[30] Parker 2004:12. And also Hong Kong before it rejoined China in 1997.

Conclusion

This chapter has explored the extent to which post-national spatialities represent the resurgence of institutions, practices and forms of organization that characterized the pre-national world.

It has argued that the most characteristic political form of capitalism as it developed and expanded was the city state. The nation state became the spatial face of capital accumulation only after World War II and in only those few countries where Fordist/Keynesian and social democratic policies were adopted. In those countries (in what became the 'developed' world), Fordist/Keynesian and social democratic policies generated and distributed wealth and material wellbeing nationally rather than within urban-based export sectors. These changes represented a departure from historical patterns of capitalist expansion. They were not a natural outcome of industrialization or rising GDP, but the result of state regulatory policies that made investment and production serve the expansion and integration of national markets.

Previous sections argued that current trends represent a resumption of earlier ones, that post-Keynesian spatial policies are really *pre*-Keynesian, that they are resurrecting pre-Keynesian structures and, specifically, the interconnected urban spaces through which capitalism operated before the world wars. In areas of the world where national states emerged with the adoption of Keynesian policies following World War II, post-national spatialities represent a return to pre-national ones. But these spatialities have continuously characterized other areas of the world where these policies were not adopted.

The argument, then, is that, though current trends of change are characterized as 'new', they are not new but only newly salient; they have not recently emerged, but only re-emerged with the adoption by governments of a variety of restructuring initiatives designed to reinstate the spatialities and institutional logics associated with the nineteenth-century imperial order. Characterizing post-national spatialities as new and historically unprecedented prevents effective analysis of their political and economic implications. It leaves their politics and possibilities, the form of political economy that they imply, shrouded in mystery and beyond the reach of political analysis and action. If the concentration of productive resources in and by world cities and the mobilization of those resources for foreign trade is a consequence of a policy shift, they are only inevitable and irreversible if people are made to believe they are.

References

Albrechts, L. and E. Swyngedouw (1989) 'Challenges for Regional Policy under a Flexible Regime of Accumulation'. In L. Albrechts, F. Moulaert, P. Roberts and E. Swyingedouw (eds.) *Regional Policy at the Crossroads: European Perspectives*. London: Jessica Kingsley, 67–89.

Arrighi, G. (1994) *The Long Twentieth Century: Money, Power, and the Origins of Our Time*. London: Verso.

Blockmans, W. P. (1994) 'Voracious States and Obstructing Cities: An Aspect of State Formation in Preindustrial Europe'. In C. Tilly and W. P. Blockmans (eds.) *Cities and the Rise of States in Europe A.D. 1000 to 1800*. Boulder: Westview, 218–50.

Braudel, F. (1982) *The Wheels of Commerce: Civilization and Capitalism, 15th–18th Century*, Vol. II. Trans. S. Reynolds. New York: Harper and Row.

(1984) *The Perspective of the World: Civilization and Capitalism, 15th–18th Century*, Vol. III. Trans. S. Reynolds. New York: Harper and Row.

Brenner, N. (1998) 'Global Cities, Global States: Global City Formation and State Territorial Restructuring in Contemporary Europe'. *Review of International Political Economy*, 5(1), 1–37.

(2004) *New State Spaces: Urban Governance and the Rescaling of Statehood*. London: Oxford University Press.

Castells, M. (1994). 'European Cities, the Informational Society, and the Global Economy'. *New Left Review*, 204, 18–32.

Castles, S. (1984) *Here for Good: Western Europe's New Ethnic Minorities*. London: Pluto Press.

Chanda, N. (2007) *Bound Together: How Traders, Preachers, Adventurers, and Warriors Shaped Globalization*. New Haven: Yale University Press.

Chang, H. J. (2008) *Bad Samaritans: The Myth of Free Trade and the Secret History of Capitalism*. New York: Bloomsbury Press.

Clout, H. (1981) *Regional Development in Western Europe*, 2nd edn. Chichester: John Wiley.

Colley, L. (2008) 'A Tale of Two Empires: Review of J. H. Elliot, *Empires of the Atlantic World: Britain and Spain, 1492–1830*'. *New York Review of Books*, 55(12), 43–46.

Connor, W. (1973) 'The Politics of Ethnonationalism'. *Journal of International Affairs*, 27, 111–21.

Cox, O. C. (1959) *Foundations of Capitalism*. New York: Philosophical Library.

Cullen, L. M. (1968) *Anglo-Irish Trade 1660–1800*. Manchester: University of Manchester Press.

Darwin, J. (2007) *After Tamerlane: The Global History of Empire since 1405*. London: Penguin.

Dobb, M. (1947)[1963] *Studies in the Development of Capitalism*, revised edn. New York: International Publishers.

Donaldson, A. (2006) 'Performing Regions: Territorial Development and Cultural Politics in a Europe of the Regions'. *Environment and Planning*, 38, 2075–92.

Elliot, J. H. (2006) *Empires of the Atlantic World: Britain and Spain, 1492–1830*. New Haven: Yale University Press.

Finer, S. E. (1997) *The History of Government from the Earliest Times: The Intermediate Ages*. Oxford: Oxford University Press.

Gellner, E. (1983) *Nations and Nationalism*. Ithaca: Cornell University Press.

Gouldner, A. W. (1977–78) 'Stalinism: A Study of Internal Colonialism'. *Telos*, 34, 5–48.

Graf, A. (1911) *L'Anglomania e l'influsso inglese in Italia nel secolo XVIII*. Turin: E. Loescher.

Gramsci, A. (1957) *The Modern Prince and Other Writings*. London: Lawrence and Wishart.

(1971) 'The Intellectuals'. In Q. Hoare and G. N. Smith (trans. and eds.) *Selections from the Prison Notebooks*. New York: International Publishers, 3–23.

Gugler, J. (2004) 'Introduction'. In J. Gugler (ed.) *World Cities beyond the West: Globalization, Development, and Inequality*. Cambridge: Cambridge University Press, 1–26.

Halperin, S. (2004) *War and Social Change in Modern Europe: The Great Transformation Revisited*. Cambridge: Cambridge University Press.

(2013) *Re-Envisioning Global Development: A 'Horizontal' Perspective*. London: Routledge.

Hannerz, U. (1996) *Transnational Connections*. London: Routledge.

Hansen, M. H. (2000) 'Introduction: The Concepts of City-State and City-State Culture'. In M. H. Hansen (ed.) *A Comparative Study of Six City-State Cultures: An Investigation Conducted by the Copenhagen Polis Centre. Historisk-filosofiske Skrifter 27*. Copenhagen: Royal Danish Academy of Sciences and Letters.

Hay, R., Jr (1977) 'Patterns of Urbanisation and Socio-Economic Development in the Third World: An Overview'. In J. Abu-Lughod and R. Hay, Jr (eds.), *Third World Urbanization*. London: Methuen, 71–101.

Hechter, M. (1975) *Internal Colonialism: The Celtic Fringe in British National Development, 1536–1966*. Berkeley: University of California Press.

Hespanha, A. M. (1994) 'Cities and the State in Portugal'. In C. Tilly and W. P. Blockmans (eds.) *Cities and the Rise of States in Europe AD 1000 to 1800*. Boulder: Westview, 168–83.

Hirschman, A. (1958) *The Strategy of Economic Development*. New Haven: Yale University Press.

Hobsbawm, E. (1990) *Nations and Nationalism since 1780: Programme, Myth, Reality*. Cambridge: Cambridge University Press.

Holland, S. (1976) *Capital Versus the Regions*. London: Macmillan.

Hoogvelt, A. (1997) *Globalisation and the Post Colonial World: The New Political Economy of Development*. London: Macmillan.

Hubbard, G. E. (1935) *Eastern Industrialization and Its Effect on the West*. London: Oxford University Press.

Jásci, O. (1929) *Dissolution of the Hapsburg Monarchy*. Chicago: University of Chicago.

Kasaba, R., K. Çağlar and F. Tabak (1986) 'Eastern Mediterranean Port Cities and their Bourgeoisies: Merchants, Political Projects, and Nation-States'. *Review*, 10(1), 121–35.

Keating, M. (1998) *The New Regionalism in Western Europe: Territorial Restructuring and Political Change*. Cheltenham: Edward Elgar.

—— (2001) 'Rethinking the Region: Culture, Institutions and Economic Development in Catalonia and Galicia'. *European Urban and Regional Studies*, 8, 217–34.

Khanna, P. (2009) 'The Next Big Thing: Neomedievalism'. *Foreign Policy*. Available at: www.foreignpolicy.com/articles/2009/04/15/the_next_big_thing_neomedievalism

Kloosterman, R. C. (2001) 'Clustering of Economic Activities in Polycentric Urban Regions: The Case of the Randstad'. *Urban Studies*, 38: 717–32.

Koebner, R. and H. D. Schmidt (1965) *Imperialism: The Story and Significance of a Political Word, 1840–1960*. Cambridge: Cambridge University Press.

Landes, D. (1969) *The Unbound Prometheus*. Cambridge: Cambridge University Press.

Lane, F. (1973) *Venice: A Maritime Republic*. Baltimore: Johns Hopkins University Press.

Lewis, M. W. and K. E. Wigen (1997) *The Myth of Continents: A Critique of Metageography*. Berkeley: University of California Press.

MacLeod, G. (2001) 'New Regionalism Reconsidered: Globalization and the Remaking of Political Economic Space'. *International Journal of Urban and Regional Research*, 25, 804–29.

MacLeod, G. and M. Jones (2001) 'Renewing the Geography of Regions'. *Environment and Planning*, 19: 669–95.

Martin, R. (1989) 'The New Economics and Politics of Regional Restructuring: The British Experience'. In L. Albrechts and F. Moulaert (eds.) *Regional Policy at the Crossroads*. London: Jessica Kingsley, 27–51.

Martin, R. and P. Sunley (1997) 'The Post-Keynesian State and the Space Economy'. In R. Lee and J. Wills (eds.) *Geographies of Economies*. London: Arnold, 278–89.

Myrdal, G. (1957) *Rich Lands and Poor*. New York: Harper and Row.

Niceforo, A. (1890) *L'Italia barbara contemporanea*. Palermo: Sandron.

Olds, K. and H. W. C. Yeung (2004) 'Pathways to Global City Formation: A View from the Developmental City-State of Singapore'. *Review of International Political Economy*, 11(3), 489–521.

Paasi, A. (2003) 'Region and Place: Regional Identity in Question'. *Progress in Human Geography*, 27: 475–85.

Parker, G. (2004) *Sovereign City: The City-State through History*. London: Reaktion Books.

Plumb, J. H. (1950) *England in the Eighteenth Century*. Harmondsworth: Penguin.

Portes, A. (1977) 'Urban Latin America: The Political Condition from Above and Below'. In J. Abu-Lughod and R. Hay, Jr (eds.) *Third World Urbanization*. London: Methuen, 59–70.

Pries, L. (ed.) (2001) *New Transnational Social Spaces*. London: Routledge.

Sabel, C. (1994) 'Flexible Specialisation and the Re-Emergence of Regional Economies'. In A. Amin (ed.) *Post-Fordism: A Reader*. Cambridge, MA: Blackwell, 101–56.

Sassen, S. (1994) *Cities in a World Economy*. Thousand Oaks: Pine Forge Press.

(1997) 'Cities in the Global Economy'. *International Journal of Urban Sciences*, 1(1), 11–31.

(2001) *The Global City: New York, London, Tokyo*, 2nd edn. Princeton: Princeton University Press.

(2003) 'Globalization or Denationalization?' *Review of International Political Economy*, 10(1), 1–22.

(2007) *A Sociology of Globalization*. London: W. W. Norton.

Schneider, W. (1963) *Babylon is Everywhere: The City as Man's Fate*. New York: McGraw-Hill.

Smith, D. M. (1971) *Victor Emmanuel, Cavour, and the Risorgimento*. London: Oxford University Press.

Swyngedouw, E. (1997) 'Neither Global nor Local: "Glocalization" and the Politics of Scale'. In K. Cox (ed.) *Spaces of Globalization: Reasserting the Power of the Local*. New York/London: Guilford/Longman, 137–66.

Tan, T. Y. (2007) 'Port Cities and Hinterlands: A Comparative Study of Singapore and Calcutta'. *Political Geography*, 26, 851–65.

Taylor, P. J. (2000) 'World Cities and Territorial States under Conditions of Contemporary Globalization'. *Political Geography*, 19(1), 5–32.

(2003) *World City Network: A Global Analysis*. London: Routledge.

Thompson, W. R. (1999) 'The Military Superiority Thesis and the Ascendancy of Western Eurasia in the World System'. *Journal of World History*, 10(1), 143–78.

Tilly, C. (1983) 'Flows of Capital and Forms of Industry in Europe, 1500–1900'. *Theory and Society*, 12(2), 123–42.

(1994) 'Entanglements of European Cities and States'. In C. Tilly and W. P. Blockmans (eds.) *Cities and the Rise of States in Europe AD 1000 to 1800*. Boulder: Westview, 1–27.

de Tocqueville, A. (1955) *The Old Regime and the French Revolution*. Garden City: Doubleday.

Weber, E. (1976) *Peasants into Frenchmen: The Modernization of Rural France, 1870–1914*. Stanford: Stanford University Press.

Wood, M. E. (2002) *The Origin of Capitalism: A Longer View*, revised edn. London: Verso.

Yeoh, B. S. A. (1999) 'Global/Globalizing Cities'. *Progress in Human Geography*, 23, 607–16.

PART II

Legacies of non-European empires in today's world

The legacy of Eurasian nomadic empires

Remnants of the Mongol imperial tradition

IVER B. NEUMANN AND EINAR WIGEN

Introduction: the problem

We should not take for granted that remnants of 'Western' imperial tradition are the only ones on display today. It is true that Europe and its settler states dominated the world economically and politically in the nineteenth and twentieth centuries. That does not necessarily mean, however, that the broad European imperial tradition succeeded in eradicating other imperial traditions. There is, furthermore, the possibility that the European tradition was itself indebted to other traditions. In this chapter, we will make the case for the relevance of what we call the Eurasian steppe tradition. We will focus on its lingering importance, and only touch on its historical role as the main other in early European state formation. We first chart the 1,500-year-long history of the steppe tradition and try to capture it by way of an ideal type, and contrast it not with an ideal type of contemporary 'Western' polities, but of nineteenth-century-style European empires. The second section is a brief discussion of how the imperial steppe tradition was obfuscated by the European political tradition on the level of discourse. We then trace the continuing importance of the steppe tradition in three areas, namely Central Asia, Turkey and Russia.

A nomadic imperial tradition

Although the pre-history of the imperial steppe tradition in Eurasia stretches back at least to the eighth century BC, and includes some predominantly Iranic-speaking polities, the first documented Eurasian steppe empire, that of the Hsiung-Nu, hails from 209 BC (Di Cosmo

We should like to thank our editors and fellow contributors as well as Bjørnar Sverdrup-Thygesen and Rune Svarverud.

2004). The best-documented and best-known empire in the Eurasian steppe tradition is the Mongol Empire. Discussions of immediate precursors are frequently referred to as 'Turko-Mongol' in the literature. So are successors, although there is a bifurcation at the very end of the living tradition. At the time of their respective demise in the late eighteenth century, the Zunghar Empire was a Mongol affair, while the Crimean Khanate was a Turkic one (that is, a Turkic-speaking dynasty of Mongol lineage).

From its very beginning, the steppe tradition was derivative of sedentary polity building. Steppe polities were based on pastoral nomadism, which emerged historically only when agriculture was in place. Furthermore, steppe empires formed in order to prey on trade routes between sedentaries, raid and, where possible, take tribute from them (Barfield 1989; also Lattimore 1940). Sedentaries were also the ones to evolve writing, and are consequently our main source on steppe empires.

This makes for a certain lop-sidedness of sources, among other things, because there is little mention in the sources of how steppe empires also served as a magnet for disgruntled sedentaries who wanted to run away from state-induced tax burdens (see Scott 2009). To take but two examples, what little we know of the Merovingian Empire demonstrates important steppe hybridization, and the hybridized nature of the Bulgar polity that emerged from the merging of Bolgars from the steppe and sedentary Slavs is well known. The Eurasian steppe tradition is the *pudenda origo* of European states (Neumann and Wigen 2013).

To the extent that there exists a scholarly consensus, scholars believe that steppe empires emerged as a result of a fixed pattern that we may call polysynthetic. Some particularly ambitious young man would establish himself as head of a group of households; such groups are usually referred to as 'tribes', and defined in terms of perceived common ancestry.[1]

If a leader and his 'tribes' proved particularly good at raiding caravans and sedentaries, he would attract ever more of the familiar 'tribes', until the momentum was there to conquer more 'tribes' with

---

[1] Scott (2009: 259) argues that tribes are a by-product of state formation, and represent those elements which are not (yet) fully incorporated as a subject of the state, such as the peasantry.

other traditional allegiances. When taken to its logical extreme – as by Chinggis Khan and his lineage, the so-called Golden Kin – the resulting empire could envelop the entire steppe and begin to conquer sedentaries on a more permanent basis. When the founder of the empire died, there was, invariably, a succession struggle. Empires rarely survived for more than a couple of generations.

Following the Hsiung-nu and the Huns, particularly successful steppe empires organized along similar lines include the Uighur and the Khitan Empires. The Uighurs, whose powers peaked in the late eighth century, were a nomadic turned sedentary people who had considerable experience in ruling sedentary populations and cities. The Khitans were a semi-nomadic Turko-Mongolian people that had established the Liao dynasty, been displaced, and returned as a key steppe force of the twelfth century (Sverdrup-Thygesen 2013).

From the Uighurs the Mongols borrowed their alphabet (and used it until about a century ago), their way of setting up a chancery and the concept of scribes. The Khitans, who were brought into the Mongol fold in 1218, had administered a loose and non-confessional steppe empire based on tribute extracted by decimally organized cavalry (Morgan 1986: 49). For this, they had used intermediaries, and these are the direct predecessors of the *darugha* used by the Mongols, the Turkish concept for which is *basqaq* (Morgan 1986: 109). The Mongol intermediaries who ran the Golden Horde in Russia in the early decades were locally known as the *baskaki*.

All empires function by the use of intermediaries. Chinggis' key tool was his imperial guard, which had at its core his classificatory brothers (*anda*) and people who had chosen to leave their tribe to follow him personally (*nöker*). The guard, which included representatives of all the Mongolian tribes ('a useful form of hostage-taking', Morgan 1986: 90), and which was in effect Chinggis' household, numbered around 10,000 at the outset of his conquests.

Although the Mongols made eminent use of heavy wooden saddles and composite bows, their key advantage in warfare was their strategy, which emphasized protracted training, advance planning, multi-strand coordination and tight discipline. Alone at the time, they concentrated their thinking not on the single combatant or on a small group of soldiers, but on the *tümen*, (Russian: t'ma), a unit ideally composed of 10,000 men, though it was officially recognized that actual tümen would be undermanned (Allsen 1987: 193). The land needed to man a tümen was also used by the Mongols as the basic administrative unit. At the height of its power, in the mid thirteenth century, the Mongol Empire, in the shape of four different polities, covered most of the known world, from the Pacific coast to Russian lands and from the high north to the waters outside Japan. India, which was not at that time a Mongol possession, was to become so under Babur.

The Mongols lay claim to universal sovereignty. They conceived the world as a Mongol Empire to be known, under Chinggis Khan's successors, as the Golden Kin. All peoples were potential members of the universal Mongol Empire. Allsen writes that these political ideas can be traced back to the Türk Khaganate, and were in all likelihood transmitted to the Mongols by the Uighur Turks. In the Mongol adaptation of this ideological system it was held that Eternal Heaven (*Möngke Tenggeri*), the sky god and the chief deity of the – shamanistic – steppe nomads, bestowed upon Chinggis Khan a mandate to bring the entire world under his sway. This grant of universal sovereignty gave the Mongols the right, or perhaps more accurately, placed upon them the obligation, to subjugate and chastise any nation or people refusing to join the Empire of the Great Mongols on a voluntary basis (Allsen 1987: 42).[2]

The key principle of organization was biological and classificatory kinship. Succession was a major challenge to the Mongol Empire, as it was for all steppe polities. As the Mongols had no fewer than three succession principles, both primogeniture, ultimogeniture and collateral seniority, it was increasingly difficult to decide who held the best claim to the imperial title. It was Chinggis Khan's family as such who held the legitimate right to rule, and each potential contender was allotted a place within the hierarchy of the state. The centre of the empire was the *khagan*'s, but the eastern bit (also known as the 'blue' portion) was allotted to one of the other brothers and the western bit (known as the 'white' and later 'golden' portion) was allotted to yet another brother. As each of these geographical areas also corresponded to a part of the army and hence also the state, this meant that each of them had a base for launching a bid for succession once the khagan had died. And such a 'bid' had its function: it was the way by which rulers gained legitimacy to rule. Showing prowess in the power struggle that

[2] The idea of a heavenly mandate was, of course, also a Chinese idea (cf. de Rachewiltz 1971: 104).

ensued following a leader's fall was proof of possession of *qut*, the Turko-Mongol concept for divine grace. Being able to play the power game necessary to win the title, and also to fight for it in battle, in and of itself legitimized the effort. There was the institution of the *kuriltay*, an inter-tribal council where representatives of all the tribes had to sanction the new leader's accession. However, *de facto* power had a legitimizing effect in itself, and kuriltays had a tendency to legitimize the most powerful, and hence most able, candidate.

The language of the fights over succession was the one of the *jasagh*, the rules of the ancestors, which were supposed to be upheld and to which respect should be paid, not least when these were used creatively. Although the custom was for the youngest son to follow his father, there was no automatic succession involved. The candidates built alliances that felt out one another until a single candidate emerged as the stronger and called a kuriltay where the leading Genghisid successors were to consecrate him (Allsen 1987: 34). After Chinggis Khan died in 1227, his youngest son Tolui took over as regent, but in 1229 it was Ögödei who made khagan. When he died in 1241, a protracted fight between the Toluids and the Ögödeians ended when Tolui's oldest son Möngke made khagan in 1251. This protracted fight was of key importance to European history, and we will return to it below.

Ideal type: steppe patrimonialism

The key thing in this chapter is to point up legacies and remnants of a non-European imperial tradition. One way of doing this is to start from a juxtaposition of an ideal type of Eurasian steppe empire to one of Western empire. Where mode of production is concerned, agriculture is the obvious base for ideal types of European-type polities, be that states or empires. The basic mode of production of Eurasian steppe empires, namely pastoral nomadism, does in fact have agricultural production as its precondition for emergence. Historically, pastoral nomadism in the steppe co-existed with some apiculture, horticulture and even agriculture, and it was not unusual for steppe marginals to spend much time on agriculture. That is of little concern to an ideal type, however.

European ideal types of empire invariably stress the importance of a territorial centre from which power radiates, at a gradient, so that the imperial presence tapers off around the edges. Such a model is dependent on there being a sedentary production that may produce a surplus that can feed the empire's administrators. Steppe empires depart from this in two major ways. First, every single household, those of local aristocrats included, pursued nomadic pastoralism. Second, due to climatic factors, the form of nomadism practised tended to be transhumant. This means that nomadic routes are followed in the summer season, while the winter season is spent in quarters. This makes for a difference in temporality where capitals are concerned, with European imperial capitals operating at full strength for most, if not all, of the year, and Eurasian steppe capitals being mainly winter residences. As a corollary, steppe empire capitals were usually located in a valley. The capital of the Mongol Empire was, for example, Karakorum on the Orkhon River, built by Chinggis Khan's son Ögödei (Purdue 2005: 23–24).

Two key traits of ideal-type European empires are the importance of middlemen, and the importance of there being specific and various bargains between the centre and each middleman, so-called heterogeneous contracting (Nexon and Wright 2006). These traits are immediately recognizable in European steppe empires as well, with the twist that middlemen had to travel to the imperial centre in order to receive their patent (*yarlik*) for rule. The two ideal types are also at one in that personal relationships between the emperor/khagan and his henchmen were important, but typically, the key henchmen of European empires would fill administrative functions (a Colbert, a Disraeli), whereas key henchmen of the khagan (*nöker, anda*) would fill a military function (Endicott 1989). The precondition of possibility for this is the different degree of functional specificity of the two types, a difference that may ultimately be traced back to the difference in mode of production. Another, and we would argue crucial, difference evolves from a much-discussed change in European polities away from basing politics primarily on loyalty to the ruler towards basing it more and more on loyalty to the polity as such.[3] There is no parallel to this development where the Eurasian steppe empires are concerned, which is why Weber characterized them as patrimonial, with *sultanism* being the purest form of patrimonialism. Khazanov (2001: 4–5) highlights the role of charisma within the steppe tradition. Weber categorizes sultanism as traditional and leaves out the charismatic. We will argue

---

[3] This tradition is often referred to as a republican one (Onuf 1998).

that particularly twentieth-century sultanism has involved a patrimonially organized state led by a charismatic leader. Both the Bolshevik and the Kemalist regimes came to power after historical discontinuities in the principles of rule. It would be meaningless to argue that they took their legitimacy from tradition. Rather, it was Lenin's, Stalin's and Kemal Atatürk's ability to do away with tradition that bolstered their charismatic positions.

European empires were what a historian of religion would call cult based, that is, based on an institutionalized community of ritual specialists, in this case, a Church. As already noted, steppe empires drew on a different aspect of religion for their legitimation. Rather than tying legitimacy to the cultic aspect, which would traditionally have meant foregrounding shamans as cultic specialists, they emphasized the ruler's heavenly mandate. Where religious legitimacy in the European case is tied to the social institution of the Church, in Eurasia it is tied to the social institution of leadership.[4]

Where middleman maintenance is concerned, there is a key difference that may be traced back to the difference in mode of production. The middlemen of European empires typically traded economic surplus for imperial protection. The middlemen of Eurasian empires, however, typically received parts of the spoils of operations such as raiding caravans and taking tribute from sedentaries in exchange for participation. A similar difference emerges where marriage patterns are concerned: European empires typically sported dynastic marriages. The Golden Kin intermarried, too, but typically, the khagan's household was wife-giving to middlemen (Kotkin 2007).

Since the loyalty of middlemen was dependent on spoils distributed by the khagan, success in war was followed by the distribution of loot. This ran into problems as soon as nomadic raids resulted in territorial conquests and actual rule over sedentaries. When one thirteenth-century nomadic leader came across the treasure chamber of a newly conquered sedentary state and was about to distribute it among his subjects, which he thought would give him everlasting fame (and thus loyalty from his middlemen), his Persian advisor suggested a different course of action:

---

[4] Note that the Byzantines tried to have it both ways, with the Basileus having a heavenly mandate *and* the Church being a legitimating mainstay of the empire. Anachronistically, this is referred to as Caesaro-Papism.

> If thou distributest a treasure to the multitude
> Each householder will receive but a grain of rice.
> Why takest thou not from each a barley-corn of silver
> That thou mayest accumulate everyday a treasure?[5]

The practice of taxing sedentary subjects, and indeed having subjects at all (rather than defining them as outsiders to be plundered) is something that sedentary (mostly Persian) advisors introduced to the steppe–nomadic rulers. This was part of a fundamentally different way of conceptualizing the relationship between ruler and ruled from what the steppe nomads had adhered to previously. This is a case of hybridity between nomadic and sedentary practices of statecraft. Since political loyalty was just as valuable as material wealth, and both less vulnerable and burdensome to nomads (treasure is heavy and can easily be plundered by other nomads), according to the ideal type, rulers seek to convert material capital into symbolic and social capital as soon as possible.

Finally, there are important systematic differences in personnel between the two types of empire, both where the elite and the people are concerned.

Elites European polities, empires included, were typically dynastic, with some of them even carrying the name of the dynasty (the Habsburgs, the Oldenburgs). Successions might be intra-dynastic, or they could be between different lineage-based dynasties (the Yorks vs the Lancasters, the Guelphs vs the Ghibellines). Eurasian steppe empires were also dynastic, but here it was an entry value for any pretender that he should belong to one specific kinship group, namely the founder kinship of the empire.

Populations The basic unit of European empires was the household, which was tied to a plot of land and often also to a village. The basic unit of steppe empires was the household, which was multi-ethnic and multilingual. These were moveable. The territoriality of European empires is typically tied to fixed areas and regions, whereas steppe empires are typically tied to interchangeable grazing lands and trekking routes. This translates into systematic differences when empires break up: European empires typically break up along territorial lines, whereas Eurasian empires break up into discrete 'tribes'.

---

[5] Sa'dī (1899: chapter 1 'Manner of Kings', couplet 18). Our gratitude goes to Ashk Dahlén for directing us to this source.

With the ascendance of that scourge of empire, nation, national originary myths will vary accordingly.

Leadership in battle   European empires were largely built by sacrificing 'other people's lives', with the monarch and aristocracy leading from the rear. While the dynasty and the aristocracy were ideally martial, they were not expected to die in pursuit of imperial goals to the same extent as were the peasants. In steppe empires war-making was the duty and the privilege of the nomads who formed the backbone of the polity, and while there was a hierarchy among them and one may reasonably assume that those further down the hierarchy were more likely to die in battle than the khagan, they were all expected to fight and potentially die. The khagan led from the front, and he led 'his own' rather than mercenaries or conquered peasants. While conquered nomads would be enrolled in the horde, sedentary subjects were assets rather than a fighting force, and were not considered to have anything to do with war (Barthold 1968: 291).

The character of the boundary populations   Eurasian steppe empires will typically envelop ever new steppe-dwelling 'tribes', until the population living closest to the sedentaries will have the choice between being enveloped or taking refuge amongst the sedentaries. Typically, a critical mass of warriors will choose the latter alternative, and will then go on to earn a living as border guards. Advancing steppe empires and their remnants will, therefore, typically stand against forces paid for by sedentaries but consisting of former steppe peoples as well as sedentaries. Border populations of European empires will typically build and man defences against the Eurasian steppe empires, whereas Eurasian empires will organize their border populations on a raiding and tribute-taking – i.e. an offensive – basis.

This discussion could easily have been expanded to cover systematic differences between sedentary and nomadic empires, but since the basic use to which we are going to put it is to demonstrate that remnants of imperial steppe tradition lead a subterranean existence in a world practically and theoretically dominated by European imperial remnants, we chose to be Euro-centric about it. We may summarize our contrasting discussion as follows:

Since the imperial family and its entourage was nomadic as distinct from sedentary, however, its legacy is somewhat more dispersed than most imperial legacies, in both a spatial and symbolic sense.

Table 5.1 *Ideal-typical traits of European and Eurasian empires compared*

	European	Eurasian
Mode of production	Agriculture	Nomadic pastoralism
Differentiation of production	High	Low
Capital active	Year-round	If capital – winter
Contract centre–periphery	Law-based	Patrimonial
Middlemen	Are tied to administration	Are tied to the khagan personally
	Are administrative	Are military
	Give spoils and women	Receive surplus and women
Religion legitimating	Cultic	Personal
Dynastic succession	Inter	Intra
Major population units	Villages/regions	Households
Military leadership	From the rear	From the front
Loyalty	Increasingly to the polity	To the ruler

Remnants of the steppe tradition: personnel

Human remnants of the Mongol Empire's four major offshoots are in evidence. The Yuan dynasty in China lasted until 1348. The Ilkhans in Persia lasted approximately as long. In the West, however, the Golden Kin stuck it out in the felt tent capital of Saray whence they could maintain a steppe-based lifestyle. Muscovy seems to have stopped paying tribute to the Khipchak Khanate sometime around 1470, and made an alliance with the western part of what was left of it in 1502. Muscovy effectively swallowed its partner, and in 1507, Sigismund of Poland-Lithuania was 'granted' the western part from its last Khan. The Khipchak Khanate was no more.

In the steppe itself, unsurprisingly, the living tradition lasted longer. The Yuan dynasty had an afterlife north of the Chinese border. In the mid fifteenth century, the Oirat Empire was a major steppe force (Purdue 2005: 59). It was followed by one last Mongol imperial steppe polity, the Zunghar Empire, which sported a new glue, Tibetan Buddhism. The first Mongol contact with Tibetan Buddhism since the thirteenth century occurred in 1566, when the Ordos Mongol Khutukhai Secen Hongtiji (1540–86) travelled to Tibet. In 1578, his successor Altan Khan gave Sodnam Gyamtsho 'the title of "Dalai Lama" (Oceanic Teacher in Mongolian),[6] and the Dalai Lama declared Altan to be the reincarnation of Khubilai Khan' (Purdue 2005: 66). One Mongolian offshoot, the Kalmyk, moved west and arrived north of the Caucasus from Inner Asia in the 1620s, causing the usual ripple effect on the steppe by pushing the grazing lands of the Nogays further west, which in turn became a factor in increasing the raids of the Nogays and the Crimean Tatars against Russian sedentaries (Khadorkovsky 2004: 132–33). By the seventeenth century, the Kalmyks were a major power in the western steppe. The living imperial steppe tradition was liquidated by the expansion of two sedentary empires, Chinese and Russian, into the steppe. And yet, there were remnants.

The Crimean Khanate was the main successor to the Khipchak Khanate, and although they remained fairly stationary around the Crimean peninsula and their capital Bakhchisaray, old steppe habits died hard. Their political organization was certainly straight out of the steppe tradition (Fisher 1970: 10). Furthermore, the Crimean continued lucrative steppe pursuits such as raiding, tribute-taking and slave trading. In 1571, Crimean Tatars attacked Moscow, and the attacks continued on a lesser scale well into the eighteenth century.

After the Russian annexation in 1784, some 50–75 per cent of the Crimean Tatar population decamped for the Ottoman Empire (McNeill 1964: 199). According to Reşat Kasaba (2009: 9; see also Fisher 1999: 181), as many as 900,000 Muslims left Crimea and the Caucasus in the eight years following the Crimean War (1853–56). In this case, the answer to where the Mongol-Turkic population went is Anatolia. That is, in fact, the answer that usually applies.

The Cossacks were another story, and present themselves as a key example of the hybridizing fallout of empire. They congealed not from pastoral households, but from runaways from all kinds of different

---

[6] Note the similarity with the title Chinggis Khan (his name was Temüjin), which means oceanic/universal khan/ruler.

polities towards frontier settlements. The steppe polities and the Cossacks both perpetuated Mongol practices, but they did so in different ways (McNeill 1964: 115–16, 118).

By the time of the Napoleonic Wars, physical remnants of the steppe tradition were reduced to territorially bounded units along the Russian–Chinese border. Contemporary examples include the state of Mongolia, Inner Mongolia in China, Buryatia and Tuvy in Russia.

Social fact remnants of the imperial Eurasian steppe tradition

Having traced the steppe polities up to their demise in the late eighteenth century, we now turn to a discussion of remnants understood as social facts (as opposed to personnel). The hitch regarding wide-ranging historical discussions like the following is always the same; the number of variables in play is so large that it is very hard to establish that any one phenomenon is a causal effect of any one set of historical patterns. The argument must remain a tentative and somewhat under-specified one, at least until more work has been done.

We begin with the most obvious case, which is Central Asia, and then proceed with the increasingly less clear-cut cases of Turkey and Russia. Before we proceed, however, we want to make note of a fourth case that is in need of further work, but that we leave out here for reasons of space and lack of expertise: the Indian subcontinent.

In terms of political tradition, both Pakistan and India were heavily influenced by the Mughal Empire. The Mughal Empire is literally the Mongol Empire, with Mughal (and Moghul) being different (and phonetically more accurate) transcriptions of the same word. This was a vast empire centred on Delhi from 1526 until the British expanded upon them, abolishing it in 1857 and claiming the title for themselves in 1876. The elite of the Mughal Empire were to a large extent Persians and Turks, but they were, like everyone else, heavily influenced by Mongol politics. The problem in determining Mongol influence is that much of the areas ruled by Mongols were ruled by Turks both before and after Mongol domination. And since Turkic and Mongol political traditions are so heavily intertwined and thus similar, it is almost impossible to tell what is a Mongol influence and what is a Turkic influence when it comes to political institutions and traditions.

Tradition in Central Asian states

Afghanistan is probably the key geographical site where sedentary–nomadic relations of the kind that emerged with the demise of the Mongols is still the order of the day. People wait to be told for whom to vote (Barfield 2010: 331). This is reminiscent of the way the *kuriltay* was an institution for confirming the most powerful khan as khagan, rather than an instrument for selecting the leader. If we believe Barfield, the Afghans took recent elections to be a way to express their loyalty to the supreme force (the Americans) by voting for the man that this supreme force wanted to rule. When the Americans did not explicitly say whom to vote for, the Afghans were at a loss. Similarly, elections in former Soviet republics in Central Asia, such a Kyrgyzstan, systematically elect the candidate supported by Moscow. This is not to say that there is no election fraud, but that the expectation on the part of the population is not that elections are instruments for selecting leaders, but merely to confirm the most powerful man as the supreme leader.

It is also no coincidence that when the Central Asian republics (as well as Azerbaijan in the Caucasus) suddenly needed a political past upon which to base their identities as sovereign states after the fall of the Soviet Union, they reached to political lineages going back to the Mongols and to the same imperial title from which the Mughals, the Muscovites and Ottomans claimed *translatio imperii*. This can hardly be called a historical accident, as many descendants of Chinggis Khan explicitly identify as such. The memory of the Mongol Empire is still something to be used for political purposes, even though in Afghanistan the Mongol invasion is still remembered for its devastating consequences for sedentary civilization. Among the Hazaras, an outlying group of people in Pakistan and Afghanistan who used to speak a Mongol language but now largely speak Iranic ones, many men can recite their genealogies going back about thirty-four generations to Chinggis Khan.[7]

In what can be termed a 'wider Central Asia', the political traditions we explore here were the main mode of conducting politics until the 1920s (Barfield 2002). In some areas, most notably in Afghanistan but also in Iran, focusing on steppe and sedentary imbrication is arguably still the most relevant way of shedding light on state–society relations

---

[7] www.freerepublic.com/focus/news/838099/posts

(Barfield 2010). In Iran, the last explicit vestiges of the power of the nomads was shattered only in the 1930s, when Shah Reza Pahlavi blocked nomadic migrations by placing army units at strategic points (Barfield 2002: 84). Yet, in terms of the state itself, there can be little doubt that a symbiosis between Azeri Turkic elements and Persians is the *modus operandi*. Turkey may seem the odd one out, with almost ninety years of uninterrupted and outright adoption of Western practices. And yet, one way to see Mustafa Kemal is as a charismatic state founder, whose charisma is used by a clan (the Kemalists) to rule with the semi-divine authority of the founder. This analogy to early Turkic states (and in particular the Ottoman) is useful as a heuristic device. Ruling (or at least trying to rule) in the name of the state founder (literally Mustafa Kemal – Kemalists) is a typical trait of Turkic state building.

With the breakup of the Soviet Union, what Peter Golden (1992: 305) terms *politiconyms* took the place of ethnonyms, with an identity as Stalinist, Kemalist, Putinist taking the place of ethnic identity as the main social marker. Moreover, we would contend that the ethnogenesis of the category Turk, as it was formulated by the modern Turkish Republic, was in fact a question of loyalty to the state, and a possibility (for Muslims) of opting in or out of the political project led by Mustafa Kemal.

This is a direct influence not only of the steppe tradition, but an innovation that came about with the demise of the Mongol Empire. The first such politiconyms were derived directly from the names of descendants of Chinggis. It is still a way to denote political loyalty in Eurasia today.

Legacy in Turkey

The Mongol polity that emerged in the 'Islamic lands' was centred on what is today Iran. It bordered the Mamluk state in the south-west, with a frontier running through Syria. Their Turkic vassals in Anatolia, the Seljuqs, had a frontier with the Byzantines running through north-western Anatolia. The polity had its origin in the campaign launched by Hülegü Khan, notorious for sacking Baghdad in 1258. The campaign was launched on the orders of Kublai Khan, Hülegü's brother and khagan. Mongol expansion in the south-west was halted by the Mamluks, a state ruled by an army composed of enslaved steppe nomads converted to Islam. As the Mongol army was to experience on several occasions, most notably at 'Ayn Jâlût, the Mamluks employed the same tactics as the Mongols, and knew the weaknesses of Mongol warfare (Amitai 1992: 139).

According to received wisdom, the Ottoman *beylik*, the Ottoman polity before it became an empire, was originally founded with a charter from the Seljuq sultan in Anatolia. The American scholar Rudi Lindner (1983, 2007) takes issue with this view, on the basis that at the time when the beylik is thought to have come into existence (1299), the Seljuqs were little more than vassals of the Ilkhanid ruler Ghazan Khan, seated in Tabriz, in what is today north-western Iran. Lindner's hypothesis that the Ottomans received their charter from the Ilkhanids in return for help in quelling a rebellion among the Mongols in Anatolia is based on little more than historical context, combined with a single coin tying Osman to the Ilkhanids minted in 1299. The other account is based merely on Ottoman chroniclers (*vakanüvis*) writing more than a century after the fact, and under completely different political circumstances. However, the Mongol connection (if there ever was one) was soon written out of official Ottoman historiography, and Ottoman chroniclers invested much in the *translatio imperii* from the Seljuqs. As the Seljuqs were also part of the same tradition, having migrated to Anatolia some two centuries earlier, but maintaining contact eastwards during this period, the connection between the Ottomans and the steppe tradition is not disputed, merely the time and manner of *translatio*. Having emerged on this frontier between the Ilkhanids/Seljuqs and the Byzantines, the Ottoman polity's mode of statecraft was highly dependent upon steppe nomadic elements.

We now turn to the attributes of the Ottoman polity seen in the light of our ideal type. First, the art of warfare and surplus extraction by the state. The military success of the early Ottoman polity has been the subject of some debate. Paul Wittek (1938) provides the baseline interpretation that the polity drew warriors motivated by religious zeal, with the practice of *gaza* being the only foreign policy available to the early Ottoman polity. While he does not mention the main mode of surplus extraction by steppe nomadic polities, the American Ottomanist Heath Lowry (2005) has argued at book's length that the Ottomans were not primarily a state dedicated to the concept of *gaza* (Holy War), nor were its *gazis*, many of whom were not even Muslims, primarily motivated by a desire to spread Islam. Their goal was booty, plunder, and slaves. (Lowry 2005: 43)

The Ottomans, at least in their very earliest phase, mobilized their army through the distribution of looted resources. It didn't take them long to establish a treasury and start taxation, but hybridity on this matter had already started among the Seljuqs in Iran in the eleventh century and the Ilkhanids in the thirteenth century.

In accordance with Wittek's emphasis on religion for military mobilization, the polity was also supposedly tied to Islam from the very beginning. Lowry, on the other hand, argues that the polity was not founded by the Turkic nomad chieftain Osman alone, but in conjunction with two other military leaders. These two were probably local Christian warlords who had recently converted to Islam. That these were later 'written out' of official Ottoman historiography as it started to be written in the fifteenth century, is easily attributable to the Ottoman dynasty's consolidation of power, and the introduction of Islam as a precondition for prestige (although not political influence). Loyalty and kinship were the key political markers in steppe nomadic tradition, not religion as such. As the Ottomans were very much part of this tradition, there is little reason that they should have avoided cooperation with local Christians.

Although he does not push the connection with steppe practices much further, Lowry concludes that the way Osman became first among equals in the polity

is reminiscent of the Turko-Mongol practice of the *Khuriltay*, the assemblies where leaders were traditionally chosen/elected in such societies on the basis of their ability. (Lowry 2005: 65)

What we see here is that, as Lowry points out, Osman was confirmed as head of what later became the 'Ottoman' polity, another example of a politiconym, by use of a kuriltay, a legitimizing device for confirming the accession of the most powerful leader. However, it should be pointed out that the criteria used for selecting a leader was to a great extent the principle of letting the most powerful tribal leader rule. In addition to this khuriltay, we see many features that are reminiscent of Mongol forms of organization. There are what we may analytically call the *anda* (the 'oath-sworn', the *comitatus*) of Osman, the classificatory brothers, who acted as military commanders. Due to the paucity of sources, we have no indication as to how Osman, the much-celebrated founder of the empire, related to his much less celebrated co-founders, other than the story of how he refused to make war on them when his biological brother suggested doing so (Lowry 2005: 68).

Another key feature of Eurasian nomadic-emergent polities is their lack of attachment to cities and particular capitals. If one excepts Iran, no empire has ever changed capital as frequently as the Ottoman Empire and its successor state Turkey. Having started as a nomadic venture in the area around Söğüt on the frontier between the Seljuqs/ Ilkhanids and Byzantines in north-western Anatolia, they established a capital in Bursa as soon as that city had fallen to their forces in 1324. The capital was then moved to Adrianople (modern-day Edirne) in 1365, and again to Constantinople in 1453. Then, when Constantinople, which was by then also known as Istanbul, was occupied by the British in 1918, parts of the state elite relocated to Anatolia and set up a competing military and later administrative centre first in Erzurum and then in Ankara. Ankara, having become a de facto counter capital in 1920, was formalized as the capital of Turkey in 1922, which it still is. Our guess is that it is only a matter of time before the capital is moved again, this time back to Istanbul.

The Ottomans never had a good claim to descent from the most prestigious lineages of the steppe, but invested much in trying to conjure up such a connection by creating genealogies reaching back to Oğuz Khan. Politics was a matter of intra-dynastic competition, with a system resembling the Mongol up until Süleyman the Magnificent in the mid sixteenth century. The Ottomans even recognized the dynasty of the Crimean Tatars (who were descended from the Golden Horde), as legitimate 'golden kin', who were accepted as legitimate heirs to the Ottoman throne, should the Ottoman dynasty die out. While no other vassal dynasty was considered appropriate as successors, it follows that the Ottomans were very much alert to the prestige of Chinggis Khan's lineage, a lineage that has no prestige according to Islamic tradition, the Mongols being considered barbarians, something that was heightened by Hülegü's sacking of Baghdad in 1258.

As the Ottomans made war in the Balkans, its campaigns became more and more reliant on siege artillery and infantry, as besieging and storming citadels and fortresses became the order of the day. The immediate result was that the martial role of the nomads decreased significantly. Moreover, the 'nomad party', centred on Adrianople, increasingly lost out in the palace intrigue in Constantinople.[8] However, the nomads were still a force to be reckoned with, and the symbolic order of the state was strongly tied to traditions emerging from the steppe, at least in times of war.

Nevertheless, although the relationship between the nomads and the sedentary central administration in Constantinople was often strained, the nomads still played a key defensive role on the frontiers until the late seventeenth century in the Balkans, in the eighteenth century in the Caucasus and the nineteenth century in the Arab-speaking and Kurdish-speaking lands to the south. The Turkish historian Reşat Kasaba argues that in the early part of Ottoman history 'maintaining a nomadic presence, especially in the frontier regions of the empire, was an important source of strength. The imperial center used these communities as tentacles of its reach into neighboring territories' (Kasaba 2009: 8). These 'tentacles' consisted not only of Turks, but also of Tatars, the very remnants of the Golden Horde. Moreover, to call the nomads of the Ottoman Empire mere 'tentacles' seems to understate the case. The nomads were a key component of the composite nomadic–sedentary state, not merely a tool that the centre used to reach into neighbouring realms. The nomads were just as much directed inwards as they were outwards. Balancing the sedentaries (and the standing army, in most cases infantry) against the nomads (the nomadic cavalry) was a central aspect of running such a state.

The Ottomans made a point of maintaining largely open and mostly unmarked borders over which merchants, nomads, and other itinerant groups and individuals continued to move. There is little doubt that Ottoman rulers saw such openness and mobility as a source of strength. They supported social structures and policies that accommodated and strengthened the interaction of different communities across the empire. (Kasaba 2009: 47)

The practices of the steppe nomads became less explicit at the core of the empire as time went on, but as a baseline for how things were done, they outlasted a steady stream of pious sultans who usually interpreted steppe practices as *haram* (in contradiction with religious law). One important such trace is in the prohibition against spilling royal blood,

---

[8] For a discussion of a case where the Sultan (Osman II) attempted to make an alliance with the Turcoman nomads on the frontier to outsmart the Janissaries in Constantinople, see Piterberg 2003.

which the Ottomans observed carefully. Princes whose very existence threatened the stability of the state through their potential as pretenders were killed by strangulation as this prevented blood-letting. But it is when it came to war that the full battery of steppe symbolism came into play (see for example Wheatcroft 2008: 13). As Wheatcroft points out, as late as the end of the seventeenth century 'Every function of the court had its travelling counterpart' (15). The court in Constantinople transformed into a nomadic entity when the sultan was campaigning, and before departure on campaign the Sultan himself moved into his tent, which was erected outside Constantinople (43). However, the ceremonial order of the army, with its *tuğ* (horse-tail banners), carrying the significance of each of the elements of the army, similar to the banners used by the Mongol and their like, seem to have had little correspondence with actual fighting formations. The fighting against the Habsburgs had taken on a dynamic of its own, creating tactics, strategies and battle formations that were unlike the type of war fought by the Habsburgs in Europe and by the Ottomans in other theatres.

If we fast forward to the early 2000s, the lack of distinction between an economic and a political sector is not unique to the steppe tradition, but it is a key aspect of how a post-steppe state is run. An Azeri academic related in an interview with one of us regarding corruption in Azerbaijan that 'one cannot say that there is corruption in the system, in Azerbaijan corruption *is* the system'.[9] What the Americans call the 'spoils system', through which a new president (or any other elected official) replaces much of the administrative staff in the parts of the bureaucracy over which he presides, is taken to its logical extreme in the post-steppe states. An example may be taken from a Turkish businessman complaining to one of the authors about the 'corruption' of AKP government in Turkey. According to him, Turkish politicians have always hired people on the basis of political and personal loyalty, but the ruling party, AKP, goes further than previous governments; now even the *çaycıs* (tea boys) at the national airline are appointed on the basis of loyalty to the AKP. While difficult to verify, it squares nicely with the AKP's other practices and therefore sounds eminently plausible. With a large party organization including a lot of people without education (many of them çaycıs), they have to distribute privileges to

---

[9] Baku, Azerbaijan, 7 January 2010.

their supporters, as this is expected in a Eurasian state.[10] While some would call this corruption (as indeed it is by some Turks excluded from the privileges), that presupposes a clear distinction between an economic and a political sector. Typical of states where the steppe tradition plays a key role, in Turkey and Azerbaijan such a distinction is secondary to rewarding political supporters economically. This is not, as it often looks from a Western point of view, corruption in the system. It is, rather, the way Eurasian states are run.[11]

The economic and political sectors are not the only parts of society in a steppe political tradition that are left undifferentiated. Intellectuals are also expected to play their role by eulogising the khagan. Turkish president Recep Tayyip Erdoğan has sought to silence all criticism by filing defamation lawsuits against almost all journalists who have criticised him. In May 2012, prime minister Erdoğan threatened to cut all funding to theatres, after one actor lampooned his daughter. He condemned what he called the 'despotic arrogance' of intellectuals (Gibbons 2012). Arrogant despots, on the other hand, seem to be expected and accepted.

Remnants in Russia

When Batu died in 1256, he had built a tent capital in Saray on the Volga (100 km north of today's Astrakhan) for his Khipchak Khanate, which came to be known locally as the Golden Horde. We have little history writing on the Khipchak Khanate, among other things because its archives were destroyed together with most of its city life by Tamerlane's nomadic invading force (emanating from Samarkand) in 1390.[12] Since the steppe-dwelling Mongols lacked expertise in running

---

[10] Note that Azerbaijan's ruler, İlham Aliyev, takes this to another level, e.g. by simply *giving* a stake in a state-owned goldmine to his own daughter; see Ismayilova and Fatullayeva 2012.

[11] Note that the relative importance attached to either principle is completely different in Turkey and Azerbaijan, with Azerbaijan, as well as the Central Asian republics, being closer to the Eurasian ideal type.

[12] The Golden Horde had been in dynastic crisis since the death of Khan Berdibeg in 1359, one reason being the swelling of the numbers of the Golden Kin (Spuler 1965: vol. II). The object of the invasion was Khan Tokhtamesh (1376–95), a previous protégé of Tamerlane's who succeeded in uniting the Golden Horde with the White Horde to its east. The White Horde had been established by the same Mongol campaign that spied out the Russian lands in 1223.

administrative apparatuses, throughout the Mongol Empire these were mostly staffed locally. In the case of the Khipchak Khanate, however, there was little by way of local administrative personnel to be found, and so the khagan relied on Khwarazm Turks (in Russian *Besserminy*). The Khipchak Khanate adopted Islam as its official religion under Özbek (1313–41), in conjunction with which they also adopted the Persian administrative *diwan* system. The mix of Turko-Mongol, and also some Persian, elements was also pronounced amongst this dominant layer of population, which came to be known as Tatar.

Russian scholars have not really theorized their polity as an empire, and sometimes even denied its imperial character (see, for example Riasanovsky 1967: 57). Traditionally, Russian scholars have also toned down the impact of the steppe on Muscovy. To quote but one typical example, in 1788 Ivan Boltin argued that

Having defeated (the Rus') principalities, the Tatars imposed tribute on their enslaved subjects one by one. They then left baskaks (officials) to collect the tribute and placed their soldiers in the towns before returning to their own lands. Under (Tatar) rule, the Russians lived by the same laws that they had lived by before, and these laws remained unchanged after the yoke was overthrown. Their morals, dress, language, the names of the people and the country remained what they had always been, with the exception of a few small changes in social rituals, beliefs, and vocabulary that were borrowed from the Tatars. (Quoted in Sunderland 2004: 38)

This is a misleading move. First, 'social rituals' are at the heart of social and political life, and so any borrowings here are of the essence. The Muscovy head received steppe people – who, in accordance with the steppe tradition, came riding to ask for a patent on land – by accepting their kowtowing and granting them the patent to rule their polity (Sunderland 2004: 16), just as the Mongols had done back in Karakorum. Furthermore, the habit of kowtowing (*bit' chel'bom*) was ubiquitous within Muscovy society itself (Zorin 1959: 140). Second, Muscovy actually started propping up its claims to being an imperial power on a par with the Holy Roman Empire by invoking its conquests of the successor states of the Kipchak Khanate. Furthermore, when Muscovy vanquished Kazan in 1552, Astrakhan in 1554 and Siberia in 1580, each time the khanate crown was taken to be displayed in Moscow (Khadorkovsky 2004: 45). The pride that Russians took in being the key successor of the Kipchak Khanate was also evident in the sixteenth-century aristocratic fashion for tracing one's ancestry back to Mongols (Halperin 1987: 113). Moscow's imperial claims were also presented in terms of diplomatic practices that definitely hailed from the Mongols, and which therefore necessarily struck European inter-locutors as Asian. As summed up by Charles J. Halperin:

> Given the importance of Russia's relations with its oriental neighbors, it is natural that Muscovy drew upon Tatar diplomatic practices in establishing its own. Accordingly, Muscovite diplomatic protocol was essentially Asian. (Halperin 1987: 92)

Here we have a concrete and, given that diplomacy is something of a master institution in global politics, crucial early example of how Muscovy, and also the Russian empire, were shaped by the steppe tradition within which the former states are steeped. To Halperin's examples we may add others, such as the intense attempts at trying to keep diplomats and other aliens in the dark about internal affairs. Diplomats were met at the border and kept from seeing the lands they travelled through on the way to the capital; once in Moscow, they were sequestered. One of the authors served as a guard and interpreter at the Norwegian embassy to Moscow in 1980. At that time, diplomats and other aliens were still required to apply for a travel permit if they wanted to drive further than 40 kilometres from Moscow. Then there were other Russian practices that were distinctly non-European, such as washing hands after shaking religiously unclean Catholic hands and refusing to eat with Catholics, basing their foreign policy apparatus on offices (*prikazy*) that were themselves modelled on early Mongol institutions, etc.[13]

Social, genealogical and anecdotal evidence aside, we turn now to an analytical discussion of the matter. Once again, we draw on the com-parison of ideal types presented above.

Where mode of production is concerned, the spread of the Russian and Soviet empires is also the history of the spread of agriculture. The turning of the Pontic Steppe from sustaining primarily nomadic pas-toralism to sustaining agriculture and the concurrent subduing of the Cossacks were firmly in place in the late eighteenth century. Although there were major pushes towards more agriculture as late as the 1970s

---

[13] Russian borrowings from the Mongols were extensive, see Vernadsky 1953: 127–30, 222–23, 333–90; cf. Halperin 1987: 90–95, 149n7; and, for a max-imalist reading Ostrowski 1998 (also Ostrowski 2000; Halperin 2000).

(Brezhnev's virgin land campaigns), remnants of nomadic pastoralism in today's Russia is a marginal phenomenon.

Where the temporality of the capital is concerned, Moscow is firmly an all-year capital. As late as two hundred years ago, in 1812, during the Napoleonic Wars (what Russians call the Patriotic War), General Mikhail Kutuzov famously abandoned Moscow and exploited the advantage offered him by the depth of the terrain to the full. Contemporaries such as de Bonald rightly commented on the nomadic character of this mode of waging war. Another poignant scene played itself out at the beginning of the war, when Russian peasants received advancing French soldiers as guests. True to steppe tradition, they tried to keep out of politics (Kharkhordin 2001).

The key imperial trait of heterogeneous contracting was in evidence throughout the Russian and Soviet periods, and still is. The Russian Empire perpetuated the steppe tradition by insisting that middlemen come to the capital to get their patent of rule throughout the eighteenth century. The key henchmen of the emperor were people fulfilling administrative functions, such as Mikhail Speranskiy. Soviet leaders were at one in being what they referred to as anti-Bonapartist, meaning that they were sceptical of military henchmen (or, more specifically, their potential for staging coups). This is a typical European, as opposed to Eurasian, trait of empire. Where the question of middlemen's loyalties is concerned, however, the Russian Empire, the Soviet Union and contemporary Russia are at one in basing politics primarily on loyalty to the ruler, as opposed to basing it predominantly on loyalty to the polity as such, in the European style. Contemporary Russia is unquestionably, and sometimes explicitly, patrimonial.

As to middleman maintenance, the Russian experience is remarkably undecided. From the late sixteenth century onwards, the Russian aristocracy was firmly suppressed by the tsars, and Peter the Great made it into a service nobility. The Russian Empire does not fit the European mould, where aristocrats tended to be key middlemen, in this regard. As a direct consequence of the nobility's weakness, experiments with 'self-government' in the latter half of the nineteenth century suffered from the lack of a clear group of middlemen.

The Soviet system, whereby middlemen sprang from the ranks of the Party, does not fit either mould. The entire question of regional autonomy has once again been a contested topic over the last twenty years, with the tendency being that the local base of middlemen is weakening.

We have, in the question of middleman maintenance, an issue that is very much alive in contemporary Russia. As regional governors have once again become presidential appointees, we are reverting to a situation where spoils (i.e. economic privileges) are divided by the political leader and given to middlemen according to their loyalty to the political leadership. Ideal-typically, we contrasted an imperial Eurasian steppe tradition where middlemen were recipients of spoils emanating from raiding and tribute to a European imperial tradition where middlemen channel economic resources to the centre. This could, in principle, lead us to see the channelling of economic resources from the centre to the middlemen as a reversion to a Eurasian pattern. When we do not want to argue in favour of this, it is because we do not find the economic side of this relationship to be essential, but rather see it as an effect of the very personalized tie between the man on top and his middlemen. The transfer of economic resources should, therefore, be seen as an aspect of Russian patrimonialism, rather than as a phenomenon that has independent explanatory power.

The expansion of the Russian Empire owed much to the centre's perceived need to keep people in, and the Soviet experience repeated the pattern with rather different ideological cadences (see Scott 2009; Lieven 2000). Since this was the expansion of a sedentary empire, the question of comparing the nature of its boundaries to those of Eurasian steppe empires seems moot.

We may conclude that, until the Napoleonic Wars, the Russian Empire owed a lot to the Eurasian steppe tradition. Since then, however, the remnants of that tradition have fallen by the wayside. There is, however, one key remnant of the imperial steppe tradition that still holds sway. During Soviet times, so-called cults of personality were stocks-in-trade of Russian politics. Today, the patrimonial nature of the Putin regime is not in doubt. Putin orchestrates campaigns that tout his physical and sexual prowess (he finds antiques at the bottom of the Black Sea and flies with cranes). Film cuts and stills of him doing judo, riding not horses but motorbikes, posing with a bare chest, etc. are widely distributed, as are his portraits. For the 2012 presidential election, one central advert sported a virgin who went to a fortune teller and was told that Putin would be 'her first'.[14]

---

[14] www.guardian.co.uk/world/video/2012/feb/29/putin-advert-russia-virgin-voters-video?newsfeed=true.

In order to thrive economically and politically, would-be chiefs and middlemen in today's Russia must pledge allegiance to the man on the top or risk confiscation. The so-called Khodorkovskiy affair is the most illustrative case in this regard. When Vladimir Putin took over as president, he invited key oligarchs – the seemingly independently rich who had emerged as key to Russian economic life during the 1990s – to a party at the Kremlin. Mikhail Borisovich Khodorkovskiy failed to turn up, and continued to argue in an independent fashion, as if his wealth were held independently of any political loyalty to Putin. Within a few years, his fortune was confiscated and he and his right-hand man ended up in prison, where they still languish. This is fully in accordance with historical patterns. Confiscation was a standard practice in the Ottoman Empire (not to mention the Soviet Union), and seems to be so in post-1991 Russia. One may even see parallels between the confiscations and nationalizations of the Bolsheviks and the lack of an established right of property within other states in this tradition. Control of the nationalized property was then entrusted to loyal supporters of Stalin in much the same way as the *timar*-holders of the early Ottoman Empire were rewarded by the state.

Political struggles in today's Russia take the shape of patrons fighting one another with the help of clients. The chain of patrons ends at the top, with Putin. This patrimonialism is, we argue, a remnant of the Eurasian steppe tradition. The point here is certainly not that the steppe is the only source of such contemporary practices, which after all may be spotted in a number of settings around the world, but that the steppe tradition is among the historical phenomena that shape the specific Russian practices in point here.

Conclusion

It would be wrong to assume that European empires are the only ones to leave their mark on today's polities. The steppe empires were among the most influential, and one may still see their legacies in many aspects of political practices and legitimizing narratives across Eurasia. It is still alive in parts of Central Asia. It has left a solid legacy in Turkey as well as remnants in Russia. The difference between these polities and European ones are often observed. The debt they owe to the Eurasian imperial steppe tradition takes us one step closer to accounting for these differences.

The polities emerging from the steppe have always been hybridized, as their very way of life has agriculture as a precondition for emergence. Steppe polities were, furthermore, dependent upon sedentaries in order to sustain themselves. This hybridization became more pronounced in the tenth and eleventh centuries, as Turkic dynasties broke through Transoxiana and became rulers over sedentary populations and, as such, dependent on sedentary bureaucrats and advisors for running the administration. Furthermore, the influence of the steppe tradition was renewed every now and then up until at least the fifteenth century, as newly formed steppe confederations launched attacks and overran these earlier dynasties. Another exercise that kept established rulers of hybridized polities in touch with the steppe tradition was the need to frame their claims vis-à-vis steppe rulers in terms that were recognized by the nomadic soldiery. These would include tropes such as the promising of more loot and the invocation of *qut*, the all-legitimizing fortune or divine will.

Given widespread hybridization, many polities who bear the marks of the steppe tradition have nonetheless put their steppe-nomadic past under erasure. This is, among other things, due to hybridization itself, for over the last two hundred years, the European tradition has fastened on how a proper polity, a state, is by definition sedentary. Other variants were treated as previous incarnations of an evolutionary sequence. It followed that an affinity to the steppe came to denote backwardness. Denial notwithstanding, we have tried to demonstrate how contemporary Eurasian states have been influenced by the steppe tradition in ways that are still tangible. While the Eurasian empires may have perished, remnants of their statecraft linger. How else can one understand the political similarities that are to a large extent geographically co-extensive with the Mongol Empire? While the aforementioned hybridity has created a wide range of differences in the local particularities, and there are different ways of relating to this past in how it is written into official historiography, the political traditions of polities ranging from the Mamluks in Egypt, via the Khazars and the Khipchak Khanate (i.e. the Golden Horde) in Russia, as well as the Mughals in India to the Mongols and the Yuan in China, make for a similarity in political traditions that can help to illuminate many similarities in the present. While a *Mongolophonie* would not have a wide membership, the legacy of a Eurasian imperial tradition is in evidence in a wide spectre of state practices and traditions in and around Eurasia.

References

Allsen, Thomas T. (1987) *Mongol Imperialism: The Politics of the Great Qan Möngke in China, Russia, and the Islamic Lands, 1251–1259.* Berkeley: University of California Press.

Amitai, Reuven (1992) ''Ayn Jâlût revisited'. *Târîh* 2, 119–50.

Barfield, Thomas J. (1989) *The Perilous Frontier: Nomadic Empires and China.* Charles Tilly (ed.). Cambridge, MA: Blackwell.

Barthold, Vasili V. (1968) *Turkistan down to the Mongol Invasion.* London: Gibb Memorial Series.

Di Cosmo, Nikola (2004) *Ancient China and its Enemies: The Rise of Nomadic Power in East Asian History.* Cambridge: Cambridge University Press.

Endicott, Elizabeth (1989) *Mongolian Rule in China.* Cambridge, MA: Harvard University Press.

Fennell, John L. I. (1983) *The Crisis of Medieval Russia 1200–1304.* London: Longman.

Fisher, Alan (1999) *A Precarious Balance: Conflict, Trade and Diplomacy on the Russian–Ottoman Frontier.* Istanbul: İsis.

(1970) *The Russian Annexation of the Crimea 1772–1783.* Cambridge: Cambridge University Press.

Gibbons, Fiachra (2012) 'Turkey's PM Threatens Theatres after Actor "Humiliates" Daughter'. *The Guardian,* 17 May. Available at: www.guardian.co.uk/world/2012/may/17/recep-tayyip-erdogan-theatre-daughter

Golden, Peter B. (1992) *An Introduction to the History of the Turkic Peoples.* Wiesbaden: Otto Harassowitz.

Halperin, Charles J. (1987) *Russia and the Golden Horde: The Mongol Impact on Medieval Russian History.* Bloomington: Indiana University Press.

(2000) 'Muscovite Political Institutions in the 14th Century'. *Kritika: Explorations in Russian and Eurasian History, New Series,* 1–2, 237–57.

Ismayilova, Khadija and Nushaba Fatullayeva (2012) 'Azerbaijan's President Awarded Family Stake in Gold Fields'. Organized Crime and Corruption Reporting Project, 3 May. Available at: www.reportingproject.net/occrp/index.php/en/ccwatch/cc-watch-indepth/1495-azerbaijans-president-awarded-family-stake-in-gold-fields

Kasaba, Reşat (2009) *A Moveable Empire: Ottoman Nomads, Migrants and Refugees.* London and Seattle: University of Washington Press.

Khazanov, Anatoly M. (2001) 'Nomads in the History of the Sedentary World'. In Anatoly M. Khazanov and André Wink (eds.) *Nomads in the Sedentary World.* Richmond: Curzon, 1–23

Kharkhordin, Oleg (2001) 'What is the State? The Russian Concept of Gosudarstvo in the European Context'. *History and Theory,* 40(2), 206–40.

Khodarkovsky, Michael (2004) *Russia's Steppe Frontier: The Making of a Colonial Empire, 1500–1800*. Bloomington: Indiana University Press.

Kotkin, Stephen (2007) 'Mongol Commonwealth? Exchange and Governance across the Post-Mongol Space'. *Kritika*, 8(3), 487–531.

Lattimore, Owen (1940) *Inner Asian Frontiers of China*. New York: American Geographical Society.

Lieven, Dominic (2000) *Empire: The Russian Empire and Its Rivals*. New Haven: Yale University Press.

Lowry, Heath W. (2005) *The Nature of the Early Ottoman State*. Albany: State University of New York Press.

McNeill, William (1964) *Europe's Steppe Frontier 1500–1800*. Chicago: Chicago University Press.

Morgan, David (1986) *The Mongols*. Oxford: Basil Blackwell.

Nexon, Daniel and Thomas Wright (2007) 'What's at Stake in the American Empire Debate?' *American Political Science Review*, 101(2), 253–71.

Neumann, Iver B. and Einar Wigen (2013) 'The Importance of the Eurasian Steppe to the Study of International Relations'. *Journal of International Relations and Development*, 16(3), 311–30.

Onuf, Nicolas Greenwood (1998) *The Republican Legacy in International Thought*. Cambridge: Cambridge University Press.

Ostrowski, D. G. (2000) 'Muscovite Adaptation of Steppe Political Institutions: A Reply to Halperin's Objections'. *Kritika: Explorations in Russian and Eurasian History, New Series*, 1–2, 267–97.

Piterberg, Gabriel (2003) *An Ottoman Tragedy: History and Historiography at Play*. Berkeley: University of California Press.

Purdue, Peter C. (2005) *China Marches West. The Qing Conquest of Central Eurasia*. Cambridge, MA: Belknap.

    (2007) 'Erasing the Empire, Re-Racing the Nation'. In Ann Laura Stoler, Caroline McGranahan and Peter C. Purdue (eds.) *Imperial Formations*. Santa Fe: School for Advanced Studies Press, 141–69.

Rachewiltz, Igor de (1971) *Papal Envoys to the Great Khans*. London: Faber & Faber.

Riasanovsky, Nicholas V. (1967) 'The Emergence of Eurasianism'. *California Slavic Studies*, 4, 39–72.

Sa'dī, Shaíkh Muslihu`d din (1899) *The Gulistan of Sa'dī*. Trans. Edwin Arnold. London: Harper and Brothers.

Scott, James C. (2009) *The Art of Not Being Governed*. New Haven: Yale University Press.

Sunderland, Willard (2004) *Taming the Wild Field: Colonization and Empire on the Russian Steppe*. Ithaca: Cornell University Press.

Sverdrup-Thygeson, Bjørnar (2013) 'A Neighbourless Empire? The Forgotten Diplomatic Tradition of Imperial China'. *The Hague Journal of Diplomacy*, 70(3), 245–67.

Vernadsky, George (1953) *The Mongols and Russia: A History of Russia, Vol. III*. New Haven: Yale University Press.

Wheatcroft, Andrew (2008) *The Enemy at the Gate: Habsburgs, Ottomans and the Battle for Europe*. London: Random House.

Wittek, Paul (1938) *The Rise of the Ottoman Empire*. London: Royal Asiatic Society.

Zorin, V. A. (1959)[1941] *Istoriya diplomatii*, Vol. I, 2nd edn. Moscow: Gospolitizdat.

6 | The modern roots of feudal empires

The donatary captaincies and the legacies of the Portuguese Empire in Brazil

BENJAMIN DE CARVALHO

Introduction

The history of the Portuguese Empire in Brazil and its influence on contemporary Brazil is a story of multiple legacies. In this chapter I explore these through a study of the initial Portuguese policy of settlement of the Brazilian colony.

Eager to defend its colonial lands in Brazil from foreign powers, between 1534 and 1536 the Portuguese Crown divided the land of the colony in longitudinal tracks, or slices, going from the coast to the imaginary line set by the Treaty of Tordesillas. Brazil was thus subdivided into 15 units that became known as *capitanias hereditarias* – hereditary captaincies. The system of hereditary captaincies would formally last only a little more than a decade, being abolished in 1549. Nevertheless, its impact on social, economic and political affairs in Brazil has been important. Each of these captaincies was given to *donatários* – members of the Portuguese lower nobility or bureaucrats close to João III – whose duty it became to administer the land, colonize it and protect it against foreign invasions (see Burns 1970; Skidmore 2010: 9–18). The donatários were in turn given the right to exploit most of the natural resources of their captaincy.

While this mode of imperial expansion and consolidation was officially abandoned in 1549, it continued in practice, albeit in more of a hybrid form, until 1753 when the last captaincies were subsumed into the public administration of the crown. The story of these captaincies makes salient three different legacies of empire. Concentrating the scrutiny of the legacies of the Portuguese Empire in Brazil to the short historical period of the capitanias does not entail a conceptual

128

narrowing of the inquiry: for the period of the hereditary captaincies in Brazil is crucial to understanding how empires have legacies, and how many of these remain long after the formal end of empires.

I will proceed with the inquiry around three specific legacies of the captaincies. The first legacy entails consideration of how these policies themselves built upon prior imperial institutions. When the Portuguese adopted the model of the capitanias in Brazil, the model had already proved successful in the smaller islands of the Atlantic. In fact, the model of imperial governance through the capitanias was itself a legacy of Roman imperial expansion.

The second legacy involves the impact of these policies on current socio-economic trends. While the model of the captaincies was officially abandoned long before Brazil gained independence in the early nineteenth century, specific modes of governance of the land were transposed onto Brazilian land legislation in 1850 and later in the 1988 Constitution, and continue to structure current socio-economic conflicts around land management and distribution in Brazil. While the captaincy model had created smaller estates in the Atlantic islands and in Portugal where land was scarce, the vast availability of land in Brazil contributed to the creation of large estates and high levels of economic inequality. Furthermore, the captaincies were granted on the explicit assumption that land was to be cultivated. Failure to do so entailed the lands being taken back. This duty to cultivate land long survived the captaincies and was adopted into Brazilian law and the constitution. Paradoxically, current claims to land distribution in Brazil meant to redress the uneven distribution of land largely rooted in imperial modes of land ownership and distribution dating back to the captaincies are themselves a legacy of an imperial mode of land ownership. A case in point is one of today's largest social movements, the *Movimento dos Trabalhadores Sem Terra* (MST) or Landless Workers' Movement which grounds its demands for land reform of large unproductive estates in the duty to cultivate (see Leira 2014).

The third and final legacy addressed here is of a more meta-historical character, and concerns the character of early modern modes of imperial governance and their legacies. Much of the current debate about lack of socio-economic development is attributed to 'feudal' legacies. Such an attribution may have two possible consequences. First, it may attribute the cause for this lack of development to 'pre-imperial' elements, remnants of which subsisted into the era of modern overseas empires. This may make it difficult to understand the causes of this lack of development by seeing the solution as the need to move beyond feudalism in a manner similar to the European 'modern' experience. Such a perspective fails to take into account the fact that these elements, as I argue here, were not feudal in character, and were in fact institutional innovations or adaptations of modern European empires. The feudal label, as I show, is misguided on two accounts: in terms of a specific historical experience, and by analogy.

The chapter proceeds in five sections. It begins by sketching out the background to the Portuguese imperial expansion in Brazil. This background is important, as it shows that the system of captaincies that was put in place was one derived from the Portuguese experience both in the Atlantic islands and at home, rather than one expressly meant to address local challenges to effective governance of Brazil. The second section addresses how early modern modes of imperial governance – which have important legacies today – were themselves legacies of earlier empires. It does so by highlighting elements of the system of donatary captaincies, which had their roots in the Roman imperial tradition. It then moves to a discussion of how the captaincies in Brazil differed from past experiences in their consequences, largely due to the vast availability of land and the difficulty of cultivating it. The fourth section examines the 'feudal' character that is often attributed to this experience, focusing on the ways in which such a label may misguide us in developing an understanding of current challenges to development. Finally, this chapter discusses these three legacies in the context of their more current impact on Brazil.

The background to the imperial expansion in Brazil

From the outset, the Portuguese seaborne empire was a commercial enterprise rather than a colonial one. A small polity lacking manpower, rather than one able to control overseas possessions through colonies of settlers, Portugal established forts, which served as bases for trading. This was also the strategy initially intended for Brazil, and it was not until the Portuguese claims to Brazil were seriously challenged by other European powers, especially the French, that Portugal turned to a strategy of colonizing larger stretches of land for agricultural production. The history of the early Portuguese colonization of Brazil is as much a history of naval competition as it is one of settling the land. For, only years after Pedro Alvares Cabral had come back from Brazil in 1501 did French privateers begin to puncture the Portuguese monopoly in the trade of brazilwood (Herring and Herring 1968: 214; on privateers, see Leira and de Carvalho 2010).

The international context in which the donatary captaincies were established, was thus one of intense competition over trade routes in the Atlantic. Portugal did not have either the manpower or the financial resources to undertake the colonization of the Brazilian coastline, nor did they have the same demographic overflow as other European states had at the time. Furthermore, in contrast to the Spanish who, just like the Portuguese, had been granted their overseas dominions by papal jurisdiction in the Treaty of Tordesillas, other European states (not party to the Treaty of Tordesillas) were challenging the Treaty on increasingly stronger grounds. The challenging situation Portugal experienced with regard to its Brazilian possessions was thus intimately linked to the religious fragmentation of the Christian republic in Europe: for though Portuguese rights to Brazil had been secured by the Treaty of Tordesillas, Protestant actors not bound by Papal authority sought to establish incursions in the long Brazilian coastline.[1] The French in particular were strong challengers of Portuguese claims over Brazil. The reason for this is to be found not only in the French desire to establish overseas trade routes, but also in legal developments of the time:

[Portugal's exclusive rights to Brazil] rested ... on papal bulls that embodied the medieval canonistic tradition of universal papal jurisdiction over the world ... this gave the pope legitimate authority to assign monopoly rights over newly-discovered seas and lands to rulers who would undertake to evangelize them. But this thirteenth-century concept soon came under attack from Thomistic critics whose ideals had recently been reinforced by the Renaissance revival of Roman law, especially the Code of Justinian. Indeed the papal position was no longer accepted by progressive scholars even in Iberia (e.g. Francisco de Vitória). Armed, then, with a more 'modern' concept of empire based on the secular law of nations (*ex iuregentium*), the French court insisted upon its right to trade freely and declined to respect any title not backed up by effective occupation. The French considered their ships and merchants free to traffic with any area of Brazil

---

[1] On the religious fragmentation of the Christian republic and its consequences, see de Carvalho 2014; de Carvalho and Paras 2014; and Leira 2007.

not actually occupied by Portuguese – which meant, in fact, virtually the entire coast. (Johnson 1987: 11)

This, added to the practical challenges of patrolling the Brazilian coastal waters, put the Portuguese under severe strain in the 1520s. Their claims to Brazil were legally recognized only by the Spanish, and the law of nations was gaining in strength (Johnson 1987: 11). An effort to bribe the admiral of France proved short-lived as well (Pickett and Pickett 2011: 14). The Portuguese crown thus came to understand in the early 1530s that the defence of its Brazilian trade interests required a colonial presence, and that coastal patrols aimed at holding off unlicensed ships were inherently insufficient.

[A] fundamental shift in policy occurred which, in effect, moved the Portuguese line of defence from the sea to the land. Instead of attempting to keep French ships from reaching the Brazilian coast, the Portuguese would instead establish a number of settlements to prevent the Indian population from direct trading with the French. At the same time these settlements would answer the French juridical challenge: Portugal could now claim 'effective possession' of Brazil. Direct royal control would cease; instead of a single colony ... a plurality of private settlements would blanket the coast ... Growing strains of crown income at this time made it useful to shift the costs of such extensive colonization to private investors. (Johnson 1987: 12)

The process of effective colonization of Brazil was therefore less the outcome of a long-term imperial drive to territorialize overseas dominions, than the pragmatic answer and institutional adaptation to practical challenges. The initial plan of the Portuguese crown was to be in charge of the colonization though a model known as 'royal exclusivity' (Augeron and Vidal 2002: 23). A small fleet under the command of Martim Afonso de Sousa reached the Brazilian coastline in early 1531 with the aim of demarcating Portuguese territory, to fend off French privateers and found settlements (Augeron and Vidal 2002: 23). But while the fleet was fairly successful in Brazil, the situation in Lisbon made it increasingly clear that the crown could not carry the important costs of settling the Brazilian coastline: 'to the increasing need for a greater naval presence in the Indian and Atlantic Oceans and the growing pressure exerted by the French in the region of Pernambuco were added the economic consequences of the Lisbon earthquake of 1531 and the financial crisis of 1532' (Augeron and Vidal 2002: 24).

The Portuguese crown felt it had to move fast and set in place a system of governance based on an institution readily at hand. This institution, the system of *sesmarias* which will be elaborated below, was in turn a type of pioneer agriculture championed by the Roman Empire and with roots in the early second century BC, when these privately owned estates were accumulated through the spoils of war and confiscated from conquered peoples (Pritchard 1969; White 1967).[2]

King Joao III therefore gave in to increasing pressures to grant colonial lands to his subjects. Martim Alfonso was consequently mandated in 1532 to demarcate or divide up the Brazilian coastline into captaincies of 50 leagues of coastline each. Upon his return to Portugal in 1533, the system of 'private exclusivity' was put into place. As a number of scholars have emphasized, this was not an institutional innovation. Rather, when forced to settle its Latin American coastline, the Portuguese crown resorted to a model of ownership and agricultural development whose roots extended back to the Roman Empire, and which the Portuguese had already successfully implemented in Madeira, the Azores, the Cape Verde Islands, as well as on the island of Fernando de Noronha just off the Brazilian shore (since 1503) (Augeron and Vidal 2002: 24).

Imperial legacies in the making of early modern empires

The first legacy addressed here is how the system of donatary captaincies built upon prior imperial practices. Though the captaincies came to have a lasting effect and influence on the social and political structure of Brazil long after the end of the colonial empire, the set of institutional structures initially set in place to govern – or rather, to populate – the Brazilian coastline in order to fend off European privateers were themselves the legacies of a specific set of governance structures aimed at defending medieval Portugal against African incursions. The Portuguese roots of the donatary captaincy system are thus to be found in Portugal's long history of *Reconquista* between 800 and 1250 (see Rau 1946). Portugal thus had a long tradition of frontier settlement:

[2] Russo (1999) has an interesting take on the legacies of the Roman latifundia on the agricultural conditions leading to the emigration from Italy in the early 1900s.

When a town or a village was established and granted a *foral*, often it was (especially if it were on the frontier) also granted a certain amount of land as its territory (*termo*), part of which was usually retained as community property while the rest was given out to individual settlers with the idea of attracting them to take root in the township. The person charged with the division of these lots among the newcomers was called the *sesmeiro* after the lots (*sesmos*) which he distributed. Not only was the *sesmaria* system used during the reconquest to populate newly conquered lands, but during the fourteenth and fifteenth centuries, long after the end of the struggle with Islam, it continued to be employed both to repopulate lands which had been abandoned for various reasons, as well as to settle the various newly discovered islands in the Atlantic. (Johnson 1972: 211)

The immediate transposition of the model to Brazil can hardly be termed a success – which also to some extent was why it was so short-lived and was replaced by more formalized institutional governance structures after only a few decades. However, as Mickaël Augeron and Laurent Vidal have emphasized, the proprietary captaincy is central in understanding other colonial imperial ventures than the Portuguese one, as it came to influence a variety of proprietary ventures throughout the Atlantic, including by the French, Dutch, English and even Spanish (see Augeron and Vidal 2002: 21).[3] As they argue, historians have tended to follow the conclusions of the Portuguese crown at the time, which had come to see the system as a failure and relegated it to the domain of a brief historical parenthesis in the direct colonization of Brazil. While the system of donatary captaincies may not have yielded the expected outcomes in terms of colonial consolidation, the original aim of securing the Brazilian coastline from regular incursions by European privateers may shed light on the geo-strategic importance (and relative success) of the captaincy system. Keeping in mind the original aim behind the establishment of the donatary captaincies in Brazil, namely 'the settlement and development of vacant territory' (Johnson 1972: 211), the captaincies on balance were not such a dramatic failure.[4]

---

[3] For instance, the English Lord Proprietor was derived from the system of donatary captaincies.

[4] While having been a neglected passage of the Portuguese Empire for long, the past two decades have seen an increased attention to the captaincies, as Augeron and Vidal point out, notably with the publication of Couto 1995; Vasconcelos de Saldanha 2001; Johnson and Nizza da Silva 1992; and Tapajós 1981.

The partition of Brazil took place between March 1534 and February 1536, as fifteen captaincies were granted to a group of twelve captains, all with strong connections to the court. These were not nobles: they ranged from soldiers of fortune to bureaucrats and a humanist historian (João de Barros). The captains were given their lots by royal gift (*doação*), in a way reminiscent of medieval Portugal (Johnson 1987: 13). As pointed out by Caio Prado, in the governance of their colonies, the Portuguese did little by way of innovation. Overall, most structures of governance were exported from the Portuguese core, and few of them adapted to different local conditions (Prado 1969: 351). Johnson puts it even more succinctly: 'The seignior-ial tradition of medieval Portugal runs unbroken throughout' (Johnson 1972: 209). As Charles Verlinden (1954) remarked, the Portuguese were already in possession of the necessary governance framework for populating colonies, which it could export first to the Atlantic islands of Madeira, the Cape Verde Islands and the Azores before Brazil (Lockhart and Schwartz 1983: 184; Diffie 1977: 310).

Imperial modes of land governance and their legacies

The second imperial legacy addressed here is how imperial institutional arrangements impact socio-economic conditions long after they are formally abandoned. Specifically, this is addressed through the institutional arrangements of the policy of donatary captaincies and the *sesmaria* model, and how many of the social challenges Brazil faces today relate to the distribution of land that can be traced back to these initial land grants.

Of importance for the way in which the sesmarias came to influence the social structure of Brazil, were some central features of the system: the lands which were to be distributed had to be empty or unclaimed; they were usually close to towns or settlement where the sesmeiro could distribute land under condition that the recipient was to work and improve them, and make the grant dependent on the recipient's fitness to undertake the task and need. The donatary captains, who were given captaincies, were all granted the power to act as sesmeiros.

The practice of sesmarias nevertheless did not lead to the same result in Brazil as they had in Portugal. Availability of land not being an immediate problem, the sesmarias did not create a class of small peasants as they did in Portugal, but instead gave enormous land holdings to a small number of families. And while the initial conditions of land grants stipulated that land could only be distributed to those who could use it, in practice this was ignored (Lockhart and Schwartz 1983: 185).

Furthermore, the land was 'ceded by an irrevocable gift, inter vivos, an unusually large number of seignorial rights in the new territory of Brazil' (Johnson 1972: 208). As noted above, since the grants were made with the intention of populating Brazil – a colony far from the imperial core – the donations were fairly lucrative. They involved among other things 'the right to enslave natives and to sell them on the Lisbon market, to create towns and nominate their magistrates, [and] receive a fifth of the profits on the brazilwood sold in Portugal' (ibid.).

However, these were not feudal grants. The captains did not hold the power to determine the obligations of the population vis-à-vis them. According to medieval Portuguese constitutional practice, the relationship between donataries and the king was regulated by a donation charter, the *doação*. This charter, however, did not regulate the relationship between lords or donataries and the inhabitants of their domains – the *senhorios*. These relations – herein mutual rights and duties – were regulated by a separate document, the *foral*. The foral 'dealt with the obligations of the inhabitants of the senhorio toward their lord, and was usually issued by him as a kind of gracious gift or mini-constitution' (ibid.: 209). While the medieval practice had been for lords to issue their forals to their vassals, a series of complaints from the population had led to a complete revision and reissuance throughout Portugal around the early 1500s. As a consequence, forals were now issued directly by the crown rather than by the lords. Relations between lords and vassals had thereby been reconfigured, the rights of lords having now become more like those of state officials rather than plenipotentiary feudal lords.

And while the donatary captains stood to make a good return on their investment in settling their captaincies, the financial burden of doing so also rested solely on them. Captains thus had to equip a fleet, find financial backers, colonists and soldiers, as well as settlers and arms (Augeron and Vidal 2002: 30). These financial burdens made the private colonization of Brazil challenging as many grantees had to sell property and even borrow funds. In some cases the financial burden of outfitting expeditions or developing and defending the captaincy were so great as to lead grantees into bankruptcy. Administering the captaincies, however, proved in most respects an arduous task. The difficulty lay largely in the lack of means available to the administrators, as the Crown provided little public resources for the task. The main impetus behind setting up the captaincy system in the first place was the lack of resources at the disposal of the Crown (Russell-Wood 1998). As seen above, private lands with duties attached to them were the solution for colonizing the lands without public investment. The distance to Lisbon increased the difficulty of governing, which again was exacerbated by frequent indigenous rebellions and foreign invasions (Capistrano de Abreu 1997: 35–51). Most captaincies, save for those of Pernambuco and São Vicente experienced difficulties, and from 1549 the captaincy system was brought under control of the new administrative institutions of the *governo-geral* as an attempt to better control them from Portugal. In spite of this, many captaincies operated even more independently of the colonial government after 1549 and until the mid eighteenth century (Russell-Wood 1992).

The private settlement of the Brazilian colony thus proved to be challenging in practice. For in addition to their duty to grant *sesmarias* or 'tenures' to ensure the agricultural and economic development of the colony, captains were 'required to levy taxes, ensure order and justice, fill public obligations (offices), organize the militia, and oversee the functioning of the municipal *camaras*, while also serving as the privileged interlocutor of the crown and its representatives' (Augeron and Vidal 2002: 28).

As the system was quickly abandoned, the main legacies of the system of proprietary captaincies may lie less in its formal remnants than in the traces of its practical applications and the hybrids that emerged from the challenges the Portuguese met when attempting to implement such a system in an overseas imperial setting.

The feudal trap: reframing early modern imperial legacies

While lack of socio-economic development in Brazil today is often blamed on pre-imperial, 'feudal' elements, the story of the Portuguese captaincies illustrates the extent to which these elements were in fact a legacy of modern European empires. As has been pointed out, while many features of the captaincies were reminiscent of feudal arrangements, analysing them in either feudal or capitalist terms makes little sense, as they were clearly not feudal arrangements. 'Unlike the classical fief, the grant was not dependent upon service, military or otherwise, but rather was given *in reward* for services, past, present, and future' (Johnson 1972: 207; emphasis added). This point resonates with James Lockhart's and Stuart B. Schwartz's argument that 'Whereas the seigneury was an archaic form that seemed to move in a direction contrary to royal centralization, these grants were not "feudal" in either law or practice. They were made as a reward for services rendered and were not dependent upon the usual feudal obligations of vassal to lord' (1983: 184).

Modern political and economic development is generally understood as starting from the fundamental move away from feudalism. The modern international system as such begins with the idea that the world is made up of different territories delineated against each other by distinct boundaries, the boundaries of modern, sovereign, political authority. When explaining lack of development, we therefore often have recourse to the binary opposition of feudal/modern (suzerain/ sovereign), showing how other parts of the world are 'still' stuck in a somewhat feudal order.

Scholars and policy makers working on development issues in postcolonial states often see the challenges of development as overcoming 'feudal' elements still present within modern post-colonial polities. A common argument along those lines is that 'endemic corruption' today may arise from 'feudal' patterns associated with a 'patron-client' form of social order.[5] Thus, while feudalism as a concept mapping a specific set of historically and geographically specific authority structures was initially linked to the medieval system of governance in Europe, references to it in contemporary analysis of development are common.

Application of the feudal framework beyond the analysis of historical trends in European history seems to have happened by analogy. On the basis of its semi-feudal features, Japan under the Shoguns started the export of the feudal label beyond medieval Europe. While the analytic usefulness of the feudal framework has been questioned by medieval historians the term today nevertheless flourishes in analyses of the developmental challenges of former non-Western colonies.[6]

---

[5] Richmond and Franks 2007: 38. See also the critique in Sabaratnam 2013.
[6] Reyes notes that dependency theorists have hypothesized that 'regions that are highly underdeveloped and still operate within a traditional, feudal system' are those that had closest ties to imperial cores (Reyes 2001).

In such a view, feudal elements are perceived as the remnants of pre-colonial arrangements that should have been supplanted by modern and capitalist liberal values. In the case of Brazil, the feudal framing has been introduced with reference to the system of proprietary captaincies. But as historians have warned, this was nevertheless not a feudal system. The feudal analysis is, at least in the case of Brazil, a fallacy. As the historian H. B. Johnson has argued, in addition to the fact that 'medieval Portugal never experienced an identifiable "feudal" tradition', none of the features of the captaincies 'remotely conformed to any viable definition of feudalism' (Johnson 1972: 203).

The second underlying assumption is more historically sensitive, and refers to the divide between understanding colonial arrangements beyond Europe as intrinsic to the development of capitalism, and understanding the modalities of rule in overseas empires as the transposition of feudal relationships beyond Europe (see for instance Gallo 1999: 199; Mauro 1971).

These assumptions pose serious problems to our understanding both of contemporary development as well as of empires and their legacies. While the first overlooks the hybrid or mixed character of colonial innovations or rule, the second overlooks the fact that the personal character of socio-political arrangements did not necessarily derive from pre-colonial arrangements. In the case of early modern Brazil, a largely capitalist drive to develop trade gave way to a more sustained effort at colonizing the land in the face of competition from other European states. Furthermore, they developed largely as the result of how colonists handled practical challenges in the colonies. While the ensuing arrangements and subsequent legacies were of a character largely favouring powerful individuals and a largely personal system, it was not feudal. References to feudalism, then, only hinder our understanding of what imperial rule consisted of, how it was implemented, and the legacies it has left.

A historical inquiry into the early colonization of Brazil showcases how many elements identified as feudal (and therefore as 'less developed' by juxtaposition to modern) were in fact innovations of modern European empires. This dovetails with Kathleen Davis' argument that 'at the very moment the colonial slave trade began to soar, feudal law and slavery were grouped together and identified as characteristic of Europe's past and of a Non-European present' (2008: 8). The legacies of these empires were not of a feudal character that needs to be overcome today in order to allow for socio-economic development, but are rather modern legacies of modern empires which from the early modern period formed part of the socio-economic structure of Brazil.

The legacies of the captaincies today

As this discussion has shown, the story of the institutional setup of the Portuguese empire in Brazil is one of past and subsequent imperial legacies; those scrutinized here are by no means exhaustive. One could, for instance, explore the extent to which the origins of Brazilian federal institutions were linked to the decentralized arrangements of the captaincies. Yet, the three legacies of empires examined in this chapter have all influenced modern Brazil, and continue to do so in important ways.

In the case of contemporary Brazil, references to the feudal challenges to Brazil's modernization abound, although generally only in passing.[7] These references are symptomatic of two broader underlying assumptions about development in colonial empires and, in contemporary debates, about the social and economic development of former colonies. An underlying assumption in these references to feudalism is that the origin of challenges to development lies in the pre-colonial histories of developing countries. References to the 'feudal' character of development here are not to feudal arrangements as a legacy of empire, but rather pre-imperial feudalism. Feudalism here refers not to specific European medieval and early modern modalities of rule, but to the pre-imperial and personal and tribal character of politics in developing countries.

The debate about feudal legacies – be they of empires or of a pre-imperial order – and their impact on development and economic distribution is fierce. Dating back to the writings by dependency theorists beginning in the 1960s, 'feudal barons' have figured centrally in accounting for the lack of development both in Brazil and in Latin America in general. Commentators on the left have tended to resort to feudal analogies in explaining the lack of economic development in

---

[7] By way of illustration, consider the following: Wiarda and Kline (1990), for instance, argue that 'The weight of the feudal and semi-feudal past, of the colonial era and its institutions, hung heavier over Latin America than over North America.' Peter Evans has claimed that 'Agriculture remained essentially feudal' (1979: 20). Mauricio Font refers to 'the "oligarchic," coffee-dominated agrarian social order, which is sometimes described as feudal' (1987: 70). Paulo Vizeu (2011) mentions '"semi-feudal" and pseudo-feudal' arrangements, while Benjamin Nelson Reames (2008: 61) uses the term 'neo-feudal' to mean the lack of permeation of the modern state.

rural parts of Brazil (see Motta 2013 for a useful discussion). These authors range from scholars such as Nelson Werneck Sodré and Alberto Passos Guimarães writing in the mid twentieth century to current commentators. Nikolas Kozloff, for instance, author of *Revolution! South America and the Rise of the New Left* paints a rather grim picture of rural Brazil: 'Far from displaying a sense of modernity, the Brazilian countryside is a lawless area with downright feudal relations, a sclerotic and ineffectual state bureaucracy and racist and elitist landowners allied to powerful politicians' (Kozloff 2011).

The point is not to dispute the fact that rural Brazil displays extreme levels of poverty and inequality. Rather, by drawing attention to the fact that these relations were the product of a specific modern experience of international imperial expansion and not the transposition of feudal social relations on more 'modern' ones, my argument has been that policies to further development should be ones designed to moderate the effects of such a mode of capitalism rather than to bring about a transition from feudalism to modernity. The feudal analogy, so often picked up by commentators as a hindrance to modern liberal development, refers to legacies of modern European empires. In this specific case, it should be noted that the 'feudal barons' referred to are not the product of a specific set of feudal relations. As discussed above, the relationship between subjects and the donataries was not of a feudal character, as it was dictated by the foral, a document issued by the crown. The socioeconomic position of certain magnates in rural Brazil, rather than being a remnant of feudalism or even a neo-feudal arrangement is the result of greatly uneven economic conditions.

More specifically, as the second section of this chapter shows, the system of the sesmarias, which was an intrinsic part of the captaincy system, was itself a legacy of earlier imperial practices. While it had worked under the Roman Empire and for the Portuguese both in Portugal and the Atlantic islands to produce smaller productive estates, in the case of Brazil where the structural land conditions were entirely different and the cost of undertaking agriculture was much higher, the sesmarias contributed to generating different results. These were addressed in the third section, which showed how different structural conditions contributed to the creation of much larger, and often unproductive, estates. This legacy still largely defines the distributive structure of land in Brazil.

For one of the most important legacies of the donatarial captaincy system was the impact the sesmaria system was to have on land holdings in Brazil – right up to the present time. One of the reasons the Portuguese transplanted the sesmaria system to Brazil was because of its effectiveness in Portugal. For the system granted abandoned land on the explicit condition that it be cultivated and made productive. While the term sesmaria originally referred to the date of the granting of the right to exploit a given piece of land, the term in Brazil came to denote the area itself. While the practice, based on the Roman *latifundia*, had been successful in Europe where the duty to cultivate the land was policed and sesmeiros forced to give up land should they fail to cultivate it, the combination of a lack of policing in Brazil and the size of the colony, where the availability of land was not a problem, led to a different socio-economic result so that the sesmarias became, in practice, the inalienable property of local noblemen regardless of the productivity of the land (Fernandes *et al.* 2012: 17). As Fernandes *et al.* point out, 'the colonial period produced a trend in which the powerful controlled large areas of land, exploiting small portions intensively while allowing peasants to clear and plant smaller plots, and passing onto future generations the dual system of under-used latifundios and over-used minifundios' (18).

These long-term legacies of the colonial granting of lands is reflected in current productivity figures of the Brazilian agricultural sector, with '74% of farmers receiving only 15% of agricultural credits and holding only 24% of agricultural land, but producing 38% of the sector's gross output. Many people working hard on a small piece of land receive little credit ... The relatively few agribusiness firms in the country claim 85% of agricultural credits, control 76% of the land area, produce 62% of gross output, and employ 26% of farm labour' (Fernandes *et al.* 2012: 13–14).

It is against this backdrop that social movements such as MST have sought to advance the land reform agenda in Brazil. For as was touched upon in the introduction to this chapter, while current land distribution in Brazil is largely the legacy of unexpected consequences of early modern imperial policies, the legal means to address these inequalities are also in their own way a legacy of that period. What had made the system of sesmarias effective in other settings had been the donataries' duty to make the land productive. This ownership 'conditional upon effective cultivation of the land' was based on the sixth century Justinian Code (Fernandes *et al.* 2012: 17). This duty to make land productive became law in the 1850 *Lei da Terra* or Land Law. While the law contributed largely to legally institutiona-lize the uneven land distribution emerging from the early colonial period, it also upheld the duty to cultivate the land (see Silva 1996). Such a provision was further adopted in the 1988 Constitution, which states that land needs to serve a social function (Article 5, Section XXIII). Furthermore, for the purpose of agrarian reform, the constitution provides for the expropriation of rural property that is not performing its social function (Article 184). The current conflict between large landowners and those associated with the MST, who demand greater justice in the distribution of land, is not only rooted in legacies of imperial policies, but is in a sense a 'remake' of an early modern conflict.

The initial policy of land granting in Portugal was structured such that competition would uphold the arrangements. Competitors would check whether lands were being cultivated both in order to keep their competition in check, but also with a view to taking over lands that were not being cultivated. As seen above, this system of checks and balances did not transfer to Brazil where land was less scarce and where the governance and judicial system of the colonies were in the hands of the landowning elite. In that sense, current references to the duty to cultivate lands, and the relative success of the MST in taking over larger uncultivated estates for redistribution (*terras devolutas*) may signal the end of the perverted effects of the sesmarias. Interestingly, the end of the unexpected legacies of the captaincies may in turn signal the emergence of a new imperial legacy: the workings of a mode of governance meant for ensuring the cultivation of lands dating back to Roman times having been adopted in different guises and at different times by a series of empires.

The legacies of empire are in that sense back with a vengeance. For perhaps paradoxically, the Brazilian justice system continues to use the sesmaria grant date as a reference point to determine ownership of land (see Motta 2009: 263–66). Where ownership is disputed, ownership is determined with reference to the original entitlement by a donatary or the crown itself, with results unvaryingly going against those seeking to defend their claims. As Fernandes *et al.* argue:

The irony of this search for legitimacy is that, despite the altered usage of the word sesmaria in Brazil, the cultivate-or-lose -demand remains legally binding. Thus, rather than confirm the patrimony of a disputed property, discovery of the original sesmaria grant almost always de-legitimizes the claim of those seeking to document their title, especially since disputed lands are almost by definition undeveloped, under-utilised ones. (2012: 19)

Conclusion

As the editors have argued in their introduction to this volume, our state system came out of a structure of empires spanning the entire globe. This has a number of implications for how we understand current politics and institutional arrangements both between polities and within them. As I have shown here, empires were also constructed on past systems of empires, and earlier imperial policies were adopted and rejected, yet continue(d) to influence the world past their workings. The story I have told here is one case of these multiple legacies. Yet, it is also a story of coexistence between different types of polities and different modes of governance. Only through understanding the specific ways in which these intertwined in the past can we hope to address the challenges their legacies still pose to current politics.

For, as historical inquiries show, we need to resist the drive to impose all-encompassing logics of action in international politics (for a parallel argument, see de Carvalho, Leira and Hobson 2011). As I have shown here, paradoxically, in the early consolidation of European empires in the Atlantic – in an era of massive sovereign centralization of political authority within Europe – the expansion of empires was undertaken along logics of governance more akin to the Roman Empire than to the state system. Thus, while Europe became the site of political innovation with the emergence of modern states and the advent of modernity, when it came to developing their overseas colonies these same governments turned to institutional modes of governance that contravened this same centralization (see the discussion in Roper and Van Ruymbeke 2002: 7).

Finally, I have pointed to the inherent problem of transposing historical concepts without enquiring into how these were specifically grounded historically. Many factors that are today routinely termed as 'feudal' remnants of pre-imperial traditional societies are, in fact, institutional innovations of modern European empires. I have pushed this analysis further as well, showing how phenomena termed as feudal were not feudal but rather hybrid institutions that emerged at the intersection of imperial practices and local challenges. Thus, the feudal label, rather than being a helpful shorthand, may in fact hinder an understanding of what the colonial empire entailed, and how it has affected social, economic and political relations after the end of empires. As such, the feudal label can mask imperial processes and hinder an understanding of how empires have impacted – and to a large extent still do impact – the contemporary world of states.

As I have illustrated here, empires have legacies at different levels, and these in turn have a wide-ranging set of effects. Rather than understanding empires as distinct from the international system of states, any inquiry seeking to understand long-term development must take as a point of departure how different systems and modes of political organization intersect, coexist and influence each other. Thus, I have showed how the partition of land in the Roman Empire in the wake of warfare was a legacy that was picked up by modern empires seeking to colonize new lands. Understanding how empires emerge and consolidate must also take into account prior imperial practices and the imprint they leave. In fact, the case shows how important are the legacies of empires, long after the formal disappearance of specific imperial polities. As I have shown here, the transposition of such a system to a continent where the structure of land was vastly different from that of the small Atlantic islands or even Roman Sicily had entirely different effects.

References

Augeron, Mickaël and Laurent Vidal (2002) 'Creating Colonial Brazil: The First Donatary Captaincies, or the System of Private Exclusivity, 1534–1549'. In L. H. Roper and B. Van Ruymbeke (eds.) *Constructing Early Modern Empires: Proprietary Ventures in the Atlantic World, 1500–1750*. Leiden: Brill, 21–55.

Burns, E. Bradford (1970) *A History of Brazil*. New York: Columbia University Press.

Capistrano de Abreu, João (1997) *Chapters of Brazil's Colonial History, 1500–1800*. Oxford: Oxford University Press.

Couto, Jorge (1995) *A construção do Brasil*. Lisbon: Cosmos.

de Carvalho, Benjamin (2014) 'The Confessional State in International
    Politics: Tudor England, Religion, and the Eclipse of Dynasticism'.
    Diplomacy & Statecraft, 25(3), 407–31.
de Carvalho, Benjamin and Andrea Paras (2014) 'Sovereignty and Solidarity:
    Moral Obligation, Confessional England, and the Huguenots'. *The
    International History Review*. Published online 13 February. DOI:
    10.1080/07075332.2013.879912
de Carvalho, Benjamin, Halvard Leira and John M. Hobson (2011) 'The Big
    Bangs of IR: The Myths That Your Teachers Still Tell You about 1648
    and 1919'. *Millennium – Journal of International Studies*, 39(3), 735–58.
Davis, Kathleen (2008) *Periodization and Sovereignty: How Ideas of
    Feudalism and Secularization Govern the Politics of Time*. Philadelphia:
    University of Pennsylvania Press.
Diffie, Bailey (1977) *Foundations of the Portuguese Empire, 1415–1580*.
    Minneapolis: University of Minnesota Press.
Evans, Peter B. (1979) *Dependent Development: The Alliance of
    Multinational, State, and Local Capital in Brazil*. Princeton: Princeton
    University Press.
Fernandes, Bernardo Mançano, Clifford Andrew Welch and Elienai
    Constantino Gonçalves (2012) *Land Governance in Brazil: A
    Geo-Historical Review of Land Governance in Brazil*. Framing the
    Debate Series No. 2. Rome: International Land Coalition. Available
    at: http://www.americalatina.landcoalition.org/sites/default/files/Frami
    ngtheDebateBrazil_0.pdf.
Font, Mauricio A. (1987) 'Coffee Planters, Politics and Development in
    Brazil'. *Latin American Research Review*, 22(3), 69–90.
Gallo, Alberto (1999) 'Aventuras y desventuras del gobierno señorial
    en Brasil'. In Alicia Hernández Chávez, Ruggiero Romano and
    Marcello Carmagnani (eds.) *Localización: Para una historia de
    América*, Vol. II. Mexico: El Colegio de México, 198–265.
Herring, Hubert and Helen Baldwin Herring (1968) *A History of Latin
    America, From the Beginnings to the Present*. New York: A. A. Knopf.
Johnson, H. B., Jr (1972) 'The Donatary Captaincy in Perspective: Portuguese
    Backgrounds to the Settlement of Brazil'. *The Hispanic American
    Historical Review*, 52(2), 203–14.
Johnson, H. B. (1987) 'Portuguese Settlement, 1500–1580'. In Leslie Bethell
    (ed.) *Colonial Brazil*. Cambridge: Cambridge University Press, 1–38.
Johnson, Harold and Maria Beatriz Nizza da Silva (1992) *O Império luso-
    brasileiro (1500–1620)*. Lisbon: Editoria Estampa.
Kozloff, Nikolas (2009) *Revolution! South America and the Rise of the New
    Left*. London: Palgrave Macmillan.

(2011) 'WikiLeaks: Feudal Social Relations in the Brazilian Countryside'. *Huffington Post*, 3 March. Available at: http://www.huffingtonpost.co m/nikolas-kozloff/wikileaks-feudal-social-r_b_830400.html

Leira, Halvard (2007) 'At the Crossroads: Justus Lipsius and the Early Modern Development of International Law'. *Leiden Journal of International Law*, 20(1), 65–88.

Leira, Halvard and Benjamin de Carvalho (2010) 'Privateers of the North Sea: At World's End'. In Alejandro Colas and Bryan Mabee (eds.) *Mercenaries, Pirates, Bandits and Empires: Private Violence in Historical Context*. New York: Columbia University Press, 55–82.

Leira, Torkjell (2014) *Brasil: Kjempen våkner*. Oslo: Aschehoug.

Lockhart, James and Stuart B. Schwartz (1983) *Early Latin America: A History of Colonial Spanish America and Brazil*. Cambridge: Cambridge University Press.

Mauro, Frédéric (1971) 'Existence et persistance d'un régime féodal ou seigneurial au Brésil'. In *L'abolition de la "féodalité" dans le monde occidental* [actes du colloque international], Toulouse, 12–16 November 1968. Paris: Éditions du Centre National de la Recherche Scientifique.

Motta, Marcia Maria Menendes (2009) *Direito à terra no Brasil: a gestação do conflito 1795–1824*. São Paulo: Alameda Casa Editorial.

(2013) 'Classic Works of Brazil's New Rural History: Feudalism and the Latifundio in the Interpretations of the Left (1940/1964)'. *Historia Critica*, 51, 121–44.

Pickett, Dwayne W. and Margaret F. Pickett (2011) *The European Struggle to Settle North America: Colonizing Attempts by England, France and Spain, 1521–1608*. Jefferson: McFarland.

Prado, Cajo, Jr (1969) *The Colonial Background of Modern Brazil*. Berkeley: University of California Press.

Pritchard, R. T. (1969) 'Land Tenure in Sicily in the First Century BC'. *Historia: Zeitschrift für Alte Geschichte*, 18(5), 545–56.

Rau, Virginia (1946) 'Sesmarias medievais portuguesas'. Dissertation, University of Lisbon.

Reames, Benjamin Nelson (2008) 'Neofeudal Aspects of Brazil's Public Security'. In M. R. Haberfeld and Ibrahim Cerrah (eds.) *Comparative Policing: The Struggle for Democratization*. London: Sage, 61–96.

Reyes, Giovanni E. (2001) 'Four Main Theories of Development: Modernization, Dependency, World-System, and Globalization'. *Nómadas: Revista Crítica de Ciencias Sociales y Jurídicas*, 4(2), 109–24.

Richmond, O. P. and J. Franks (2007) 'Liberal Hubris? Virtual Peace in Cambodia'. *Security Dialogue*, 38(1), 391–408.

Roper, L. H. and B. Van Ruymbeke (2002) 'Introduction'. In L. H. Roper and B. Van Ruymbeke (eds.) *Constructing Early Modern Empires: Proprietary Ventures in the Atlantic World, 1500–1750*. Leiden: Brill, 1–20.

Russell-Wood, A. J. R. (1992) *Society and Government in Colonial Brazil, 1500–1822*. London: Ashgate.

(1998) *The Portuguese Empire, 1415–1808: A World on the Move*. Baltimore: Johns Hopkins University Press.

Russo, John Paul (1999) 'The Sicilian Latifundia'. *Italian Americana*, 17(1), 40–57.

Sabaratnam, Meera (2013) 'Avatars of Eurocentrism in the Critique of the Liberal Peace'. *Security Dialogue*, 44(3), 259–78.

de Saldanha, Vasconcelos (2001) *As capitanias do Brasil. Antecedentes, desenvolvimento, e extinção de un fenomeno atlantico*. Lisbon: Comissão Nacional para as Comemorações dos Descobrimentos Portugueses.

Silva, Ligia Osorio (1996) *Terras devolutas e latifundio: efeitos da lei de 1850*. Campinas: Editoria da Unicamp.

Skidmore, Thomas E. (2010) *Brazil: Five Centuries of Change*. Oxford: Oxford University Press.

Tapajós, Vicente (1981) *O regime das capitanias hereditárias*. São Paulo: Companhia Editora Nacional.

Verlinden, Charles (1954) *Précédents mediévaux de la colonisation en Amérique*. Mexico: Instituto Panamericano de geografía e historia.

Vizeu, Fabio (2011) 'Rural Heritage of Early Brazilian Industrialists: its Impact on Managerial Orientation'. *Brazilian Administration Review*, 8(1), 68–85.

White, K. D. (1967) 'Latifundia: A Critical Review of the Evidence on Large Estates in Italy and Sicily up to the End of the First Century AD'. *Bulletin of the Institute of Classical Studies*, 14, 62–79.

Wiarda, Howard J. and Harvey F. Kline (1990) *Latin American Politics and Development*. New York: Westview Press.

7 | Imperial legacies in the UN Development Programme and the UN development system

CRAIG N. MURPHY

The organizational structure, activities and routines, and original staff of the United Nations system – and, in particular, the UN *development* system – were, to a significant degree, legacies of late nineteenth-century inter-imperial cooperation. This cooperation, along with the pre-UN international institutions it spawned, was critical to the imperial governments' strategies of pursuing the most rapid industrial development possible while remaining separate political systems. To encourage growth of the industries of the second industrial revolution, the imperial powers (joined by a few smaller European states) established inter-imperial institutions (rules and organizations) to create and secure a global market for industrial goods. These institutions survived the Great War and the depression, and were re-chartered at the end of the Second World War as the UN system. The organizations of the UN system soon gained fundamentally new capabilities to serve the non-industrialized world, or, at least to serve powerful groups there. The cascading decolonization that began at the war's end eventually made 'the UN system' and 'the UN *development* system' (its operations in the less-industrialized world) all but equivalent. From the beginning, the main mechanism coordinating the UN development system has been the UN Development Programme (UNDP) and its immediate predecessors whose original organizational routines and staff came from the wartime institutions that managed the economies of the Allies' colonies from North Africa to India as part of the war effort, and from men and

This chapter is an expanded revised version of the first two sections of Craig N. Murphy, 'Evolution of the UN Development System' in Stephen Browne and Thomas G. Weiss (eds.), *Post-2015 UN Development: Making Change Happen* (London: Routledge 2014), 35–40. We are grateful to the editors and the publisher for permission to republish.

women who had administered the later, more progressive stages of Roosevelt's Good Neighbor policy in Latin America.

The eminent theorist of global political economy and multilateral cooperation, Robert W. Cox, often describes today's UN as kind of cooperative imperialism, a system of 'poor relief and riot control . . . the debased consequences of what was [once] a great project' (e.g. Dale and Robertson 2003: 21).This chapter describes the imperial history of the UNDP and the UN development system and concludes by considering how this particular legacy of empire could ever have been (and still can be) considered a 'great' project.

The UN, the UN development system and UNDP

The topic of this chapter, the UN system, is perhaps best synopsized by its current organizational chart; a chart that the UN Secretariat warns is neither 'official' nor 'all inclusive' and lists 109 separate organizational entities.[1] Oddly, some observers might argue, it includes the Trusteeship Council, which has not met for 20 years, and it excludes the International Criminal Court (established in 2002), which, like the World Trade Organization and International Atomic Energy Agency (that are included), is somewhat separate from the UN but has a constitutional relationship to one of the six UN 'principal organs' named in the UN Charter of 1945. Other things about the chart that many readers might question are much less problematic to most experts on the UN. The system, as defined by the chart, incorporates organizations that many journalists and a few scholars regularly treat as different from, or even as deeply antagonistic to, the UN proper: for example the World Bank and the International Monetary Fund (IMF), but they have always, in fact, been two of the now 15 'Specialized Agencies' of the UN, the most-privileged of the 100-plus UN entities. Moreover, the chart includes more than a few entities (most of which are Specialized Agencies) that were established long before the UN Charter was written. The oldest is the International Telecommunications Union (ITU), founded in 1865 as the International Telegraph Union and all, like the ITU, were incorporated into the UN at its founding.

---

[1] 'The United Nations System', available at: www.un.org/en/aboutun/structure/pdfs/un-system-chart-b&w-sm.pdf

Scholars of the UN distinguish between the 'first' United Nations – the club of national governments that these organizations serve – and the 'second' UN: the people who work for the various organizations that member governments have established as part of the UN system. This chapter focuses on this 'second' UN. The second United Nations is a field-based organization. There are about 35,000 UN staffers who sit in the headquarters' buildings in New York, Washington, DC (home of the World Bank and IMF), Geneva (where ITU and many older organizations sit) and other European and North American cities. There are some 136,000 civilians who work for the UN in the UN's 140 country-level offices and the regional offices that serve them. There are also, (as of January 2013) 93,000 uniformed peacekeepers seconded to the UN by national governments.[2]

Looked at through the lens of the UN staff and what it does, the UN system is all about the developing world. Almost all of the peacekeepers work there, and more than 97 per cent of them come from developing countries, too. All but two or three of the civilian field offices are in the developing world[3] or in the poorer countries of Eastern Europe and 81 per cent of the civilian field staff is locally recruited. Staff at the headquarters of UN organizations, almost all of which are in Europe and North America,[4] includes a higher percentage of people from the developed world. Nevertheless, most of their work involves research

---

[2] All personnel statistics are rounded to the nearest 1000. Statistics on peacekeepers as of 31 January 2013, 'Rankings of Military and Police Contributions to UN Operations', available at: http://www.un.org/en/peacekeeping/contributors/2013/j an13_1.pdf. Statistics on civilian field staff as of 31 December 2010, 'Head Count of Field Staff', UN System Chief Executives Board for Coordination, High-Level Committee on Management, CEB/2011/HLCM/HR/24/Rev.1, 12 December 2011, p. v including footnote e. Statistics on headquarters' staff as of 31 December 2010, 'Personnel Statistics', UN System Chief Executives Board for Coordination, High-Level Committee on Management, CEB/2011/HLCM/HR/13, p. 1, supplemented by overlooked data on the World Bank, from http://web.worldbank. org/WBSITE/EXTERNAL/EXTABOUTUS/0,,contentMDK:20101240~menuP K:1697052~pagePK:51123644~piPK:329829~theSitePK:29708,00.html and on the IMF from, www.imf.org/external/about/staff.htm. The current number of country offices is taken from www.undg.org/unct.cfm? module=CountryTeams&page=RcEmailReport.

[3] Those in Belgium, Turkey and possibly Russia are the exceptions.

[4] The exceptions that appear on the current UN organization chart are the UN Environmental Programme, headquartered in Nairobi, and the four economic commissions for the developing regions headquartered in Addis Ababa, Bangkok, Beirut and Santiago.

for, or coordination of those in the peacekeeping missions and country offices. Today, 'the UN system' and 'the UN development system' refer to much the same thing.

It certainly wasn't originally intended to be this way and it didn't start out this way. When the UN Charter was negotiated, the European colonial powers wanted it to buttress and preserve empire (Mazower 2009). Of course, the system that was actually created more reflected the war aims and post-war promises of the wartime United States – originally 'the United Nations' was Roosevelt's name for the anti-fascist alliance (Plesch 2011: 1) – than those of the European powers, but supporting the people and governments of the non-industrialized world was not a top US priority in 1945, either. Moreover, if we listened only to the speeches in New York given by the representatives of the most powerful countries, the UN doesn't even sound like a development organization today. The priorities of the most powerful states are maintaining the structure of the global economy that has contributed to their power, managing their conflicts with other power-ful states and minimizing the threats to international peace that impinge upon their national interests, not the particular problems of the developing world. Nevertheless, the UN development system plays a significant global role by addressing those problems. The more than quarter-million people who work for it directly or are seconded to it have a form of power – a capacity to do things – that differs from that of the first UN. Moreover, the staff's authority to act in the field is amplified by the prestige of the United Nations and the ideals to which it is connected.

UN ideals also draw around the second UN a much larger 'third' United Nations

composed of actors that are closely associated with the world organization but not formally part of it. This 'outsider-insider' UN includes nongovernmental organizations, academics, consultants, experts, independent commissions, and other groups of individuals. These informal networks often help to effect shifts in ideas, policies, priorities, and practices that are initially seen as undesirable or problematic by governments and international secretariats. (Weiss, Carayanis and Jolly 2009)

The third UN also carries out many of the tasks that member govern-ments assign to the second UN, but then don't provide the funds that would allow the staff to carry them out. There is nothing particularly new in this. Both the League of Nations and the earlier Public International Unions (the organizations like the ITU that were the original form of inter-imperial cooperation) relied on the sponsorship of aristocratic benefactors and on the foundations established by Carnegie, Ford and Rockefeller, as well as on the staffs of non-governmental organizations (NGOs) to help carry out the work assigned to the intergovernmental agencies.[5]

Since the 1980s, reliance on the third UN has grown. This trend has intersected with an increasing tendency to carry out UN operations in the developing world in cooperation with other 'partners' – donor governments and local governments – who provide much of the funding. These partnerships often lead to strange ways of referring to the UN's specific role; for example, when Helen Clark, the head of the UN Development Programme, recently told an interviewer, 'UNDP is the lead agency in the UN development system and it's a very big program in its own right, with something like $4.5 to $5 billion going through its books every year' (quoted in Defontaine 2013). Well, yes, 'going through its books', but only about $1 billion of that amount is from regular, un-earmarked contributions from wealthier UN members to poorer countries. The rest comes from various partnerships with donor governments, national governments in the developing world and the third UN.[6]

It is hard to say who is really in charge of this widely dispersed and extremely complex UN development system. Officially, of course, it is various member governments, but given the organizational complexity of the system, the members' influence is dispersed through dozens of governing boards that oversee different agencies. The complexity of the system of oversight often leads member governments to complain that the system is out of their control, which is the primary reason that both 'donor' (i.e. 'wealthy, aid-providing') governments and 'developing' governments pursue 'partnerships', with earmarked contributions, as a way to gain leverage over a relatively independent staff and a complex system that supposedly shares a single purpose, but that has no central authority (Weinlich 2014).

If one asks, 'Does anyone coordinate all the disparate work of the UN development system?' there is one clear answer: in the same

---

[5] This is a theme throughout Murphy 1994.
[6] 'UNDP Institutional Budget Estimates for 2012–2013, Report of the Administrator', DP/2011/34, 30 June 2011, p. 9.

interview, UNDP Administrator Helen Clark correctly pointed out that UNDP 'has the role of coordinating and leading the UN development system, and so when you are the leader of UNDP, you also chair the UN development system of all the agencies and the funds and the programs for the UN' (quoted in Defontaine 2013). Until 1998, when the office of Deputy Secretary General was established, the UNDP Administrator was also the number two person in the Secretariat and usually led the coordinating group of the chief executives of the largest UN agencies.[7] In practice, this continued at least until 2006 when Mark Malloch-Brown, a protégé and close friend of Secretary General Kofi Annan, served first as UNDP Administrator, then as Annan's Chef de Cabinet, and finally as UN Deputy Secretary General.

UNDP's role as the coordinator of the UN development system is even stronger in the field, where the lead UN officer in every developing country has almost always been from the Programme even though a 1997 reform made it possible for career officers in other agencies (such as UNICEF and the UN Fund for Population Activities) to become a UN Resident Coordinator. Almost all of those who actually serve in those roles still come from UNDP,[8] a practice that causes some resentment in other agencies, but nothing compared to the deeper resentment of the non-UNDP 'Special Representatives of the Secretary General' (SRSGs) who, also in the 1990s, began coordinating UN activities in the (relatively small number of) countries with peacekeeping missions. Former UNICEF chief Carol Bellamy explains, 'The lack of understanding and respect, not for UNICEF, but for the development process and the country teams ... in a lot of these SRSGs or whoever the hell they were, was much more worrisome than an occasional boring, pompous, Resident Coordinator' (quoted in Murphy 2006: 293). Not surprisingly, since the 1990s, Secretary Generals have increasingly chosen their Special Representatives with country-coordinating responsibilities from UNDP as well.

[7] Today, the mechanism is called 'the Chief Executives Board for Coordination'. Its membership includes 'the United Nations [proper]; 15 Specialized Agencies established by intergovernmental agreements; 2 Related Organizations – World Trade Organization and the International Atomic Energy Agency; and 11 Funds and Programmes created by the United Nations General Assembly'. CEB, 'Who We Are', www.unsceb.org/content/who-we-are.

[8] UN Development Group, 'RC Email Report'. Available at: www.undg.org/unct.cfm?module=CountryTeams&page=RcEmailReport

What is UNDP? The Programme that officially took on that name in 1966 had existed as part of the UN since the post-war organization began. From the beginning, the UN Secretariat coordinated 'technical assistance' offered to developing countries by the Secretariat itself and by the separate UN Specialized Agencies including the ITU, Food and Agriculture Organization (FAO), World Bank, International Monetary Fund (IMF) and even the International Trade Organization – an agency that had been meant to be the larger structure for the General Agreement for Tariffs and Trade but never officially came into existence (Murphy 2006: 53–54). Such assistance involved sending experts in every field in which national governments might be involved – from fish farming to public finance – on short-term 'missions' to start programmes and train local counterparts. There could be dozens of experts in one country at any time. Their work was coordinated by a representative of the Secretary General in the nation's capital, the 'Resident Representative', appointed by the technical assistance section of the Secretariat – the role that became today's UN Resident Coordinator.

The UN's original (1946) programme of technical assistance was given a major boost by US President Truman's December 1948 'Point Four' pledge to assist the underdeveloped countries through 'a co-operative enterprise in which all nations work together through the United Nations and its Specialized Agencies wherever practicable' (Heppling 1995: 23). In 1949, the UN's programme gained a new name, 'the Expanded Programme for Technical Assistance' (EPTA). The significant new US funding – followed by smaller amounts from US allies, the Soviet Union and its allies, and neutrals such as Sweden – meant that the UN was able to expand its system of country offices from three countries in 1948 (Haiti, Iran and Pakistan), to 15 in 1952, to 45 (almost all independent developing countries) in 1958. The UN added new country offices in every new state that achieved decolonization. The early 1960s wave of decolonization meant that there were a total of 72 in 1966 (Garcia 1966: 20). By then, as has been the case ever since, there were country offices in the vast majority of UN member states.

In 1958, the UN General Assembly also created a (temporarily) separate agency, the UN Special Fund, to finance 'pre-investment' technical assistance: the search for 'bankable' projects to be funded by the low-interest development facility, desired by the UN's growing majority of developing states, which the United States insisted be placed under the World Bank (where the US had an effective veto) rather than under the General Assembly (Murphy 2006: 58). In 1966, the UN majority voted that EPTA and the Special Fund be merged to become UNDP.

To summarize this and the rest of a history that is really only slightly more complex: UNDP became and remains the coordinator of the UN development system because it was that in the beginning and it was able to remain in that position as the system grew due to (1) the funding provided by donor countries, (2) the interest of the Specialized Agencies and other parts of the UN in providing technical assistance, and (3) the growth, through decolonization, of the developing world.

Structures, procedures, staff and impact on the development enterprise

A historian who consults the paper archives of any UN country office or the UNDP paper files in New York will find records that look very similar to the earliest records of the ITU, the Universal Postal Union, or any of the other global-level intergovernmental organizations founded in the nineteenth century. There will be the same kind of financial accounts, budgetary procedures, minutes of meetings (written in the same 'not quite verbatim' style), pre-meeting agendas and circulation slips attached to all those records with statements about the records' confidentiality. Those slips will be addressed to administrative officers with similar titles. Even the schemes for numbering documents are very similar. Similar records will be found in the archives of 'private' international regulatory standard-setting organizations founded before the First World War, such as the International Electrotechnical Commission. There is a good reason for this: all these organizations came out of the same bureaucratic and ideological movement. Historians and world systems sociologists write about the shared origins of today's global organizations in the nineteenth-century emergence in Europe of modern state institutions and of epistemic communities developing fundamentally new forms of systemic expertise in government, both in the metropole and in the colonies (Murphy 1994: 53–54, 62–70).

Historian Mark Mazower writes of the illusive nineteenth-century dream of '"Science the Unifier" of humankind' that motivated all of the

Public International Unions as well as the private standard setters.[9] Sociologists Frank J. Lechner and John Boli outline the late nineteenth-century European origins of global technologies and institutions that have sustained a modern, rationalist 'world culture' (Lechner and Boli 2005: 109–35). Lechner and Boli see the unfolding of this culture as the process that explains the emergence of today's rationalist states and global organizations (both public and private). Mazower, on the other hand, is fascinated by all the failed nineteenth-century experiments in applying system and science to global affairs – the schemes for universal languages and catalogues meant to cover every possible form of cooperative human endeavour. For Mazower, this world culture is captivating, but ultimately of much less consequence.

For those of us concerned with the UN system as it is today, the interesting organizations are not the failed nineteenth-century international experiments, but those that survived. Why did they? The reason is certainly not just because the surviving institutions were manifestations of an emergent world culture they shared with the failures. Many years studying the ecology of international regulatory standard-setting and service-providing global organizations have convinced me that the surviving institutions were those that allowed their nineteenth-century founders – primarily the governments of Europe's great powers, the architects of the contemporary 'new' imperialism – to create and protect the larger market areas for industrial goods in which the new industries of the second industrial revolution could flourish (Murphy 1994: 48–151; see also Murphy 2005 and 1998). These market-creating institutions included telegraph and postal unions, similar organizations that linked Europe's railways and roads, systems for establishing new industrial standards and protecting intellectual property (especially in the important new emerging industries that grew out of the new fields of electrical and chemical engineering) and mechanisms for establishing and maintaining rules to facilitate international trade in industrial products. There were, of course, alternative ways in which industrialized countries could have been linked together to create market areas large enough for the new industries to survive in. Late nineteenth-century European leaders were familiar with the success, on a smaller scale, of the economic and political integration efforts in the United States, Germany, Italy and Switzerland that

---

[9]   This is the title of Mazower 2012, chapter 4 (94–115).

had encouraged earlier waves of industrialization. However, late nineteenth-century domestic politics pulled every major European power in two directions, both towards the deeper unification of the continent that could have fostered the new industries and towards the competition among empires that demanded the continent remain divided (Murphy 1998; cf. Stead 1899). Unification of the market area for industrial goods via inter-imperial cooperation through the Public International Unions was a compromise that satisfied both forces.

Mazower is certainly correct to emphasize the ultimate, horrendous failure of late nineteenth-century rationalist inter-imperial coopera- tion. Nevertheless, throughout the quarter century before the First World War that cooperation did succeed in economic terms: it gave the European imperial core the new electrical and chemical industries (and the related early consumer products industries) and all the eco- nomic growth that came with this 'second industrial revolution'. Not surprisingly therefore, both in the interwar years and after the Second World War, the leaders of the victorious powers preserved and strengthened the market-creating international institutions that they had developed before 1914, in anticipation of a new industrial era in which new industries would be created within an even larger market area that would include the United States (the most powerful of the victors), Japan and all the economically dependent territories of the non-communist industrial powers, the area that came to be called the 'Global South' or earlier, 'the Third World'.

The victorious powers also strengthened and added to another small set of surviving experiments in international government, what can be called the 'market-securing' or 'market-taming' international insti- tutions such as the International Labor Organization (ILO) and the pre-League predecessor to the FAO, the International Institute of Agriculture (IIA). Both organizations were created to ease the concerns of groups that might be harmed by the internationalization of indus- trial economies that the early market-creating institutions assured. The ILO aimed to prevent the 'race to the bottom' in wages and labour standards that troubled industrial workers who confronted new inter- national competition. The IIA was meant to work in the same way, by empowering farmers with information so they would not be cheated by more knowledgeable middlemen, and would be encouraged to adjust their products and methods of cultivation to meet the demands of a global market (Murphy 1994: 98). After the Second World War, the victors also created the more effective, if less formal, international institutions of what political scientist and UN policy maker John G. Ruggie calls 'embedded liberalism'; the exceptions to the liberalization of trade within the industrialized world that they allowed in order to protect the welfare state and the interests of farmers in the Global North (Ruggie 1982).

Throughout the interwar period, the League of Nations also experimented with giving other potential victims of economic globalization a stake in an increasingly liberal world order. A largely ineffective system of internationally monitored colonialism, the mandate system, helped administer the colonies that had been stripped from Germany. More significantly, a few governments in the non-industrialized world were offered League of Nations technical assistance to encourage 'development'.

At the time of the League, 'development' was understood as something that normally happened within the colonial world. Historians Frederick Cooper and Randall Packard write, 'What was new in the colonial world of the late 1930s and 1940s was that the concept of development became a framing device bringing together a range of interventionist policies and metropolitan finance with the explicit goal of raising colonial standards of living' (Cooper and Packard 1997: 4). Embracing 'development', Cooper and Packard argue, was a way for colonial governments to relegitimize empire, which was being challenged by nationalists, labour movements and others who questioned colonial rule.

The language used to describe the League's assistance, which is still used by the UN development system (and in fact, in almost all international development work) reflected this colonial enterprise. The League sent an unprecedented technical assistance 'mission' to China in 1931 to recommend reform of the country's entire education system (League of Nations Mission of Educational Experts 1932). The League's missionaries represented the newer religion of applying science to problems of government – in this case, through the scientific discipline of public education – rather than the old Protestants and Catholics who had built the new schools and hospitals in Europe's colonies before the 1930s. But, as Cooper and Packard point out, the same change was taking place in Europe's colonies at the same time.

This precedent of the League's technical assistance to an independent China became a model for a group of key Allied officials who, at the end of the Second World War, moved directly from colonial administration in wartime Asia and Africa into the top economic positions within the UN Secretariat. Perhaps the most important was the British foreign service officer David Owen, the first person hired into the UN Secretariat in 1945.

Owen had spent much of the war in an Allied office called 'the Middle East Supply Centre' (MESC) in Cairo, which was tasked with creating more autarchic, but still prosperous economies throughout the liberated colonies and dependent nations from Morocco eastward to India in order to free up the ports of the southern Mediterranean to supply a southern front through Italy. The successful scheme was the brainchild of a young Australian logistical genius, Robert Jackson, who was deferred to by his commanders due to the earlier success of his plan to defend and supply Malta, which was crucial to the victory in North Africa. Owen worked under Jackson at the MESC. Both continued to play central roles in the UN development system until they died (Owen in 1970, Jackson in 1991).

Jackson went from MESC to command of the wartime and immediate post-war United Nations relief efforts in Europe and parts of Asia and Africa through the UN Relief and Rehabilitation Administration (UNRRA). In terms of staff and resources, UNRRA was a larger operation than anything ever mounted by the UN since (Murphy 2006: 37). Jackson's most important later role was to author a famous (or infamous) 1969 internal critique of the UN development system (Jackson 1969), known by its nickname 'The Capacity Study'. The study worried that the UN development system – with its scores of parts and lacking a central 'brain' – had very little capacity.

While Jackson went into the field with UNRRA, Owen went to New York to hire the other staff of the UN Secretariat, negotiate agreements linking all of the Specialized Agencies to the Secretariat and committing all of them to provide technical assistance, send out the first UN development missions, establish the first country offices and maintain the coordinating mechanism (the EPTA) in New York. Historians tend to attribute most of the UN development systems' institutional innovations to Owen, but his friendly competitor Jackson often disagreed: 'Resident Representatives, what were they? Nothing more than my country representatives of MESC. I mean, they're merely carrying on that concept' (Jackson 1990, fols 58–9).

Others who were there at the founding of the UN agree that Jackson's organization of MESC, which was then taken to UNRRA, became the template for the organizational practices of the entire UN system. Richard Symonds, who worked in the colonial government in India throughout the war and then came to UNRRA before a long career at the UN explains:

Working together in UNRRA were a number of people, particularly British and American, who were shortly afterwards to be appointed to key administrative posts in the United Nations and the specialized agencies. With this shared background of mistakes as well as achievements, they were able to agree on common personnel, salary, pension, and other arrangements which have been an important element in holding together the UN system. (Symonds 2005: 26)

One area where there is no disagreement is about Owen's over-whelming influence over the staffing of the UN Secretariat, especially when it came to his primary interest, development. Cambridge historian Richard Toye and Oxford economist John Toye argue that the early UN's hiring practices were completely 'patrimonial'. Owen, who initially served under a weak Secretary General (Trygve Lie) and then under someone who largely defined his role as external (Dag Hammarskjöld), was both willing and able to surround himself with like-minded people, albeit people from every continent and almost every country (Toye and Toye 2004: 61). The impact of Owen's central role in hiring – which continued in UNDP, at least, through the late 1960s – remained almost 50 years later when I led a small research group that conducted hundreds of interviews with current and past UNDP staffers. I rarely met anyone whose personal connection to Owen was more than two degrees away. This early patrimonial hiring contributed to a strong, unified culture within the staff of UNDP, a culture that influenced, but does not dominate, the rest of the UN development system.

Owen's EPTA (and then UNDP) became the incubators of development cooperation throughout the UN system because originally the Secretariat in New York had little or no technical expertise with which it could provide technical assistance. The Secretariat became, instead, the coordinator of technical assistance provided by the specialized agencies: knowledge of the education system provided by the UN Education, Scientific, and Cultural Organization (UNESCO); medical expertise provided by the World Health Organization (WHO); help designing civil aviation systems provided by the International Civil Aviation Organization (ICAO), etc.

Initially, the Agencies cooperated not out of any deep concern for eliminating poverty or reducing global inequality. Quite the contrary, there is overwhelming evidence of a lack of interest in those issues among the early staff of every Specialized Agency except UNICEF.[10] However, in the 1950s and 1960s, taking on technical assistance was the only way that the agencies found that they could grow. For every seven technical assistance experts that they placed in the field, the Secretariat would pay for one new professional position back at the agency's headquarters. As a result, by the late 1960s, almost every agency within the UN system had its primary focus (at least in terms of its staff and funding) on the developing world, just as it does today.[11]

UNDP ideas

While the separate organizations of the UN development system eventually ended up with somewhat divergent understandings of the problem and the purpose of 'development', UNDP's strong organizational culture has meant that the system's coordinator has remained tied to the worldview that Owen (and Jackson and their early colleagues) brought to the organization in the 1940s. Perhaps the best way to understand those ideas is to recall the previously mentioned early League of Nations technical assistance programme to China, which took the late-colonial idea of 'development' to an independent country by promoting major policy interventions (in this case, in education) with an explicit goal of raising standards of living. A 1996 critical history of education in modern China remarks, 'Terms of reference are not always the same, but the issues elaborated in the [League's resulting] report are clearly identifiable antecedents of those that defined the Third World's decades of development between 1960 and

---

10   A point made throughout Black (1986), the first full-length history of the
      organization; see especially the foreword by Sir Robert Jackson.
11   This is the central theme (and central objection to the workings of the UN's
      development system) in Jackson 1969.

1980 ... [and are] a benchmark against which to evaluate China's precommunist education system' (Pepper 1996: 37).

The fact that the report still seemed like a 'benchmark', even in 1996, was in part a consequence of the peculiarity of the ideas embraced by the League's experts, led by R. H. Tawney, a Christian socialist and education reformer in his own country, Great Britain. The group were not the typical Eurocentric apologists for empire involved in 'development' in the 1930s. While their methods of investigation and the procedures that they recommended might be very similar to those of bureaucrats of the colonial state, their goals differed.

David Owen was very much a man like Tawney. One of Owen's formative experiences came in the three years immediately before the war (1936–39) that he spent with a young economist, Hans Singer, and a historian of the same age, Walter Oakeshott, working on a study organized by William Temple (then Archbishop of York and later Archbishop of Canterbury) and John Maynard Keynes on the impact of the Great Depression on the everyday life of Britain's long-term unemployed. The three young men, 'lived with unemployed families in the [northern English] counties – from the coal mine sectors, the textile sectors, the automobile industries, or key works that had reduced activity – to report back on their concerns, on the effect of long term unemployment on family life, [and] on children, especially in unemployed families'.[12] Owen recruited Singer, 'on the steps of Church House in London where the preparatory meeting for the UN took place, where he [Owen] had just started' to be the second person to join the UN Secretariat. In 2005, when Singer recalled the early UN he said that the lessons he and Owen had learned in the north of England in the 1930s were the same lessons the Argentine Keynesian economist, Raul Prebisch, was learning at the same time as he tried to battle the Depression, and the same lesson that the Brazilian ambassador to the UN Roberto Oliveria de Campos kept reiterating in New York throughout the 1940s: to deal with human tragedies created by an international economy that no single state could control, the world needed a new kind of economic cooperation.[13] When the Brazilian

---

[12] Hans Singer, interview with CNM, 8 July 2005.
[13] Ibid. It was striking that Singer broke in the middle of his account of his first work with Owen in the 1930s to insist that Prebisch was reaching the same conclusions at the same time and when he came to describing his first UN job he said, 'because it was developing countries, I supposed my first job would be to

ambassador rose at the November 1946 session of the General Assembly's economic committee to support Owen's first technical assistance programme to Asia and the Americas, he represented a country that had given nearly 1 per cent of its national income to UNRRA for war-ravaged Europe based on a principle of international solidarity that had been championed by Keynes and his American co-designer of the IMF and World Bank, Harry Dexter White.[14] In 1948, supporting Owen's plans, Campos recalled Latin American support for UNRRA, arguing that now the same principle required that the UN in 1948 focus on 'their own children's needs' (Black 1986: 75).

Eric Helleiner's careful study of debates about international inequality within the governments of the Allied powers throughout the Second World War confirms that while early innovations in international development assistance may have used tropes and organizational models that came from colonial administration, they were intended to serve a slightly different purpose. For example, at the Bretton Woods Conference, where the majority of states represented were 'developing' country members of the wartime alliance (members of the wartime 'United Nations' from Latin America), the USA was represented by officials, such as White, who had been centrally involved with a later, more progressive stage of Franklin Roosevelt's Good Neighbor Policy in Latin America. 'To be sure', Helleiner argues, 'US officials supported international development in the 1940s for a number of strategic and economic reasons. But they were also influenced by the ideology of the New Deal with its interests in social justice, poverty alleviation, and interventionist economic policy' (Helleiner 2010: 42).

I have argued elsewhere that UNDP's dominant views about the particular way in which these goals and policy mechanisms should be

---

learn something about developing countries, and, because developing countries were largely Latin American, I was working with the Brazilian ambassador Roberto Campos', and then explained Campos' long frustration with what he considered to be amnesia about the global lesson of the 1930s.

[14] United Nations 1946: 89 (actual debate: 20 November 1946). Earlier, Brazil claimed that its government had given 10 per cent of its national income to UNRRA, a claim not challenged in the debate, United Nations 1946: 12 (actual debate: 25 January 1946). Authoritative figures can be found in UNRRA 1947: 55. Jackson attributes the one per cent UNRAA aid target to Harry Dexter White in consultation with Keynes (1969: 4).

mixed has changed over time. They began with an understanding of 'development as engineering' in which prosperity (and equity) are most achieved by effective planning, logistics and the application of the 'best' techniques – ideas associated with the imperialist MESC and the young Robert Jackson. Today – especially in the work of UNDP's Human Development Office, which publishes the many global, national and local Human Development Reports – the emphasis is on 'development as freedom' associated with democratic social planning and the work of Amartya Sen and his colleague Mahbub ul Haq, who first articulated the concept of 'human development' (Murphy 2006: 41–50).

This trajectory could not have been predicted at the beginning, even though Haq, Sen and their closest colleagues all acknowledge that the origin of the human development idea is in the work of their most important teacher in the 1950s, Barbara Ward, and Ward was Robert Jackson's wife (Murphy 2013). However, there is no reason why spouses, even if they are both preeminent leaders in the same profession, should share a worldview. Jackson may have considered his views compatible with Ward's. Perhaps along with Owen, Jackson considered his top-down, engineering-like, 'one best way' approach to development to be something required by crises – by war and by the humanitarian disasters that UNRRA faced in the war's wake. Moreover, even if his worldview was shaped by empire, he was never an apologist for empire. After the war, he embraced one of the first principles to which Owen committed the EPTA, the 'right of each requesting government itself to decide what help it needs and in what form' (Joyce 1965: 44); and Jackson followed the principle with complete integrity, becoming one of the most deeply respected advisors of many of the most prominent of the anti-colonial leaders, especially of Kwame Nkrumah (Murphy 2006: 130–38). Nonetheless, 'development as freedom' means more than deferring to post-colonial governments, and, in that way, the culture that Owen brought to UNDP may have played the critical role.

Just poor relief and riot control?

The ideas of 'human development' and 'development as freedom' are rooted in a particular, Western tradition; they centre on the concept of a heroic, self-actualizing individual that is not found in all of the world's major philosophical and religious traditions. Today, many critiques of the imperialist origins of UNDP's ideas and practice focus on this fact. I am sympathetic to those critiques, although I am not sure that they will have any impact (Murphy 2013: xx). I am less sure about the critique of the UN system as an originally progressive project that has been debased into multilateral cooperation that supports a form of imperialism.

Perhaps there is a more productive way to frame the question: we know that international development cooperation has remained a central activity of the United Nations system since the Cold War ended and that the development ministries of most wealthy countries remained active and well funded even as the post-Cold War economic crises deepened. This suggests that international development cooperation plays some essential function in the global political economy. It is a part of global governance that, if it did not already exist, we would have to invent.

What might that function be? There are at least two suggestions in the political science literature. David Halloran Lumsdaine sees international development as the external manifestation of the charitable force that secures the modern welfare state. As the democratic governments in industrial societies come to see their primary role as one of making life better for all their citizens, some force of consistency or guilt makes such governments and their citizens willing to sacrifice to improve the lot of people everywhere. Because of something inherent in human beings – a sense of compassion, perhaps – we cannot maintain wealthy, egalitarian states without extending some kindness to a larger world (Lumsdaine 1993). This is an argument that seems compatible with the case I have made above about the sources of UNDP's ideology in the organizational culture that came to it from men like Owen, albeit men who also brought in, or reinforced organizational forms derived from their colonial experience.

In contrast, Robert W. Cox suggests a different view, that international development cooperation serves to quell international dissent against global capitalism. Cox's evidence includes the way in which, after the Cold War, UN 'humanitarian' activities replaced a kind of development cooperation once that had much greater ambitions:

Global poor relief and riot control now tops UN priorities, displacing development assistance which had the top spot during the 1950s and 1960s. Poor relief takes the form of humanitarian assistance. Riot control takes the form of peace keeping or peace enforcement. Famine requiring humanitarian aid can often be traced to consequences of a globalization that favors food production for world markets over local self-sufficiency. UN military intervention, intended to maintain public order where local government authority, has become a back up for NATO (i.e., US-) commanded military action against 'rogue states.' In these ways the United Nations serves as a subordinate adjunct to centralized global military power. (Cox 2002: 86)

Of course, international development cooperation may *both* provide necessary support to a coercive form of global power and provide an essential moral safeguard to the locally egalitarian welfare states that occupy one part of our contemporary global order. That is the hypothesis that I hope this chapter will encourage us to amplify and explore.

References

Alexander, Yonah (1966) *International Technical Assistance Experts: A Case Study in UN Experience.* New York: Praeger.

Black, Maggie (1986) *The Children and the Nations.* New York: Unicef.

Cooper, Frederick and Randall Packard (eds.) (1997) 'Introduction'. In Frederick Cooper and Randall Packard (eds.) *International Development and the Social Sciences: Essays on the History and Politics of Knowledge.* Berkeley: University of California Press, 1–41.

Cox, Robert W. (with Michael G. Schechter), (2002) *The Political Economy of a Plural World: Critical Reflections on Power, Morals and Civilization.* London: Routledge.

Dale, Roger and Susan Robertson (2003) 'Interview with Robert W. Cox'. *Globalisation, Societies, and Education,* 1(1), 13–23.

Defontaine, Catherine (2013) 'The Development Agenda: An Interview With UNDP Administrator Helen Clark'. *The Nation,* 12. Available at: www. thenation.com/article/173627/development-agenda-interview-undp-ad ministrator-helen-clark#.

Garcia, Adriano (1966) *International Cooperation and Development: The United Nations Development Programme Resident Representative System.* Quezon City: University of the Philippines Law Center.

Helleiner, Eric (2010) 'Global Governance Meets Development: A Brief History of an Innovation in World Politics'. In Rorden Wilkinson and Jennifer Clapp (eds.) *Global Governance, Poverty, and Inequality.* London: Routledge, 27–45.

Heppling, Sixten (1995) *UNDP: From Agency Shares to Country Programmes, 1949–1975.* Stockholm: Ministry of Foreign Affairs.

Jackson, Robert G. A. (1969) *A Study of the Capacity of the United Nations Development System,* 2 vols. Geneva: United Nations.

(1990) Transcripts of Interviews. Oxford, Bodleian Library, MS Eng. c. 4678.

Joyce, James Avery (1965) *World of Promise: A Guide to the United Nations Decade of Development.* Dobbs Ferry: Oceana Publications.

Lechner. Frank J. and John Boli (2005) *World Culture: Origins and Consequences.* Oxford: Blackwell Publishing.

League of Nations Mission of Educational Experts (1932) *The Reorganization of Education in China.* Paris: League of Nations International Institute of Intellectual Cooperation.

Lumsdaine, David Halloran (1993) *Moral Vision in International Politics: The Foreign Aid Regime, 1949–1989.* Princeton: Princeton University Press.

Mazower, Mark (2009) *No Enchanted Palace: The End of Empire and the Ideological Origins of the United Nations.* Princeton: Princeton University Press.

(2012) *Governing the World: The History of an Idea.* New York: Penguin.

Murphy, Craig N. (1994) *International Organization and Industrial Change: Global Governance since 1850.* New York: Oxford University Press.

(1998) 'Globalization and Governance: A Historical Perspective'. In Roland Axtmann (ed.) *Globalization in Europe.* London: Pinter Publishers, 144–63.

(2005) 'The Dialectic of Liberal Internationalism'. In Craig N. Murphy (ed.) *Global Institutions, Marginalization, and Development.* London: Routledge, 32–53.

(2006) *The United Nations Development Programme: A Better Way?* Cambridge: Cambridge University Press.

(2013) 'The Role for "Human Security" in an IR that Can Learn from Difference'. In Mustapha Kamal Pasha (ed.) *Globalization, Difference, and Human Security.* London: Routledge, 17–26.

Pepper, Suzanne (1996) *Radicalism and Educational Reform in 20th Century China: The Search for an Ideal Development Model.* Cambridge: Cambridge University Press.

Plesch, Dan (2011) *America, Hitler and the UN: How the Allies Won World War II and Forged Peace.* London: I. B. Tauris.

Stead, William T. (1899) *The United States of Europe.* New York: Doubleday and McClure.

Symonds, Richard (1990?) 'Bliss Was It in That Dawn: Memoirs of an Early United Nations Career, 1946–1979'. Oxford, Bodleian Library, MS Eng. c. 4703.

Toye, John and Richard Toye (2004) *The UN and the Global Political Economy*. Bloomington: Indiana University Press.

United Nations (1946) *Summary of the Meetings of the Second Committee of the General Assembly, First Session, Second Part*. Lake Success: United Nations.

UNRRA (1947) *Report of the Director General to the Council*. Washington, DC: UNRRA.

Weinlich, Silke (2014) 'Funding the UN Development System'. In Stephen Browne and Thomas G. Weiss (eds.) *Post-2015 UN Development: Making Change Happen*. London: Routledge, 75–94.

Weiss, Thomas G., Tatiana Carayanis and Richard Jolly (2009) 'The "Third" United Nations'. *Global Governance*, 15, 132–47.

PART III

The future legacies of the American Empire

8 | Foreign bases, sovereignty and nation building after empire

The United States in comparative perspective

ALEXANDER COOLEY

Introduction

Commentators and scholars routinely refer to the vast global network of US military bases and security installations as a contemporary American 'empire'.[1] They view American commanders as modern proconsuls, make comparisons to Roman military power, express concerns about the militarization of US foreign policy and draw attention to US interference in the domestic affairs of its base hosts (Kinzer 2006). But viewing the US basing network as an actual modern imperial system poses significant theoretical challenges. As Christopher Sandars suggests, since World War II the governing arrangements of US overseas military facilities have resembled more of an informal or 'leasehold empire', relying on the legal consent of hosts, security contracts and quid pro quo to maintain the American presence (Sandars 2000). Further, with some important exceptions, the United States in the Cold War and post-Cold War era has not exercised the degree of political control over its base hosts as a colonial power would, rendering it vulnerable to unilateral renegotiations, growing domestic political opposition, exit threats and even evictions from base hosts.[2]

---

[1] For representative examples, see Gerson and Birchard 1991; Johnson 2004 and 2000; Lutz 2009; and Bacevich 2011. Kaplan 2005 accepts the analogy for its positive connotations.

[2] For example, US forces have been evicted from their bases in Ecuador (2007), Uzbekistan (2005), Philippines (1991), Thailand (1976), Libya (1970), France (1966) and Morocco (1956). In other cases, including Spain, Greece and Turkey, host countries terminated agreements over major facilities, but allowed a reduced presence on other sites. On the dynamics of such 'base politics', see Calder 2007; and Cooley 2008. On the applicability of the empire analogy, see Cooley and Nexon 2013.

There is, however, a more fundamental and formal connection between US empire and the overseas military basing presence that is often neglected in the so-called American empire debate: many of the USA's most important overseas basing relationships are themselves imperial legacies, legally originating in the transition of an overseas base host from an imperial periphery or occupied polity to an independent, nominally sovereign state. In my previous work with Hendrik Spruyt, we have argued that in many cases of imperial disengagement, former metropoles struck deals to retain the use of strategic military and economic assets in former colonies by employing hybrid forms of governance such as territorial leases (Cooley and Spruyt 2009; Spruyt 2005).

In this chapter, I advance two related arguments about military basing agreements as enduring imperial legacies and their relevance for current international relations debates. First, I argue that in an array of cases involving the USA, the granting of basing rights by the former colony was a core feature of the original decolonization bargain. Washington only acquiesced to granting the independence of former colonies and occupied states when it was satisfied that it had taken the necessary steps to secure generous basing rights and military access; these were publicly secured for defence purposes, but frequently allowed for US political intervention and interference in a host country's domestic affairs. Consistent with Halperin and Palan's observation that transitions from empires to states are often incomplete, these decolonization bargains initially institutionalized continued sites of US imperial control through the granting of unrestricted basing rights, but did so within the legal and normative framework of state independence or, more precisely, exceptions that were carved into the constitutions of these new nominally sovereign base hosts. As a result, empire initially endured in the form of basing rights, though it did so under a new legal rubric.

Second, I contrast the political reception of these 'conditional independence' agreements in different eras, showing how prevailing international norms about state sovereignty impacted the political and legal standing of US overseas basing contracts. Prior to World War II, US basing agreements were consistent with other forms of comprised sovereignty and hierarchy that characterized the territorial expansion of the USA, as well as with the broader prevailing norms of colonial governance and trusteeship in the international system.

As decolonization accelerated through the 1950s and 1960s, the norm of national sovereignty strengthened. As a result, these foundational neo-imperial basing rights agreements were redefined, renegotiated and more narrowly specified by more assertive and legally capable base hosts. In certain cases, independent base hosts used their improved bargaining leverage to unilaterally abrogate these foundational accords or even evict American forces from their territory. Thus, basing agreements have evolved significantly in the post-imperial era and are now characterized by a patchwork of different legal and institutional assemblages and formulas.

In exploring the political evolution of basing rights as an imperial legacy, I also seek to recast some of the analytical assumptions developed in the new hierarchy literature in international relations. Within this research programme, scholars posit that relationships between polities can vary along the anarchy–hierarchy continuum, with imperial rule constituting hierarchy, interstate relations anarchy and clientelism located somewhere in between (Lake 2009, 1999 and 1996; Nexon and Wright 2007; and Nexon 2009). Indeed, David Lake's seminal book on international hierarchy uses official data on overseas US troop deployments as its main measure of the degree of hierarchy that characterizes American bilateral security relations with its clients (Lake 2009).

The imperial basing legacies examined in this chapter suggest that newly independent base hosts simultaneously established dual logics of both anarchy and hierarchy. As Halperin and Palan suggest in the volume's introduction, these dual embedded logics did not just supplant previous imperial rule, but rather constitute an important hybrid organizational form in their own right. Formally, newly independent base hosts acquired sovereign powers of decision making, yet they also consented legally to a foreign military presence within their territory that often subjected these nominal powers to external approval or veto. Accordingly, treating these states exclusively either as sovereign actors or as neo-imperial subjects risks overlooking the important connections and political tensions that arose from these parallel political logics and their respective legal foundations.

I begin with a stylized account of how US overseas basing rights were formally linked to processes of decolonization and de-occupation, both bilaterally and through the involvement of third parties. Next, I compare prevailing norms of sovereignty before and after World War

II and explore how these differentially impacted the political reactions, both in the home and host, to these enduring basing legacies. Finally, I examine the relevance of the US experience to other cases of conditioned French and British decolonization, finding important similarities in diverse settings such as French agreements in Africa and the UK's disengagement from the Middle East and Cyprus.

Acquiring bases: the spoils of empire and war

Typically, post-World War II the US basing rights have been secured either by contract or as a direct result of colonial or military occupation. However, prior to World War II, the USA acquired many of its most prized strategic bases – many of which endured for over a century – from its imperial expansion at the turn of the twentieth century.

The spoils of empire: Cuba and Panama

Much scholarship considers the Spanish–American War of 1898 as the pivotal marker in the United States' rise as a bona fide imperial power.[3] In reality, the USA had held a number of overseas territories, islands and possessions for some time, but the acquisition of the Philippines, Puerto Rico, Northern Marianas, Wake Island and Cuba thrust the USA into larger-scale colonial management and planning (Hunt 1979). Not coincidentally, in all of these acquisitions, as well as in Hawaii, US military planners quickly established enduring military facilities. Briefly consider the two critical cases of US basing rights in Cuba and Panama.

In Cuba, where US officials had declared during their intervention in a campaign that already had been nearly won by Cuban nationalists, that the US did not seek 'sovereignty, jurisdiction or control' over the island, US planners from the outset sought a legal basis to guarantee both enduring basing rights and domestic political control before allowing for the island's nominal independence (Hansen 2011 and Pérez 1991). Immediately following its intervention, the United States began consolidating the military facilities it had acquired at the deepwater harbour of Guantánamo Bay in the southeast of the island. Cubans had shunned Spanish rule only to be forced to accept US

---

[3] Lafeber 1998 [1963] suggests that this period of American imperialism was not the aberration in US foreign policy as previously assumed.

occupation. The infamous Platt Amendment, inserted into the nascent Cuban Constitution in 1902, granted US officials the right to lease or buy naval bases on the island as well as to intervene in domestic Cuban affairs. The provisions were presented at the Cuban Constitutional convention as a strict condition to end US military rule and were approved by a contentious 16–11 vote (with 4 abstentions). A year later, Cuba was granted its formal independence. Platt was eventually revoked in 1934, on the stipulation that the United States be granted a perpetual lease over Guantánamo, which 110 years later continues to operate as an extra-sovereign space, without host country consent, under US military control.

Around the same time in Panama, the United States coercively tied the granting of sovereign independence to the Central American country to obtaining exclusive rights over the newly completed Canal Zone. Following decades of US involvement and small-scale interventions in what had been the Colombian province, the failure of successive French companies to complete the canal construction prompted US planners to renew their interest in the territory (Lindsay-Poland 2003). In 1902, the US and Colombian Foreign Ministers drafted a treaty that granted the USA exclusive Canal Zone rights through a 100-year lease, but the treaty was rejected by the Colombian government as an unacceptable violation of sovereignty.

A few months later in November 1903, the US forces intervened to decisively assist separatists, allowing them to declare an independent Panama. In exchange, the new Panamanian government was forced to accept an even more lop-sided accord than the rejected US–Colombian protocol. The hastily signed new treaty, ratified by the Panamanian legislature after Washington threatened to withdraw its naval forces that were still deterring Colombian forces, guaranteed the USA the right to build and operate a canal over 500 square miles on the isthmus in perpetuity, as well as authorized the expropriation of additional lands for the construction of military installations necessary for the security and maintenance of the Canal Zone.[4] Article 136 of the new Panamanian constitution, like the Platt Amendment in Cuba, granted the USA the right to use its forces to keep the peace throughout the country.

---

[4] For an inventory of US facilities, see Lindsay-Poland 2003, 28–29.

Post-World War II de-occupation and neo-colonial basing rights

The expansion of the US basing network during World War II proved decisive in the US and Allied victory. Most of these facilities (Iceland, Greenland, Portugal) were retained after the war, while the formal de-occupation of defeated Japan, Germany and Italy was similarly tied, in various ways, to establishing the legal basis for the enduring presence of US and Allied forces.

In the Philippines, where the USA had governed as a colonial power from 1898 to 1942 (Kramer 2006), Manila was granted its sovereignty on 4 July 1946, but the price was acquiescing to an extensive set of US basing rights. The 1946 Treaty of General Relations – which explicitly excluded US basing facilities from the sovereign transfer – was accompanied by the hierarchical 1947 Military Bases Agreement (MBA) under which the US military was granted a 99-year lease of rent-free access to 16 facilities, including Clark airfield and Subic Bay naval station. The US military retained the right of complete freedom of movement throughout the country, maintained criminal jurisdiction over US soldiers and was awarded the right to administer the city of Olongapo, host to the Subic Bay facilities.[5]

But perhaps no other overseas base host has attracted as much political and scholarly attention as that of the Japanese island of Okinawa, host to 75 per cent of US military facilities in Japan. Following the Battle of Okinawa, US officials had established a number of facilities and developed the island into a hub for East Asian activity. As a condition for granting occupied Japan its sovereignty in 1952, Tokyo agreed to cede administration of the island (Article III) to the US military under the formula of 'residual sovereignty', which implied, but did not specify, the island's return to Japan at some point in the future (Eldridge 2001).

From 1952 to 1972, the US military administered and governed the island through the US Civilian Administration of the Ryuku Islands (USCAR), which operated in parallel to a local government but retained the power to veto all domestic legislative decisions.[6] The foundational 1960 USA–Japan Mutual Security Treaty, still in effect

---

[5] See Table 4.1 in Cooley and Spruyt 2009, 123.
[6] On US military motivations to keep Okinawa and the evolution of US military administration, see Yoshida 2001; and Sarantakes 2000.

today, also differentiated between US authority and sovereign basing rights on Okinawa, allowing the USA unrestricted rights on Okinawa as well as extraterritoriality for all crimes committed by US personnel, as opposed to the Japanese main islands where greater restrictions were agreed to. Reversion to Japan was finally achieved in 1972, after a decade of reversion protests and escalating demonstrations (Wakaizumi 2002). As a result of this special history many Okinawan politicians regard the enduring US military presence not only as an actual colonial legacy, but also as a symbol of the prefecture's inequality within Japan itself (Johnson 1999).

In the other wartime cases, most notably Germany and Italy, the United States used its wartime authority to craft broad discretionary powers for retaining an extensive military presence, codifying them both in de-occupation treaties and new security cooperation agreements such as bilateral defence treaties and NATO agreements (Duke 1989). A unique case remains that of US bases in the UK that have been governed by informal agreements and norms, not an explicit set of legal arrangements (Duke 1987). A similar large network of US bases in Korea has endured since the ceasefire of the Korean War.

Third party transfer and basing rights

One final variation on the US 'bases-for-decolonization' theme involved overseas military facilities that were either transferred or whose establishment was sanctioned by third–party ruling colonial powers. The most important of these deals was the UK–USA 'lend-lease' deal of 3 September 1940 (also known as 'destroyers-for-bases') under which the USA acquired 99-year leases over bases on the possessions of Antigua, Bahamas, Aruba-Curacao, St. Lucia, St. Thomas, Trinidad, British Guiana, as well as temporary access to Bermuda and Newfoundland. The facilities were used to stage supplies between North America and Europe during World War II, and after the war became a backbone of the US global basing network (Sandars 2000, 42–47).

In the mid-Atlantic Azores, the USA acquired rights to critical basing facilities for anti-submarine operations through Britain's invitation in 1944, just one year after Portugal had allowed Britain to establish a presence on Terceira under the centuries-old Anglo-Portuguese alliance (Herz 2004). Tellingly, during the 1960s, Portuguese Prime Minister António de Oliveira Salazar himself would wield US basing rights as a bargaining chip over the Kennedy Administration's initial pressure on Lisbon's colonial policy, threatening Washington with eviction if it did not oppose international demands in the United Nations for Portuguese decolonization (Cooley 2008, 161–163; Rodrigues 2004). In Morocco, US officials were granted rights by France to construct a series of large airbases in 1951, but following independence in 1956 and United States intervention in Lebanon in 1958, the Moroccan government evicted US forces and the facility closed in 1963.

Perhaps the most politically controversial of these third-party transfers – and another acute example of independence conditioned on basing rights – occurred on the island of Diego Garcia, part of the Chagos group in the Indian Ocean (Vine 2009). In 1965, by decree, Britain separated the Chagos from colonial Mauritius (and other nearby islands from the colonial Seychelles) as a condition of granting its independence. The islands were designated as part of the new British Indian Ocean Territory (BIOT) and, just one year later, Britain granted the United States the right to use the islands and construct military facilities. Over the next few years, the 1,500–2,000 Chagosian inhabitants of the islands were removed, first by having food and medical supplies restricted, and then in 1973, by force. The base now is perhaps the most important single overseas US military facility, hosting a harbour that can accommodate an aircraft carrier task force, a large runway that can host heavy bombers and refuellers, surveillance and intelligence facilities, and, by some accounts, a 'black site' detention facility used by the CIA.[7]

Questions of sovereignty and the political evolution of basing rights

The second concern of this chapter is to explore the domestic political reception and legal standing of US bases, as imperial legacies across these different periods. Here, changing norms of sovereignty played a critical role in the status of these basing accords.

---

[7] On the island's immense strategic value, see Erickson *et al.* 2010.

The US basing network in the age of empire and wartime

Prior to World War II, US authorities pioneered and adopted a number of novel legal categories to codify the denial of sovereignty in their newly acquired territories. The Spanish–American War was accompanied by the acquisition of a number of additional Pacific islands and territories and followed by military interventions and occupations in Central America and the Caribbean, including campaigns in Mexico, the Dominican Republic, Haiti, Honduras and Nicaragua.

The issue is not just that the USA, contrary to its self-perceived exceptionalism, was rapidly amassing overseas territories, colonies and islands as part of a concerted new imperialism (Kramer 2011). Rather, as a result of these acquisitions US officials were forced to generate a number of new legal categories through which these colonies, territories and islands, many of them hosting military assets, could be reconciled with US law and emerging international legal norms governing the obligations of colonial powers. As Burnett argues:

American imperialism also consisted of efforts to impose limits on expansion: to draw lines around what counts as properly 'national' territory (as opposed to, say, territory 'belonging' to the nation but not fully part of it), and even to circumscribe national power, for purposes of reducing the number of contexts in which the government must take up the responsibilities that come with such power. Burnett 2005, 781

Thus, categories such as 'unincorporated territory', 'incorporated territory' and 'appurtenance' were created to designate these new acquisitions as neither foreign nor part of the United States, but as nevertheless belonging to the USA. These categories sought to avoid the responsibilities associated with both sovereignty and imperial tutelage, as the latter was increasingly regarded internationally as incurring obligations and responsibilities on behalf of the colonial power. The important new naval facilities constructed on the ambiguously sovereign sites of Puerto Rico, Guam, Cuba and Hawaii were important elements of the US global basing network and many of these facilities, including the extra-constitutional site of Guantànamo Bay, still endure under special legal categories of association.

In such a climate of 'sovereign ambiguity' and surging global empire, the nearly farcical independence-for-basing deals thrust on

Cuba and Panama at the beginning of the twentieth century – while certainly resented domestically – were neither out of step with prevailing international norms of limited sovereignty, nor with other US coercive legal practices in the Western hemisphere. Indeed, as Jonathan Hansen recounts in his overview of contemporary US debates over the Platt amendment and its implications for the meaning of sovereignty and independence, a *New York Times* editorial chided Platt's critics for harbouring 'extravagant notions of the future political status of Cuba', qualifying that the sovereignty of a state must be 'subject to the general peace and public order of nations' (Hansen 2011, 139). The arbitrator and guardian of the 'public order', was, of course, the United States.

Sovereignty norms and the political evolution of basing rights after World War II

Shortly after the wartime basing arrangements were codified, it became clear to US policy makers that the emerging post-war international political environment would threaten the status of its overseas basing arrangements. State sovereignty as a universal organizing principle institutionalized the notion that the legality of any foreign military presence in peacetime depended on obtaining the consent of the host country (Woodliffe 1992). In turn, sovereign consent to the US presence inevitably became a topic of domestic political debate and political campaigning in base hosts, as well as a natural target for rising nationalism and populist appeals. Periods of democratization, particularly in the wake of authoritarian rule, proved especially politically contentious for the status of US basing accords (Cooley 2008). Finally, the rise of the Soviet Union and global competition for basing access heightened perceptions that base hosts under superpower courtship held considerable bargaining power.[8]

As early as the 1950s, across a number of different overseas hosts such as Japan, Panama, Philippines, Portugal, Libya, Korea, Iceland, Spain and Turkey, host leaders demanded – and usually

---

[8] As Vine 2009 argues, some naval planners in the 1950s, specifically citing what they considered to be the deteriorating political environment for US deployments, formulated the 'strategic island' concept, through which important US facilities would be relocated to sparsely or non-populated islands that would be immune to such political developments.

received – renegotiated basing rights deals.[9] These imposed greater restrictions on American military activities, shortened long or perpetual leases, more clearly designated the property rights over these installations and introduced new Status of Forces Agreements that, at least in theory, replaced the extraterritoriality previously granted to US troops with some elements of joint or 'concurrent' jurisdiction, such as those codified in the NATO SOFA.[10] For example, in the Philippines the 1959 Bohlen-Seranno amendment to the 1947 MBA ceded 117,000 hectares of territory, including the town of Olangapo, back to Philippine authorities, shortened the original 99-year lease period to 25 years (effective in 1966), established a Mutual Defense board to address local grievances and placed restrictions on the stationing of intercontinental missiles.[11]

Along with the almost universally politically charged issue of criminal jurisdiction over US personnel, political clashes and tensions also emerged over the use of bases in support of operations not part of the common defence – so-called 'out of area' missions. For Asian hosts such as Japan and the Philippines, the basing issue was especially sensitive during the Vietnam War, while in Europe, base hosts vehemently objected to the use of the bases for periodic US military operations in the Middle East (Lundestad 2003: 142–67).

As a typical example, Turkish officials, following a string of high-profile violations of Turkish sovereignty, insisted in the renegotiated Defense Cooperation Agreement of 1969 on explicit Turkish government consent for any non-NATO use of the bases.[12] Of all its European hosts in 1973, only Portugal and West Germany offered US forces the necessary basing platform to assist in its airlift support for Israel, an accommodation Lisbon paid for afterwards when it was targeted by an Arab oil embargo.[13]

---

[9] One of the best sources on this issue remains the executive report written for the White House by Frank Nash (Nash 1957). On how these tensions played in the European context, see the country case studies in Duke and Krieger 1993.

[10] On the political tensions generated by USA–host country SOFAs, see Stambuk 1963. On the purpose and evolution of SOFAs, see Delbrück 1993; Erickson 1994; and Egan 2006.

[11] Table 4.1 in Cooley and Spruyt 2009: 123.

[12] Cooley 2008: 114. Also, the Cuban Missile Crisis 1962 and the USA's tacit trade off of the Jupiter missiles also upset Turkish defence officials.

[13] Similarly, in 1986, only the United Kingdom allowed US bombers to use its territory for the Libyan bombing campaign, which necessitated Spanish-based

Thus the rise of nationalism, the onset of decolonization and increased democratization in host countries created a new awareness of the sovereign imbalances that characterized most of these foundational basing agreements. Beyond renegotiation, another technique of political management, especially popular in European hosts such as Germany, Italy, Iceland and Turkey, was to insist on labelling the bases as 'NATO' installations, as opposed to US installations, thereby publicly emphasizing their multilateral purpose.[14]

Rent for bases

Basing rights also become commodified, allowing host country elites to divert attention from their imperial origins and reframe their utility as sources of economic and military assistance. Even some long-standing hosts such as the Philippines, Panama and Portugal, beginning in the 1960s, demanded a substantial quid pro quo for extending US basing rights. Under a long-standing policy, US officials have always refused to officially pay 'rent' for facilities, instead emphasizing the common security purposes and bundling separate economic and security assistance agreements with formal basing accords. Nevertheless, new categories of foreign assistance such as the Foreign Military Sales (FMS) and Foreign Military Financing (FMF) were fashioned to disburse military and economic assistance disproportionally to overseas US base hosts, often as part of 'defence cooperation' packages that accompanied basing rights renegotiations (Harkavy 1989: 340–356).

Yet, the transactional nature of US bases is exactly what rulers over the 1970s and 1980s in Spain, Turkey, Philippines, Panama and Greece invoked to justify the alleged national benefits that accrued from these basing deals, especially when membership in the US security umbrella was insufficient to justify the ongoing military presence (Clarke and O'Connor 1993). Large base-related rents also allowed authoritarian rulers such as President Ferdinand Marcos of the Philippines to secure

bombers to touch base in East Anglia before taking off for the Libyan Gulf. For an inventory of these access decisions for southern European hosts, see Cooley 2008: 204.

[14] On the logic of the NATO cases, in contrast to the East Asian system, see Hemmer and Katzenstein 2002. On the importance of multilateralism for legitimizing US bases in Italy, see Monteleone 2007.

their regimes and fund their patronage machine and security forces (Bonner 1988). These basing rights packages reached their peak in the late 1970s and 1980s, as hosts would use information about other packages to drive up their demands with US negotiators (McDonald and Bendahmane 1990). In the late 1980s, for example, the USA was effectively paying the Philippines $480 million a year for basing rights.

Post-Cold War developments and US failure in Iraq

The post-Cold War era has seen a mix of political trends over basing rights. Since 1991, basing issues in Europe – with a few exceptions – are no longer 'hot button' questions of national sovereignty, and instead have been relegated to the status of technical issues in security cooperation. Tellingly, although the CIA ghost flight scandal of the 2000s revealed that US forces and contractors had used a web of European-based military facilities and airfields to illegally detain and transport prisoners (almost all of whom were formally under European supervision and control), few host governments chose to conduct active formal investigations (Grey 2006).

Outside Europe, the facilities in Panama and the Philippines were finally closed, the former upon the expiration of the Canal Zone lease in 1999 and the latter following the Philippine Senate's failure in 1991 to ratify an accord that would have extended the US lease on Subic Bay. The status of the US presence in Okinawa also exploded back on to the global media and political agenda in 1995 when three US servicemen raped a twelve-year-old girl. The 2000s witnessed a renewed attention to basing rights as part of the Global War on Terror. This included opening new, smaller facilities in areas including Africa (and the accompanying creation of AFRICOM, a new regional command), the Black Sea and Central Asia, all of them obtained through contract and some form of quid pro quo.[15] The decade also witnessed the networking of a global transnational network of anti-base activists and campaigns across these tradition-ally segmented base hosting sites and regions (Lutz 2009 and Yeo 2009).

---

[15] Cooley 2008: 217–48. On the Global Defense Posture restructuring of the 2000s, also see Feith 2004; and Campbell and Ward 2003.

But the most compelling, if unexpected, illustration of the contemporary tension between state sovereignty and basing rights was Washington's unsuccessful attempt to secure long-term basing rights in Iraq. During 2003 and 2004, US officials and analysts freely drew analogies to models of American wartime occupations of Germany and Japan, distilling lessons learned and possible models for long-term legal arrangements to govern the US military presence (Dobbins *et al.* 2003). 2008 Republican Presidential candidate Senator John McCain referred to the 'Korean' model as a blueprint for US forces in Iraq, potentially allowing for tens of thousands of troops to be stationed in large bases by mutual consent.[16] However, in December 2011, the last combat troops of the USA withdrew from the country under the terms stipulated by the 2008 USA–Iraq Status of Forces Agreement.

As it turns out, just four years after the US occupational body, the Coalition Political Authority, transferred nominal sovereignty back to Iraq in 2004, Iraqi officials succeeded in placing US forces on a more restrictive legal footing. The public outrage in the wake of the US military scandals of Abu Ghraib and the 2007 massacre of civilians in Nisoor Square by the security contractor Blackwater further stiffened Iraqi resolve to regulate the activities of US contractors. Over the course of the 2008 negotiations, Iraqi authorities marshalled domestic political opposition, invoked norms of international sovereignty and pointed to other examples of US security deals, to maintain an uncompromising stance on a deadline for US withdrawal that surprised even experienced American negotiators (Skye 2011).

The resulting SOFA accord rescinded the almost unrestricted rights and access enjoyed by the US military, placed US security contractors under Iraqi law, relocated US forces outside of population centres and mandated complete withdrawal by 2012.[17] Although US-based critics of the Obama Administration lashed out at US negotiators for failing to secure even long-term basing rights, the failure of the 'de-occupation for bases' model to endure in Iraq testifies to the significantly altered international normative and legal contexts that distinguished 2011 from 1945.

---

[16] See Taylor Martin 2008.

[17] For a perspective that examines the Iraqi side of the 2008 negotiations, see Al-Rikabi 2010.

Basing rights and decolonization in comparative perspective: France and the UK

How well do these arguments and observed trends about US base hosts apply to other cases of imperial power disengagement and bargaining over basing rights? In this third section, I assess how basing rights were embedded in French and British decolonization agreements. I find similar patterns of evolution in the cases of French relations with former African colonies, with more limited – though still instructive – examples in the British case. Though Russian basing relations with its former satellites have been governed by many of the same governance forms, such as leases, the sudden unravelling of the Soviet Union as a result of centrifugal dynamics, rather than political bargaining, render the bases-for-decolonization formula broadly irrelevant to the post-Soviet space, though a number of other Soviet legacies, as Ortmann observes elsewhere in this volume, endure (Kotkin 2003).

French basing rights and patterns of African decolonization

A broad look at French decolonization in Africa reveals that the decolonization-for-bases formula was central to French disengagement across the continent. However, the stability of these initial agreements varied across the Northern African and Sub-Saharan clusters. France granted Tunisia its independence in 1956 and agreed to withdraw all troops except for those at its base at Bizerta, which was leased and whose precise sovereign status was left open-ended (Cooley and Spruyt 2009: 58–68). In Algeria, after seven years of war, the Evian Accords of 1962 enshrined a 'bases-for-independence' formula that both sides had come round to accepting after insisting on exclusive sovereignty for most of the conflict. In essence, France granted Algeria its independence in exchange for maintaining basing right at the naval station of Mers-el-Kébir for fifteen years, as well as joint production of Algeria's hydrocarbons.

Although they facilitated disengagement, both the Algerian and Tunisian foundational agreements proved short-lived, as growing host nationalism, the decolonization norm and weakening French influence prompted newly independent elites to demand the complete withdrawal of French forces. In Algeria, in 1965 Houri Boumedienne came to power on a platform of economic nationalism and reducing dependency on France in the security and oil sectors. After Boumedienne's nationalizing of all hydrocarbon production and courting of other foreign partners, France saw its relational power diminish; after an unsuccessful attempt to sanction Algiers, Paris withdrew its naval presence at Mers-el-Kébir in 1967, ten years before the lease's expiration. In Tunisia, negotiations over the future legal status of Bizerta became intertwined with Tunisian demands for access to the Sahara. Unable to reach an accord, fighting broke out in 1961 with France holding the base by force, while inflicting hundreds of casualties and occupying surrounding areas. The standoff on what was now formally sovereign Tunisian territory proved a politically and internationally untenable position for Paris, which withdrew all its troops by 1963.[18]

Further south, 1960 was a key year for French colonial disengagement from the sub-Saharan region, as fourteen former sub-Saharan African colonies were granted independence. Of these, Paris secured post-independence basing rights in seven new states, retaining military bases in Senegal (Dakar), Madagascar (Diego-Suarez), Cameroon (Fort Lamy), Chad (Ndjamena), Côte d'Ivoire (Port Bouet), Gabon (Libreville) and Central African Republic (Bangui). In 1977, Djibouti, host to a major set of installations, was also granted independence under the classic formula, while Réunion as a French Department also hosted major bases. Basing rights were usually specified in the Mutual Defence Agreements and/or Military Assistance Agreements that also provided technical assistance, training and hardware (Chipman 1989). In almost all of these cases, France enjoyed unrestricted use rights, retaining the right freely to move troops outside of designated basing areas and, in most cases, intervene domestically to restore political order.

Except for Chad, all of these base hosts successfully renewed these foundational basing rights in the early 1970s.[19] Madagascar was a partial exception, where an attempt to curtail French basing rights and restrict troops to the naval base at Diego Suarez during

---

[18] Woodliffe observes that a key pressure on the French decision to completely withdraw in 1963 was a UN General Assembly declaration that recognized 'the sovereign right of Tunisia to call for the withdrawal of all French armed troops on its territory without consent' (1992: 77).

[19] Though French troops would return in 1986 for Operation Epervier and then again in 2007 under the MINURCAT mission.

renegotiations led to a complete French withdrawal in 1975. France closed its facilities in Cameroon and the CAR in 1997, dissolved its basing agreement with Côte d'Ivoire in 2009, while in Senegal it handed back its bases in 2011. Currently, France retains a formal basing presence in Djibouti, Gabon and Réunion, as well as an ambiguous presence under UN auspices in Chad.[20]

Compared with the North African cases, French basing rights in the south were more extensive and often welcomed by host country elites, mainly because they served to bolster their patrimonial rule given their weak internal capabilities. An additional reason for their endurance appears to have been the relatively lower levels of nationalism in the south compared to the North African cases. The most politically controversial aspect of the French Sub-Saharan bases was their frequent use for interventions into their hosts' domestic and regional affairs. Between 1962 and 1995 France used the bases for nineteen different interventions – not including its participation in UN operations – including missions to prop up ruling regimes, quell riots, defend groups of French nationals and suppress rebellions.[21]

Britain's gradual imperial retreat

With a few important exceptions, Britain proved to be more pragmatic than France or the United States about securing and maintaining basing rights from its foreign imperial positions. Where it could it also tried to condition the granting of independence on maintaining basing rights. However, following World War II, Britain's imperial decline led to a steady retrenchment from most of its imperial outposts, as most of its facilities were voluntarily ceded.

In both of its large Middle East mandates, British officials made the granting of independence contingent on securing basing rights. The 1930 Anglo-Iraqi Treaty – drawn up as the legal foundation for Iraqi independence in 1932 – granted British forces nearly unrestricted basing rights for twenty-five years and mandated that British advisors consult in government affairs. The agreement generated deep opposition among many Iraqi political actors, through periods of political

---

[20] For inventories, see Hansen 2008.
[21] For a list up until 1986, see the chart in Chipman 1989: 124. To these I've added interventions in Gabon (1990) and Djibouti (1991).

turbulence and series of domestic coups in the 1930s and 1940s, and even served as a historical warning to Iraqi negotiators with the United States in 2011. Similarly, in Transjordan, Britain was granted basing rights in the 1946 agreement that ceded its mandate, with a treaty establishing a joint security force and military assistance.

Closer to home, the granting of dominion status to the Irish Free State in 1922 was conditioned on the UK maintaining control over the deep-water ports of Berehaven, Cobh and Lough Swilly, though these too were ceded in 1937, when Ireland became a republic (Canning 1982). More broadly, after World War II, Britain maintained 'main support areas' across former Dominions in Australia, Canada, Sri Lanka and the more controversial Simonstown base in South Africa. But the overall trend during the 1950s and 1960s was voluntary disengagement, while the debacle of Suez accelerated plans for imperial retrenchment and encouraged more confrontational stances towards the British presence. For example, Britain initially had planned to retain facilities in Aden after the promised independence for 1968, but violent clashes in 1967 led to a full withdrawal by British forces that year.

One important exception was the island of Cyprus, which was granted independence in 1960 only after Cypriot authorities agreed to cede the sovereign areas of Dhekelia and Akrotiri under the Treaty of Establishment (signed by Britain and Cyprus and also guaranteed by Greece and Turkey).[22] Governed by the UK Ministry of Defence, the status of these facilities on 99 square miles of the island has never changed or been converted to a lease status; they have remained sovereign UK territory through the intercommunal violence of the 1960s, the 1974 Turkish invasion and partition, the introduction of international peacekeepers and Cyprus's 2004 accession into the European Union (Constantinou and Richmond 2005). A similar conditional transfer characterized the granting of Malta's independence in 1964, though in this case the agreement was more voluntary as UK officials secured a large naval base through a Defence Cooperation agreement for ten years (renegotiated in 1972) in exchange for a £51 million rental payment.[23]

Tellingly, the most important UK overseas military facilities now lie not on overseas states, but within a handful of enduring British

---

[22] The provisions of the Sovereign Base Areas are located in the Treaty Annexes.
[23] Dowdall 1972. British forces were fully withdrawn in 1972.

Overseas Territories where the presence of UK forces both guarantees and constitutes UK rule (Aldrich and Connell 1998). In Gibraltar and the Falkland Islands, where the UK still maintains substantial naval and air force deployments, UK forces secure local populations against the territorial claims of neighbouring Spain and Argentina, respectively. UK personnel also serve in Diego Garcia and Ascension Island – the major staging area for the 1982 Falklands military campaign – alongside much larger contingents of US personnel, even though in both cases the islands formally remain UK territory.

Looking forward, a fascinating looming possible case of decolonization and basing rights may soon be upon us should Scotland separate from the United Kingdom. As Malcolm Chalmers and William Walker first observed, the facilities on which the UK's lone remaining independent nuclear capability rests, the seaborne Trident system, is almost entirely based at Faslane and Coulport in Scotland (Chalmers and Walker 2001). With no realistic relocation alternatives available, and assuming an independent Scotland would be denuclearized and sign the Non-Proliferation Treaty, London and Edinburgh would have to conclude a series of agreements that would allow for exclusive UK control over these facilities and their operations. The authors anticipate that a type of base lease would be the only realistic way to govern such an arrangement and that Scotland would be pressured to acquiesce to it in order to gain Westminster's backing for its prompt membership in the European Union and NATO.

Conclusions: bases as evolving sovereign legacies

Many of the key nodes in the global network of US military bases are, in fact, enduring legacies of US empire or wartime occupation. In a range of base hosts, governments were only granted their sovereignty by acquiescing to codify an enduring American military presence. Such arrangements lie at the very intersection of the distinctions that IR scholars make about relations under hierarchy anarchy and under hierarchy. US bases not only were a tangible imperial legacy that endured into the 'post-imperial' era, but also their formal legal logics often clashed with the constitutional and contested politics of these new independent states. As the editors of this volume suggest, the very political contestation over US basing agreements and their terms was both a legacy of 'incomplete transition' from the imperial era and a point of national definition and sovereign assertion on behalf of base hosts.

Varying international norms of sovereignty and host country consent also played an important part in the political evolution of these foundational basing agreements. As the USA acquired overseas territories and possessions at the turn of the twentieth century, it constructed new legal designations and offered qualifications for how its sovereign clients in the Western hemisphere could govern. Following World War II, such hierarchical arrangements became increasingly more difficult to maintain, as the political backlash within US host states targeted the terms of these agreements and the forces of nationalism and democratization saw US facilities as much as symbols of sovereign violation as security arrangements.

The failure of US officials in 2011 to secure extended basing rights in Iraq testifies to the now straining compatibility between a foreign power maintaining formal overseas bases and the exercise of state sovereignty in its host. As such, the current expansion of informal basing arrangements, cooperative security locations, tacit cooperation, use of military contractors, covert action and the use of drones are all, to some extent, reactions to the political difficulties generated by designating a facility a formal overseas base with clear and transparent legal roles. As such, this growing non-formalized US global military footprint may be more difficult to detect, debate and regulate than classical basing accords. Going forward, this amalgamation of informal overseas US military activities arguably constitutes a more significant political legacy of American empire than the formal basing agreements that this chapter has examined.

References

Al-Rikabi, Jaffar (2010) 'Iraq and the Theory of Base Politics: Cooley, Institutionalism and Culture'. MA Dissertation, Georgetown University.

Aldrich, Robert and John Connell (1998) *The Last Colonies.* Cambridge: Cambridge University Press.

Bacevich, Andrew (2011) *Washington Rules: America's Path to Permanent War.* New York: Metropolitan Books.

Ball, Desmond (1980) *A Suitable Piece of Real Estate: American Installations in Australia.* Sydney: Hale & Iremonger.

Bonner, Raymond (1988) *Waltzing with a Dictator: The Marcoses and the Making of American Policy.* New York: Vintage Books.

Burnett, Christina Duffy (2005) 'The Edges of Empire and the Limits of Sovereignty: American Guano Islands'. *American Quarterly*, 57(3), 779–803.

Calder, Kent E. (2007) *Embattled Garrisons: Comparative Base Politics and American Globalism.* Princeton: Princeton University Press.

Campbell, Kurt M. and Celeste Johnson Ward (2003) 'New Battle Stations?' *Foreign Affairs*, 82(5), 95–103.

Canning, Paul (1982) 'Yet Another Failure for Appeasement? The Case of the Irish Ports'. *International History Review*, 4(3), 371–92.

Chalmers, Malcolm and William Walker (2001) *Uncharted Waters: The UK, Nuclear Weapons and the Scottish Question.* East Linton: Tuckwell.

Chipman, John (1989) *French Power in Africa.* Oxford: Blackwell.

Clarke, Duncan L. and Daniel O'Connor (1993) 'US Base Rights Payments after the Cold War'. *Orbis*, 37(3): 441–57.

Constantinou, Costas M. and Oliver P. Richmond (2005) 'The Long Mile of Empire: Power, Legitimation and the UK Bases in Cyprus'. *Mediterranean Politics*, 10(1), 65–84.

Cooley, Alexander (2001) 'Imperial Wreckage: Property Rights, Sovereignty and Security in the Post-Soviet States'. *International Security*, 26(3), 55–67.

(2008) *Base Politics: Democratic Change and the US Military Overseas.* Ithaca: Cornell University Press.

Cooley, Alexander and Daniel Nexon (2013) 'The Architecture of Empire: Globalization and the Politics of US Overseas Basing'. *Perspectives on Politics*, 11(4), 1034–50.

Cooley, Alexander and Hendrik Spruyt (2009) *Contracting States: Sovereign Transfers in International Relations.* Princeton: Princeton University Press.

Delbrück, Jost (1993) 'International Law and Military Forces Abroad: US Military Presence in Europe, 1945–1965'. In Simon W. Duke and Wolfgang Krieger (eds.) *US Military Forces in Europe: the Early Years, 1945–1970.* Boulder: Westview, 83–115.

Dobbins, James, John G. McGinn, Keith Crane, Seth G. Jones, Rollie Lal, Andrew Rathmell, Rachel Swanger and Anga Timilsina (2003) *America's Role in Nation-Building: From Germany to Iraq.* Santa Monica: RAND.

Dowdall, J. (1972) 'Mintoff's Malta: Problems of Independence'. *The World Today*, 28(5), 189–95.

Duke, Simon (1987) *US Defence Bases in the United Kingdom: A Matter for Joint Decision?* Basingstoke: Macmillan.

(1989) *United States Military Forces and Installations in Europe.* Stockholm and New York: SIPRI and Oxford University Press.

Duke, Simon and Wolfgang Krieger (eds.) (1993) *US Military Forces in Europe: The Early Years, 1945–1970.* Boulder: Westview Press.

Egan, John W. (2006) 'The Future of Criminal Jurisdiction over the Deployed American Soldier: Four Major Trends in Bilateral US Status of Forces Agreements'. *Emory International Law Review*, 20, 291–344.

Eldridge, Robert D. (2001) *The Origins of the Bilateral Okinawa Problem: Okinawa in Postwar US–Japan Relations, 1945–1952.* New York: Garland.

Erickson, Andrew S., Ladwig C. Walter III and Justin D. Mikolay (2010) 'Diego Garcia and the United States' Emerging Indian Ocean Strategy'. *Asian Security*, 6(3), 214–37.

Erickson, Richard J. (1994) 'Status of Forces Agreements: A Sharing of Sovereign Prerogative'. *Air Force Law Review*, 37, 137–53.

Feith, Douglas J. (2004) 'Prepared Statement before the House Armed Services Committee'. 23 June. Available at: http://merln.ndu.edu/merl n/pfiraq/archive/dod/sp20040623-0522.pdf

Gerson, Joseph and Bruce Birchard (eds.) (1991) *The Sun Never Sets: Confronting the Network of Foreign US Military Bases.* Boston: South End Press.

Grey, Stephen (2006) *Ghost Plane: The True Story of the CIA Torture Program.* New York: St Martin's Press.

Hansen, Andrew (2008) 'The French Military in Africa'. Council on Foreign Relations, 8 February. Available at: http://www.cfr.org/france/french-military-africa/p12578.

Hansen, Jonathan M. (2011) *Guantánamo Bay: An American History.* New York: Hill and Wang.

Harkavy, Robert (1989) *Bases Abroad.* Oxford: Oxford University Press and SIPRI.

Hemmer, Christopher and Peter J. Katzenstein (2002) 'Why Is There No NATO in Asia? Collective Identity, Regionalism and the Origins of Multilateralism'. *International Organization*, 56(3), 575–609.

Hunt, Michael H. (1979) 'Resistance and Collaboration in the American Empire, 1898–1903'. *Pacific Historical Review*, Special Issue, 48(4).

Johnson, Chalmers (ed.) (1999) *Okinawa: Cold War Island.* Cardiff, CA: Japan Policy Institute.

(2000) *Blowback: The Costs and Consequences of American Empire.* New York: Owl Books.

(2004)*The Sorrows of Empire: Militarism, Secrecy and the End of the Republic.* New York: Metropolitan Books.

(2007)*Nemesis: The Last Days of the American Republic*. New York: Metropolitan Books.

Kaplan, Robert D. (2005) *Imperial Grunts: The American Military on the Ground*. New York: Random House.

Kinzer, Stephen (2006) *Overthrow: America's Century of Regime Change from Hawaii to Iraq*. New York: Henry Holt.

Kotkin, Stephen (2003) *Armageddon Averted: The Soviet Collapse, 1970–2000*. New York: Oxford University Press.

Kramer, Paul A. (2006) *The Blood of Government: Race, Empire, the United States and the Philippines*. Chapel Hill: University of North Carolina Press.

(2011) 'Power and Connection: Imperial Histories of the United States in the World'. *American Historical Review*, 116(5), 1348–91.

Lafeber, Walter (1998) *The New American Empire*. 35th anniversary edition [1963]. Ithaca: Cornell University Press.

Lake, David A. (1996) 'Anarchy, Hierarchy, and the Variety of International Relations'. *International Organization*, 50(1), 1–33.

(1999) *Entangling Relations: American Foreign Policy in its Century*. Princeton: Princeton University Press.

(2009) *Hierarchy in International Relations*. Ithaca: Cornell University Press.

Lindsay-Poland, John (2003) *Emperors in the Jungle: The Hidden History of the US in Panama*. Durham, NC: Duke University Press.

Lundestad, Geir (2003) *The United States and Western Europe since 1945: From 'Empire' by Invitation to Transatlantic Drift*. Oxford: Oxford University Press.

Lutz, Catherine (ed.) (2009) *The Bases of Empire: The Struggle against US Military Posts*. New York: NYU Press.

McDonald, John W. Jr. and Diane B. Bendahmane (1990) *US Bases Overseas: Negotiations with Spain, Greece, and the Philippines*. Boulder: Westview Press.

Monteleone, Carla (2007) 'The Evolution of a Pluralistic Security Community: Impact and Perspectives of the Presence of American Bases in Italy'. *Journal of Transatlantic Studies*, 5(1), 43–85.

Murphy, Sean D. (1991) 'The Role of Bilateral Defense Agreements in Maintaining the European Security Equilibrium'. *Cornell International Law Journal*, 24, 415–36.

Nash, Frank (1957) *United States Overseas Military Bases*. White House Report. Washington, DC [Declassified February 1990].

Nexon, Daniel (2009) *The Struggle for Power in Early Modern Europe: Religious Conflict, Dynastic Empires and Institutional Change*. Princeton: Princeton University Press.

Nexon, Daniel and Thomas Wright (2007) 'What's at Stake in the American Empire Debate'. *American Political Science Review*, 101(2), 253–71.

Pérez, Louis A. (1991) *Cuba under the Platt Amendment, 1902–1934*. Pittsburgh: University of Pittsburgh Press.

Rodrigues, Luís Nuno (2004) 'About Face: The United States and Portuguese Colonialism in 1961'. *Electronic Journal of Portuguese History*, 2(1), 1–10.

Sandars, Christopher T. (2000) *America's Overseas Garrisons: The Leasehold Empire*. New York: Oxford University Press.

Sarantakes, Nicolas Evan (2000) *Keystone: The American Occupation of Okinawa and US Japanese Relations*. College Station: Texas A&M Press.

Skye, Emma (2011) 'From Surge to Sovereignty'. *Foreign Affairs*, 90(2), 117–27.

Spruyt, Hendrik (2005) *Ending Empire*. Ithaca: Cornell University Press.

Stambuk, George (1963) *American Military Forces Abroad: Their Impact on the Western State System*. Mershon Center: Ohio State University Press.

Taylor Martin, Susan (2008) 'Keeping Troops Overseas isn't as Trouble Free as John McCain Says'. *Tampa Bay Tribune*, 20 April.

Vine, David (2009) *Island of Shame: A Secret History of the US Military Base on Diego Garcia*. Princeton: Princeton University Press.

Wakazumi, Kai (2002) *The Best Course Available: A Personal Account of the Secret US–Japan Okinawan Reversion Negotiations*. Honolulu: University of Hawaii Press.

Woodliffe, John (1992) *The Peacetime Use of Foreign Military Installations under Modern International Law*. Dordrecht: Martinus Nijhoff Publishers.

Yeo, Andrew (2009) 'Not in Anyone's Backyard: The Emergence and Future of a Transnational Anti-Base Network'. *International Studies Quarterly*, 53(3), 571–94.

Yoshida, Kensei (2001) *Democracy Betrayed: Okinawa under US Occupation*. Bellingham: Center for East Asian Studies, Western Washington University.

9 | Empire, capital and a legacy of endogenous multiculturalism

HERMAN MARK SCHWARTZ

Empire, capital and endogenous multiculturalism

Do empire and capitalism produce different kinds of multiculturalism? And how did empire and capitalism interact to produce the multicultural societies we see everywhere today? Imperial and capitalist multiculturalism do differ, but not as much as one might expect, and not just because modern capitalist society emerged out of several imperial powers. It is tempting to see today's multiculturalism as a lingering feature of capitalism's impure origins in the world that preceded it. But both empire and capitalism contain contradictory and endogenous tendencies towards homogenization and differentiation that grow out of generic political and economic logics. Homogenization and differentiation each lower both governance costs and transaction costs in the mobilization of labour forces. The precise mix differs from place to place, as a function of the imperial centre's relative strength, population density in newly conquered territory and the onset of industrialization.

I tease out some of these differences by comparing labour mobilization and migration in late Qing China, the British tropical empire before and after the industrial revolution and the US Empire. Thirty million people migrated from Han China into Manchuria in the nineteenth century. This came close to producing the same kind of culturally homogeneous population and production practices that existed on the south side of the Great Wall. In essence, it replicated prior Sung and Ming dynasty expansion during the previous millennium. The British Empire in tropical Asia sponsored fairly large migrations to relatively empty areas, including roughly 19 million Indians to

Thanks to the project participants, Brian Balogh, Richard Bensel, Peter Katzenstein, Audie Klotz, Jeffrey Kopstein, Kees van der Pijl and Srjdan Vucetic for comments and criticism on earlier drafts. All errors remain mine.

Burma. Finally, the USA saw a massive land rush, with roughly 600,000 slaves and then 30 million voluntary migrants displacing lightly settled natives (Weaver 2003; Belich 2009). Most migration occurs as chain migration, and in all three migrations imperial policies constructed these chains. With a few salient exceptions, imperial policies typically produced multicultural societies in order to facilitate political control and to bring new territory into their economic ambit. Thus there is no reason to suspect that the American Empire will produce some kind of culturally homogeneous future.

These cases show that in some sense we have 'empire all the way down', because empire is a logic of governance that can accommodate different forms of economic organization, one of which is capitalism. Multicultural societies are precisely one way to have commercial or capitalist activity comport with empire and vice versa. While we might expect capitalism to produce a mixture of deracinated individuals mixing in new urban environments, even these give rise to group identities, albeit of a new sort, rather than the homogeneous fields of abstract capital and labour that both Marx and the neo-classical economists posit. For their part, empires must balance *divisa et impera* against the risk that peripheral identities become a cause for rebellion. The imperially organized capitalism that emerged in the 1800s (or 1500s?) faces both problems.

Empire, identity power and markets

Ancient empires' multiculturalism emerged out of second-best solutions to the problems of optimizing among revenue extraction, internal security and external security (Lieven 2004: 133; see also van der Pijl 2007). First, the ancient world presented any would-be empire with a multitude of languages, customs and religions. Identities and loyalties were strongly local in the absence of the homogenizing power of mass literacy and the press (Anderson 1983). The lack of shared identity created both problems and advantages for empires as they sought to expand.

Typically, successful empires built off an ethnically and linguistically coherent core (Lieberman 1992, 2003). But expanding empires negotiated two different kinds of difficulties thrown up by differences between that core and later conquests. The degree of linguistic and cultural similarity between the core groups and newly conquered groups necessarily grew with distance from that original core, increasing the difficulty of securing compliance. Intermarriage, hostages, an attractive culture and a desire for self-preservation could bring newly conquered elites into administrative compliance with central elites, but did not necessarily obliterate their specific culture (Mann 1986). And what about peasants? The second-best solution of letting village headmen collect taxes reinforced village solidarity and customs to the detriment of any coherent imperial identity. The optimal solution, commercialization, permitted direct taxation, but also did little to encourage adoption of central norms. Multiculturalism thus emerged directly from imperial expansion. This multiculturalism was diverse across production units (i.e. villages), but relatively speaking, homogeneous within them.

Given enough time, empires could homogenize deviant groups. The consolidation of a meritocratic bureaucracy in China gave local elites a pathway into the state, but only if they adopted the norms and language of the central state. In turn, these elites helped pass along a common written language and other cultural norms that brought outlying peasant groups closer to the core group's identity. In the absence of widespread literacy and cheap printed materials, this passive process of cultural isomorphism could take a long time. China attained something close to cultural homogenization only over two millennia, despite being able to move and replicate its peasantry on its open external and internal frontiers.

The need to generate cash to pay for hard power made identity salient. For virtually all empires, the only or largest source of resources was surplus agricultural production. But taxing that resource put empires into direct conflict with landowners, who also sought control over that surplus via rents. Successful empires – such as the Chinese empires – were those that could prevent landowners from becoming an aristocracy, subordinate those landowners to central state authority and capture the bulk of the surplus for the centre. Replacing aristocratic control over peasants, the law, and violence with central control required powerful civilian and military bureaucracies.

In turn, these centrally directed bureaucracies posed a dual challenge that affected the kind of multiculturalism that emerged. First, how to fund them? Second, how to prevent actors lower down the hierarchy from seizing control over those bureaucracies and using them to challenge the imperial centre? The latter problem reinforced elite

homogeneity, but carried some risks. Homogenization of the bureaucratic elite lowered the transaction costs for running an empire, but it
also lowered the transaction costs for potential internal challengers
trying to build a coalition against the centre. The typical formula for
avoiding challenges was to divide and rule. Thus the Chinese dynasties
separated civilian and military authorities, and rotated each across
China's many counties. This separated control over violence from the
means to fund that violence and limited bureaucrats' ability to develop
a regional power base.

Funding bureaucrats required money, not only because money was
easier to move than taxes in kind – after all, both military and civilian
employees needed to eat, which meant that the agricultural surplus
eventually had to find its way to those employees – but also, in the ideal
case, money created a kind of firewall between both bureaucracies and
the peasantry. Direct collection of the agricultural surplus meant that
the civilian or military bureaucracy might put roots down into that
peasantry, begin acting like landlords and think of the surplus as a rent
payable to them. A fully commercial economy, based on money taxes,
insulated the peasantry from potential personal loyalties to the bureaucracy and limited the claims that landowners could make on peasants.
The problem instead became one of extracting money from peasants
and landowners. Peasants could be squeezed through state monopolies
on salt and other centrally controlled necessities. Here more homogeneity across peasant villages made them more likely to respond to
millenarian calls for a tax revolt.

Empires used control over imported luxuries to extract additional
revenue from landlords and their own bureaucrats, though Pearson
(1991: 41–116) disagrees. This also helped prevent the emergence of a
final potential challenge to its power: merchants. Local merchants, who
simply circulated local goods up to and down from wholesale markets,
were not a political threat. Rather, they were crucial to monetization at
the level of the peasant economy (Fox 1971). But long-distance trade,
with its potentially huge profits and prestige, might create a mercantile
elite that threatened state power directly or, through its ability to bid
for the loyalty of military elites, indirectly.

The Chinese dynasties expended considerable energy controlling
trade. The Chinese tribute system, and its associated periodic bans on
freebooting mercantile activity, centralized the inflow and outflow of
high value, scarce goods. Reciprocally, it empowered southeast Asian

kingdoms on the other side of the exchange (Reid 2004: 23–25, 27). China thus did not get an ethnically heterogeneous mercantile class, although many mercantile communities existed at the fringes of the empire.

But elsewhere, the inner dynamics of long-distance trade combined with weaker imperial centres to produce ethnically differentiated long-distance merchant communities. These ethnically distinct communities were a second-best alternative, relative to central control, for most empires (Reid 2004; Trocki 2004). Ethnically distinct mercantile communities resolved two problems at once. For imperial centres, the ethnic (or religious) barrier between an existing or potential aristocracy based in land helped the centre divide and conquer its opponents. If merchants got too powerful they could be expelled. At the same time merchants could not buy their way into control over land-based resources and become a hereditary aristocracy. A distinct ethnic or religious identity lowered transaction costs for these mercantile communities and allowed them to function (Grief 1989). Their identities barred them from political power, but made them indigestible to their imperial hosts.

Empires aspired to homogeneity. Multicultural populations emerged out of empires' second-best choices about routines for organizing, expanding and retaining political power. Even China, over most of its history, was relatively heterogeneous. For other empires the core ethnic lines divided highland from lowland and central from peripheral peasant populations; peasants from aristocracies; aristocracies from long-distance merchants.

What about capitalism as a way of organizing economic activity? By definition, capitalism produces diversity through an expanding division of labour and urbanization (Simmel 1971: 251–93). Unlike empires, this diversity exists within and across production units. We might suspect that in the long run this should produce a homogeneous population. After all, the exploitation of newly emptied lands allowed capital to operate freely as pure disembodied capital in what Kees van der Pijl (2007) sees as a homogeneous Lockean space. But in fact the market-based logics of capitalism reinforce diversity in the population because of the transaction costs in markets for both labour and capital. Opening up production in new lands created a need for labour to complement that capital. In a classic contradiction, a relatively homogeneous and pure capital pulled ethnically, religiously and racially disparate populations into these empty spaces, as well as creating some ethnically based forms of capital accumulation.

First, peasant resistance to full time participation in open labour markets means that these markets usually arise out of violence. It is not coincidental that all of our empires used slavery to start production and to bring labour supplies into new production zones. Coercion tends to bring discrete bodies of workers to new places where their ethnic or religious identities solidify. Second, voluntary migration relies on chain migration to overcome the transaction costs in relocating. This also creates compact communities with a coherent ethnic identity. Capitalism tends to mobilize populations via market coercion. Capitalist economies tended to have voluntary and quasi-voluntary migration. But this usually took the form of chain migration. Capitalist migrations thus produced self-sustaining communities of novel ethnic groups in target societies. These groups in turn banded together for self-defence, producing new ethnic identities out of individuals who otherwise would have had familial or village identities. Capitalist migration thus produced something like the old imperial communities, but on a mass basis and in new locations. The economic and social logics underlying chain migration (and the quantitatively much more important phenomenon of sojourning) thus produce variegated ethnic populations rather than the homogeneous ones that abstract theories of capitalism envision. This was even more true during the transition from ancient empire to modern capitalism, during the nineteenth century. Finally, anonymous capital markets are vulnerable to all sorts of market failures. Well into the modern period, some kind of shared identity and social context lubricated the extension of credit even in relatively developed economies. Thus, like empire, capitalism produces multicultural societies partly because it recycles material created by empire and partly from its own endogenous logics.

Manchuria and the expansion of a classic ancient empire

Chinese expansion into Manchuria presents the limiting case for multiculturalism as a natural outcome of empire. Recall that China presents us with something close to all empires' preferred end state: a relatively homogeneous peasant population with its lower transaction costs for social control and in revenue extraction; a landowner class exposed to market pressures and disconnected from the imperial bureaucracy;

separate civil and military bureaucracies; and central control over long-distance trade. Migration to Manchuria illustrates the normal pattern of imperial expansion into a relatively unpopulated area (Perdue 1987), reproducing, in cellular form, the Han population and production patterns of northern China. Yet, even here local elites shaped a heterogeneous society, and conflict with other empires coerced or induced migration of millions of Koreans and thousands of Japanese and Russians.

The Qing dynasty that ruled China from 1644 to 1911 originated in Manchuria, north of the Great Wall. Ecological considerations (the inability to grow rice so far north) and political considerations (retaining a sense of identity among the Manchu, i.e Qing elite) led the Qing to bar permanent Han Chinese migration across that border until the late ninteenth century. The Manchu preferred a sojourning labour force for their estates (Amrith 2011: 51). But Russian expansion into Siberia and then the Japanese intervention in Korea motivated the Qing to try to populate Manchuria to pre-empt its rivals.

Sojourners could not deter external rivals. Thus from the 1860s onward, the controls on migration disappeared as the Qing sought to boost the Chinese population. A massive land rush occurred. Roughly half a million Chinese moved annually from northern Chinese provinces, and particularly Shandong and Hebei, into Manchuria (Gottschang 1987: 461). As McKeown notes, in the absence of this land rush, 'Manchuria might not be a part of China at all today' (2004: 182) Net, about 8 million people moved permanently over the period from 1890 to 1940; gross about 30 million moved. Japanese occupation of Manchuria induced and coerced a further 2 million Koreans to migrate across the Yalu. Finally, 500,000 Japanese and 140,000 Russians had settled in Manchuria by 1930 (Gottschang 1982: 11, 13).

Yet the Qing's geopolitical motives needed an economic complement to succeed. The possibility for soybean cultivation sustained expansion into Manchuria. By 1929 Manchuria would account for 60 per cent of global soybean production and soy had become China's largest export (Gottschang 1982: 17; Kung and Li, 2011: 569). Finally, railroad construction also furthered both imperial and economic aims, as new Russian and Japanese railways lowered the cost of migration the same way steamboats did in southeast Asia and the Atlantic. Migrants moved in the classic pattern of chain migration. Much of the outmigration was enabled by existing family chains (Amrith 2011: 53–54). But brokers and gentry, who already had ties to the bureaucrats and estate owners controlling Manchuria, organized a substantial portion (Bix 1972: 426). Unlike labour brokers in southeast Asia (see below) or southern China, these lenders typically advanced peasants the cost not only of passage but also enough money to start production on a plot of land. They wanted to move family farmers in addition to transient labourers. By contrast, labour brokers and the state organized Korean migrants to Manchuria. The Japanese state hoped to use Koreans as an industrial labour force and a counterweight to the dominant local Chinese population (Park 2000).

Migration into Manchuria thus recreated different versions of traditional imperial patterns of ethnicity and economy. As Bix notes, 'before the twentieth century, the functioning of Manchuria's agricultural economy continually reproduced the type of class system based on peasant indebtedness that was an integral feature of its genesis' (1972: 443). At the bottom was a relatively homogeneous Chinese population. Above them lay two (sometimes three) contending governmental elites and their associated technical cadres. Finally, much like Protestant settlers in Ireland, a second ethnic group coexisted uneasily with the Chinese majority. War and revolution would displace the non-Chinese governmental elites (including the Manchu/Qing) and part of the minority peasant population, leaving Manchuria essentially ethnically homogeneous in the modern period. The post-revolutionary state would complete the process of creating a national identity using the usual tools of myth and media. But in the absence of intrusions from other empires, the Qing Empire might have produced an ethnically homogeneous population in Manchuria.

The British South and Southeast Asian Empires

The British Empire in Asia produced divided populations; what Furnivall (1948: 303–12) labelled 'plural societies'.[1] Initially this empire had a population much like those in the ancient empires described above, but falling freight costs made it possible to pioneer export production in relatively unpopulated areas of southeast Asia. Imperial authorities mobilized immigrant labour to exploit the new opportunities. As Furnivall noted, 'The first condition of the economic

---

[1] Space considerations prevent discussion of similar patterns in the Dutch Empire.

development of backward areas is an adequate supply of labour ....
[For Western enterprise] the Government must provide this labour'
(1948: 341). Compared with later migrations to the USA and, to a
lesser extent the rest of Anglo-America, the British state was much
more involved in generating and organizing this migrant flow. I discuss
Indian flows into Burma as these constitute the largest such flow: 60 per
cent of external Indian migration.

Despite its precociously modern form as a joint stock company, the
British East India Company (and its formal state successors) duplicated
the normal routines practised by barbarians after conquering a settled
population. Indeed, Lieberman (2008: 770) considers them as the
maritime equivalent of the inner Asian nomads. The British reproduced
typical imperial patterns at first with respect to monopolization of
long-distance trade, the use of mercantile and fiscal intermediaries,
communal self-governance and coercive extraction from a settled peasant population. Given how diaphanous their control really was until
the steam engine revolutionized transportation, it had little choice. Was
this much different from the Mughals or Seleucids?

As with earlier ancient empires, the British tried but were only
partially successful in monopolizing long-distance trade for their own
state organized traders and their ethnic peers. The Empire tolerated the
continuation and abetted the spread of Indian and particularly Chettiar
(or *Chettyar*) and Gujarati merchants into local commerce and some
aspects of long-distance trade. The British could hardly do otherwise,
given the density of pre-existing trade networks in the Indian Ocean
and South China Sea (Chaudhury 1985). At the same time, Chinese
traders – meaning Teochiu, Hakka, Hoklo and other distinct language
groups rather than any uniform group – had already constituted many
mercantile networks in the South China Sea. Indeed, in many places,
and in particular the Mekong delta and adjacent regions, Chinese port
polities were the nuclei of new kingdoms, with the degree of Chinese
dominance a function of local levels of organization (Reid 1992; Cooke
and Li 2004).

In Southeast Asia the British conceded communal self-governance to
both groups, imitating the communal millet system in the Ottoman
Empire. The British relied on the Chinese to run the Straits Settlements
in the nineteenth century. Chinese tin-mining *kongsi* in the peninsula
were already well established and self-governing. The British also relied
on Indian administrative personnel to rule Burma after it came under

full British control. The empire thus produced a typical minority middleman population between themselves and the majority population. But the artificiality of this can be seen in the degree to which the pre-steam engine Chinese populations indigenized themselves. China was perpetually short of women, and formally banned the out-migration of women (Moch 2007). The overwhelmingly male Chinese émigré population rapidly intermarried, producing the distinctive *Baba*, *Peranakan* and *Lookjin* groups in the Straits, Indonesia and Thailand. This facilitated trade but simultaneously marked off these communities from the larger society.

So the British produced something much like a traditional agrarian empire in littoral and oceanic Asia. They ruled with the consent of relatively undisturbed local elites, extracted revenue by delegating tax-farming and strategic monopolies to a typical minority middleman group and selectively enslaved outsiders for use on military and transport projects. Corvée and compulsory cultivation by the peasant population supplemented this.

This changed with the shift to a more modern, high-volume economy that rails and steam ships permitted. Steam power accelerated settlement of 'empty spaces' just as it did in Manchuria and the Anglo-American temperate zones. Expansion occurred in 'empty places' in the lower Irrawaddy delta of Burma (i.e. closer to the Indian Ocean). Similar processes occurred in Sumatra and Borneo in the Netherlands East Indies, the Chao Phraya river basin in Thailand with sponsorship from the Thai royal family, and the Mekong delta in Cochin China, but I will not consider them here.

The British expanded their control of Burma steadily from 1850 to 1885. They initially brought in Indians as slave labour and then, once they had established a position in the coastal regions, as administrators. Early British penetration of Burma also rested on traditional Indian banking networks, particularly the Nattukottai (or Nakarattar) Chettiar. These communities had been trading with the eastern Indian Ocean littoral since the later Chola Kingdoms of 1070–1279 (Adas 1974: 393; Rudner 1994). From the early 1870s to 1920, annual rice output rose from 0.5 million tons to 3.5 million tons (Furnivall 1948: 85). Only a massive inflow of labour to clear jungle and settle the land could make this possible. But the supply of convicts was too small to accommodate this expansion, and the unreliability of 'convict labour [meant it] was not always cheap' (Furnivall 1948: 46). Thus, as rice exports expanded, the British sponsored a land rush of mostly Burmese peasants, but also some Indians (mostly from coastal Telugu-speaking areas), into the jungles of the lower Irrawaddy. In turn this drove an expansion of permanent Indian migration to urban areas, and particularly Rangoon (Yangon).

Although the Indians were a supplement to the Burmese, roughly 12–15 million Indians – about half of all Indians who migrated from 1850 to 1940 – ended up going to Burma. They arrived in large numbers because the majority were seasonal workers for harvest, or even more so to clear fields and build dykes essential for production of paddy rice (Amrith 2011:32). Unlike in Assam and Ceylon, but as with Chinese tin miners and Tamil plantation workers in Malaya, this seasonal labour was heavily male. Women did not come along, inhibiting family formation and settlement. Even so, the Indian population of Burma rose steadily to about 1 million – 7 per cent of the total population – by 1931 (Furnivall 1948: 117). But the huge disparity between the flow and stock of immigrants shows the difference between this migration and the ones in Manchuria and Anglo-America. Put simply, the British wanted a labour supply for lower Burma, but not one that might set off communal battles over land. By contrast, Indian migration to booming urban areas did not create competition with the less literate and less urban Burmese population. Sojourning was greater in Burma than elsewhere.

Although Burma was administratively part of India, the British regulated labour flows there the same way they regulated Indian flows to Malaya. Unlike the state-subsidized migration of Europeans to Anglo-America (with the partial exception of the United States), Brazil and Argentina, the British relied on private, 'voluntary' migration. Formal indenture operated mostly with respect to transport to non-Indian Ocean destinations and accounted for less than 10 per cent of total Indian migration (Northrup 1995: 156). The less obvious forms of bound labour in the *maistry* (Burma), *tundu* (Ceylon)and *kangani* (Malaya) systems allowed labour brokers and plantation foremen to return to their home or nearby villages and recruit workers by advancing them cash against future labour. Theoretically these migrants were interrogated at their port of departure by a magistrate as to the degree to which their labour contract was voluntary. Practically, much of this supervision was political theatre (Amrith 2010), but all three systems produced cohesive communities of in-migrants.

Vast inflows of Indian seasonal labour enabled an equally vast expansion of rice production by Burmese peasants, with 3 million moving to the lower Irrawaddy. Here too the British imperial authorities created a new market in land to match the market in labour, bringing 5 million new acres into production. From 1852 onwards the British replaced the non-contractual, use-oriented system of land rights with a contractual, mortgage-based system (Adas 1974: 387–88). British government encouraged smallholding, but left smallholders vulnerable to Chettiar and Burmese lenders. Smallholders couldn't really borrow in the open market so they would execute a kind of mortgage with moneylenders, handing over their deed against an oral contract that this transfer was a mortgage. Moneylenders would then just register the deed in their own name (Furnivall 1948: 92). By 1930 only 27 per cent of land in lower Burma was still held by peasant proprietors, although most of this was held by Burmese lenders (Furnivall 1948: 87; Adas 1974: 398–99). Increased burdens on the Burmese peasantry eventually produced an inflow of Indians willing to accept a lower standard of living and thus higher rents than established Burmese family farmers.

Adas notes that capital followed labour in the build-up of Burmese rice production (1974: 389–90). Brute physical labour cleared the jungles, production began and only then did Chettiar, Burmese and Chinese moneylenders arrive. But from 1880 onward these intermediaries were essential for production, as the cost of inputs began a steady rise. This is the inverse of the Anglo-American pattern, where capital arrived first and input prices typically fell.

Imperial policy in the British tropical empire thus produced a more heterogeneous society than did migration into Manchuria, but one in which different ethnic groups mapped onto specific broad classes. Furnivall puts it this way, although his plural society model is too stark: 'from the very earliest days of British rule there evolved a mixed community with a racial differentiation of functions' (Furnivall 1948: 46). Put less strongly, imperial policy and a modernizing economy interacted to transform part of a settled subsistence peasantry into a smallholding family farming population. That population relied on European colonial enterprise for its transport and on a mostly immigrant population for its finance. These imperial policies left behind societies in which large parts of the population could be seen as non-native on the advent of independence, and in which relatively stark occupational differences made groups associated with business, and in particular moneylending, vulnerable to nativist appeals and communal violence (Chirot and Reid 1997).

Anglo-America

Anglo-America is the suburban sprawl of the global economy (Schwartz 2012). That is, Anglo-America had a political economy in which land development created both sides of the balance sheet simultaneously, and out of nothing. Capital emerged from mortgage debt on relatively depopulated lands whose streams of income were largely in the future, rather than from current streams of income. In turn, this new capital drew in a corresponding pool of labour to validate itself. In-migration driven by land development thus induced a series of disparate migrant streams from Europe and elsewhere. This continual stream of heterogeneous groups in turn generated a constant renegotiation of internal racial and cultural boundaries in America. In most of Anglo-America, and certainly in America itself, no single ethnic group dominates, and with a few important exceptions, a Southeast-Asian style polarization across two or three large groups that encompass most of society is absent. Instead, American multiculturalism is as much about mutual tolerance in the shared pursuit of goods as it is about moving past enmity to some notionally true, shared identity.[2]

As in Burma and Manchuria, geopolitics and economics intertwined. The new states in North America sought to populate the land in order to control it. But it was precisely the new inflows or people that drove up land values for incumbent landowners. Nothing surprising here: Alexis de Tocqueville had already identified the strong connections between land, migration and the state in 1831 (de Tocqueville 1945).

'Gobernar es poblar': immigration into North America

Anglo-American North America possessed two novel and related features as compared to the older empires: first, expansion into non-proximate areas that were essentially devoid of population; second, the construction of a new form of modern state by local elites rejecting the constraints imposed by what was essentially a classical empire.

---

[2] I thank Brian Balogh for this point.

Both novelties rested on modern markets in land, and equally important, modern capital markets around land. In turn, these novelties
drove a massive and unprecedented immigration mirroring the equally
large-scale flight from modernizing economies in absolutist Europe.
Immigration occurred in sequential waves that generated recurrent
conflict between older and newer groups of immigrants. Where
British engrossment of Ireland produced a backwash of immigration,
terror and a national liberation movement, immigration into North
America produced nativism, hybrid identities and a *jus soli* understanding of citizenship.

The North American population was already multicultural at the
time of American independence. Although Britons and, of course,
Africans constituted by far the largest ethnic groups, Germans
accounted for about 8 per cent of the non-African population at the
time of the Revolution, and more Germans than English (albeit not
Britons) emigrated to the colonies in the 1700s (Taylor 2001: 317–20).
There were substantial Dutch, Swedish and Irish populations and they
lived in geographically concentrated settlements conducive to rebellion. The same was true of various non-Anglican religious groups.
British restrictions on westward movement and immigration were
intolerable to expansion-minded American elites. Expansionists won
the Revolution, which in part was a civil war between themselves and
those loyalists who fled to upper Canada. The lesson the British took
away from this conflict was to try to produce more homogeneous
populations in their other settler colonies.

Conscious of its inability to coerce compliance, the new American
state created a system of property relations precisely in order to generate voluntary adhesion to itself. Contrary to Alexander Hamilton's
desire for a visible and active European-style state, the United States
built 'a government . . . out of sight' (quoted in Balogh 2009: 3). But out
of sight did not mean out of mind. America was no libertarian paradise
in which order emerged spontaneously from voluntary market transactions. This framework favoured debt-financed expansion of agricultural production and debt-financed agricultural production favoured
continual inflows of new immigrants.

Where European state building homogenized people, the US state
building homogenized space through massive internal improvements,
the Public Land Survey System and a new legal framework for transfer-
ring land from the state to individuals. The new state then let

individuals operating inside this framework work out the optimal pattern of production. Markets homogenized individuals as producers, and those producers offered up loyalty to the new state. 'Homesteaders (and homeowners) into Americans' characterized the United States rather than 'Peasants into Frenchmen'; survey and regulation preceded settlement and production rather than being imposed on extant and heterogeneous populations. This differed from, and eventually destroyed, a different model of labour flows built on slaves. At the same time it tapped into distinct flows of immigrants, who then constituted geographically distinct communities within the United States.

The new American state had a different attitude towards land, (immigrant) labour and governance from that of the original British imperial state. Unlike the old imperial state, the new American state had to compete with Britain (via Canada), with its own possibly independence--minded westward-bound settlers and, to a lesser extent, with France and Spain for settlers' loyalty (Taylor 2010; Hatter 2011). Much as in the original Thirteen Colonies, the key issue was access to land. Settlers would align themselves with whoever offered them secure tenure, more land and self-governance, and as a century of events from Bacon's Rebellion in Virginia (1676) through to the American Revolution (1776) had confirmed, settlers were likely to abandon or destroy elites who tried to stem their westward outflow. Wakefieldism – limiting access to land so as to assure landowning elites a steady supply of cheap labour – worked better in theory than in practice.

The new United States bid for settler loyalty with land, rather than coercing loyalty. It did so in competition with the British, who offered free land to settlers in the Ontario peninsula in Canada (Taylor 2010). Neither state could project enough pure military force into the region to control it without first securing the loyalty of the existing settler population, and those loyalties were in play (Taylor 2010; Balogh 2009: 66; Hatter 2011; cf. Emmanuel 1972, more generally on settler societies). Successful imposition of a regulatory structure favouring settlers in the United States reversed the population flow into Canada.

Internal and external security thus rested on the new state's ability to deliver land to migrant and immigrant settlers, and in the south, to control slaves. As with European states, this required revenues and military force. But the new state had different relative proportions for these. Where European states confronted established land-owning nobilities in Europe and dense peasant populations in much of Asia, the new US federal state could pre-empt ownership of most trans-Allegheny land. Federally owned land in the Northwest Territory amounted to 200 million acres, and the Louisiana Purchase, Texas and California comprised an additional 1 billion acres (Gates 1989: 52; Balogh 2009: 143). Land sales provided on average 13 per cent of Federal revenue from 1806 until 1846 (Dewey 1915: 216–17). By contrast, customs and excise taxes and state monopolies provided the bulk of European state revenues. But land could not be sold unless there was labour to work that land.

And why expand at all? As in Burma, successive increases in British and then European import demand drove the frontier outward. For example, cotton production rose from 3,000 bales in 1790 to 4.5 million bales in 1860, moving steadily across the southeast from Georgia to Louisiana (Schwartz 2010: 128). Each increase thus brought in train an expansion of extensive production at the frontier, an intensification of production in former frontier zones and rising labour demand in both. But in the US south and west, conquest (the expulsion of Native Americans) created only the possibility for new production units, and those units lacked labour and any prior improvements. Creating a labour force, buying land from the state and putting up basic structures required borrowing in advance of production.

The federal state abetted local states' efforts to create access to this borrowing by permitting free banking (Hammond 1934, 1936, 1948; Sylla 1972: 214–15). Would-be planters, particularly in Louisiana, Mississippi, Arkansas and Florida, founded banks to extend themselves mortgages. By 1860, seventeen of thirty-three states had free banking, and another four a modified form (Bodenhorn 2002: 262). Credit enabled land sales, which rose from an average of 359,000 acres per year in 1800–1814, to 5.5 million acres in 1819 and eventually 20 million in 1836; a huge interstate market in slaves followed. But all of this activity was based on expectation rather than established production. It required credit creation, rather than simple credit intermediation. The southern states were able to 'bootstrap' development in a kind of Ponzi scheme that funded mortgages on land whose stream of income lay in the future, by using state bonds whose revenues ultimately also relied on that future stream of plantation income. The contemporaneous Secretary of the Treasury, William Crawford, acknowledged this bootstrapping, saying many banks were incorporated 'not because there was capital seeking investment . . . but because men without active capital wanted the means of obtaining loans, which their standing would not command' (quoted in Gates 1989: 57–8).

Expanding debt on one side of the balance sheet had a corresponding asset in the expanding number of slaves. Slaves in the abstract are a form of capital good. In 1805 the estimated value of the US slave population was $300 million. By 1860 it had risen to $3 billion, implying a rising price per head (Gunderson 1974: 922). The roughly 700,000 slaves present in the New United States in 1790 grew to nearly 4 million by 1860 (Fausto 1999: 20). This burgeoning slave population created a mobile labour force that could be redistributed as production moved westward towards the Mississippi River. The results of this dispersal are still visible in census maps for the United States, where the old cotton south remains heavily demographically African-American (Figure 9.1).

Settlement of the non-slave territories in North America produced an even more heterogeneous mixture of ethnic groups. Each new increment of frontier expansion drew in a new wave of immigrants, and a new predominant ethnic or national group. The same cotton boom that propelled slave agriculture across sub-tropical America also caused the Northwest Territories to boom on the basis of secondary demand. Immigrants constituted one-sixth of total white population growth during the 1830s–40s boom (Zolberg 2006: 128–9). But this immigration deepened the existing ethnic heterogeneity of the North, as only 25 per cent of immigrants were British. Instead, Rhineland Germans and Irish provided a third each. Expansion of the wheat production frontier into Illinois, Wisconsin and Kansas likewise expanded to Francophone Europe and Scandinavia, the catchment zone for new immigrants driving the British share down to 20 per cent (Zolberg 2006: 129).

By populating lands emptied of Native Americans, these immigrants enabled borrowing against that land. That borrowing validated the same kind of bootstrap investment in infrastructure that had occurred in the South. The Federal and 'provincial' states provided infrastructure more aggressively than did European states (Balogh 2009: 126–29; Callendar 1902; Bensel 2000). In the North, states provided about 40 per cent of all railroad capital in the 1830s (Dunlavy 1991: 12). Revenue and infrastructure were organically connected, as indicated above. The Federal General Survey Office was housed in the Treasury Department rather than at a ministry of the interior. Land and infrastructure were also organically connected. A federal land grant funded

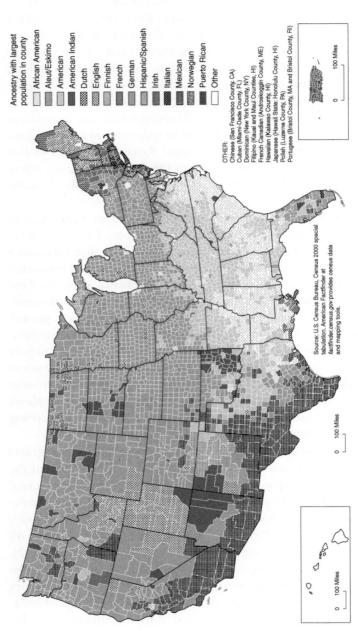

Figure 9.1 Largest ethnic group by county, 2000 Census

Ancestry with largest
population in county

- African American
- Aleut/Eskimo
- American
- American Indian
- Dutch
- English
- Finnish
- French
- German
- Hispanic/Spanish
- Irish
- Italian
- Mexican
- Norwegian
- Puerto Rican
- Other

OTHER:
Chinese (San Francisco County, CA)
Cuban (Miami-Dade County, FL)
Dominican (New York County, NY)
Filipino (Kauai and Maui Counties, HI)
French Canadian (Androskoggin County, ME)
Hawaiian (Kalawao County, HI)
Japanese (Hawaii State: Honolulu County, HI)
Polish (Luzerne County, PA)
Portugese (Bristol County, MA and Bristol County, RI)

Source: U.S. Census Bureau, Census 2000 special
tabulation. American Factfinder at
factfinder.census.gov provides census data
and mapping tools.

0 ___ 100 Miles

0 ___ 100 Miles

0 ___ 100 Miles

construction of the Illinois Central Railroad, which was intended to connect the Upper Mississippi at Galena, Illinois to the Gulf of Mexico at Mobile, Alabama. This system was generalized in the 1862 Pacific Railway Bill.

The land grant railroad system tied an immigrant population, land and state together. The federal state wanted a railroad network that would tie the entire continent together. By giving fledgling railroad firms alternating sections of land along their planned routes, the federal government put the onus of land development on the railroad company. Railroads could not make money unless the land adjacent to the rail generated sellable commodities to be carried by the system, nor could they raise capital without mortgaging their land grant. So both land and infrastructure were organically connected to immigration. The Illinois Central Railroad received 2.6 million acres of land, but these had to be sold within ten years or forfeited at auction. So the ICR offered seven years credit to settlers and small down payments to buyers. It did so through its own land development company, which distributed advertisements in Europe and engaged agents to seek emigrants (Gates 1968; Gates 1989; Zolberg 2006: 131).

Railroad and export expansion were thus tightly connected to immigration. Each geographic expansion of production brought a new, non-random wave of immigrants. Chain migration meant that immigrant waves clustered in specific locations. Put simply, immigrants from a given region in Europe tended to migrate to US regions that already had migrants from their family, village or province. This produced the large-scale regional clusters of distinct immigrant communities still visible a century later in the USA (see above in Figure 9.1).

The American Empire thus differs from the Asian empires in two important dimensions. In terms of sovereignty, the state's control over society was less coercive and much more indirect (with the important regional exception of the slave states). The state ruled by establishing frameworks in which market contestation and voluntary migration would produce the outcome the state desired. Second, America attracted a huge but sequential variety of immigrants. Those immigrants came in order to validate the exploitation of new lands opened up through land grants. These two distinct features were intertwined, as those land grants were a form of indirect state building or economic planning. The nature and timing of land development combined with imperial policy to take in a multicultural population from the start.

Nonetheless, this multiculturalism differs in terms of its sheer diversity from that found in either Manchuria or the British and Dutch empires in Asia.

Conclusion

The arrival of the industrial revolution and capitalism might have been expected to produce more homogeneous populations than those created by empires. The relentless logic of the market should override granularity and build homogeneous populations of workers to match abstract capital on the other side of capitalism's central polarity. Yet this did not happen. First, capitalism grew out of older agrarian empires. Those empires ruled through *divisa et impera*, separating potential aspirants for power from the resource bases for power. The more patrimonial an empire was, the more likely that this strategy produced distinct mercantile communities separate from the mass of peasants on the one side, and the aristocracy on the other. Highly developed, bureaucratic empires, oddly enough, had less need for a strategy of ethnic division and could rely on more functional divisions of labour. But most empires were not as well developed as the Chinese empire. As a result, most empires ended up as ethnically diverse societies with fractures between and among highland and lowland, and central and peripheral peasant populations; between peasants and aristocracies; between aristocracies and long-distance merchants.

The transitional empires Europeans built carried these divisions over into modernity. British (and Dutch) industrial capitalism built on the foundations of their older empires in Asia and on the recycled foundations of older still kingdoms and sultanates. These empires inherited and reproduced prior ethnic divisions of labour through deliberate policies. Even when, and perhaps especially when, they had a relatively blank canvas on which to draw up new economies, these empires drew on specific streams of ethnically segregated economic actors. In the temperate zones that became Anglo-America, imperial policy also structured the ethnic make-up of the labour force. The endogenous dynamic of land development drew in ever-new streams of migrants from ever-new catchment zones in Europe (and Asia to a lesser extent). After US independence, the British tried to produce ethnically homogeneous societies to assure solidarity with imperial rule (McMichael 1984). In the limiting case, this produced the relatively homogeneous

New Zealand that existed up until the 1980s; the major, if blurred, cleavage lay between settlers and indigenous Maori. Deliberate policies of exclusion, rather than the market, produced homogeneity relative to the United States.

In the United States, state policy was more open to non-Anglo immigrants, and labour could only muster opposition to Asian immigrants. Here, markets produced a multicultural society. The relentless drive to bring land into the market for cultivation and thus to create capital via mortgages, drew in about 60 per cent of European emigrants and sedimented them layer on westward layer. In the Anglo-Dominions, imperial policy and labour strength precluded this kind of sedimentation until after World War II, and everywhere, chain migration encouraged finer and finer forms of occupational segregation. The multiculturalism of the modern world thus emerged from patterns laid down in the old agrarian empires, reinforced by market dynamics that the more successful modern empires unleashed. The multiculturalism of the agrarian empires does differ in degree from modern multiculturalism, because modern communications technology and literacy promote new identities faster. Ancient empires also differ in kind, in that their multiculturalism was diverse across production units (i.e. villages), but, relatively speaking, homogeneous within them, while that produced by capitalism is diverse within production units. Still, that diversity has emerged in part because capitalist economic logics and practices recycle human materials from the older and transitional empires, and because the logic of chain migration enforces heterogeneity on the labour force that capitalism brings to its inner and outer frontiers.

References

Adas, M. (1974) 'Immigrant Asians and the Economic Impact of European Imperialism: The Role of the South Indian Chettiars in British Burma'. *The Journal of Asian Studies*, 33(3), 385–401.

Amrith, S. (2010) 'Indians Overseas? Governing Tamil Migration to Malaya 1870–1941'. *Past & Present*, 208(1), 231–61.

(2011) *Migration and Diaspora in Modern Asia*. Cambridge: Cambridge University Press.

Anderson, Benedict (1983) *Imagined Communities: Reflections on the Origin and Spread of Nationalism*. London: Verso Books.

Balogh, B. (2009) *A Government out of Sight.* Cambridge: Cambridge University Press.

Belich, J. (2009) *Replenishing the Earth: The Settler Revolution and the Rise of the Anglo-World, 1783–1939.* New York: Oxford University Press.

Bensel, R. (2000) *The Political Economy of American Industrialization, 1877–1900.* Cambridge: Cambridge University Press.

Bix, H. P. (1972) 'Japanese Imperialism and the Manchurian Economy, 1900–31'. *China Quarterly,* 51, 425–43.

Bodenhorn, H. (2003) *State Banking in Early America: A New Economic History.* New York: Oxford University Press.

Callender, G. S. (1902) 'The Early Transportation and Banking Enterprises of the States in Relation to the Growth of Corporations'. *The Quarterly Journal of Economics,* 17(1), 111.

Chaudhuri, K. N. (1985) *Trade and Civilisation in the Indian Ocean: An Economic History from the Rise of Islam to 1750.* Cambridge: Cambridge University Press.

Chirot, D. and A. Reid (1997) *Essential Outsiders: Chinese and Jews in the Modern Transformation of Southeast Asia and Central Europe.* Seattle: University of Washington Press.

Cooke, N. and T. Li (2004) *Water Frontier: Commerce and the Chinese in the Lower Mekong Region, 1750–1880.* Lanham: Rowman & Littlefield.

Dewey, D. R. (1918) *Financial History of the United States.* London: Longmans.

Dunlavy, C. A. (1991) 'Mirror Images: Political Structure and Early Railroad Policy in the United States and Prussia'. *Studies in American Political Development,* 5(1), 1–35.

Emmanuel, Arghiri (1972) 'White Settler Colonialism and the Myth of Investment Imperialism'. *New Left Review,* 73, 35–57.

Fausto, B. (1999) *A Concise History of Brazil.* Cambridge: Cambridge University Press.

Fox, E. W. (1971) *History in Geographic Perspective: The Other France.* New York: Norton.

Furnivall, J. S. (1948) *Colonial Policy and Practice: A Comparative Study of Burma and Netherlands India.* Cambridge: Cambridge University Press.

Gates, P. W. (1968) *The Illinois Central Railroad and its Colonization Work.* New York: Johnson Reprint Corp.

(1989) *The Farmer's Age: Agriculture, 1815–1860,* New York: M. E. Sharpe.

Gottschang, T. R. (1982) *Migration from North China to Manchuria: An Economic History, 1891–1942.* Ann Arbor: University of Michigan Press.

(1987) 'Economic Change, Disasters, and Migration: The Historical Case of Manchuria'. *Economic Development and Cultural Change*, 35(3), 461–90.

Gunderson, G. (1974) 'The Origin of the American Civil War'. *The Journal of Economic History*, 34(4), 915–50.

Hammond, B. (1934) 'Long and Short Term Credit in Early American Banking'. *The Quarterly Journal of Economics*, 49(1), 79.

(1936) 'Free Banks and Corporations: The New York Free Banking Act of 1838'. *The Journal of Political Economy*, 44(2), 184–209.

(1948) 'Banking in the Early West: Monopoly, Prohibition, and Laissez Faire'. *The Journal of Economic History*, 8(1), 1–25.

Hatter, Lawrence (2011) 'Channeling the Spirit of Enterprise: Commercial Interests and State Formation in the Early American West, 1763–1825'. PhD Dissertation, University of Virginia.

Kung, James Kai-sing, and Nan Li (2011) 'Commercialization as Exogenous Shocks: The Effect of the Soybean Trade and Migration in Manchurian Villages, 1895–1934'. *Explorations in Economic History*, 48(4), 568–89.

Lieberman, V. (1993) 'Local Integration and Eurasian Analogies: Structuring Southeast Asian History, c. 1350–c. 1830'. *Modern Asian Studies*, 27(3), 475–572.

(2008) 'The Qing Dynasty and Its Neighbors'. *Social Science History*, 32 (2), 281–304.

Lieven, Dominic (2004) 'Empire on Europe's Periphery'. In Alekseĭ I. Miller and Alfred J. Rieber (eds.) *Imperial Rule*, Vol. I. Budapest: Central European University Press, 133–50.

McKeown, Adam (2004) 'Global Migration 1846–1940'. *Journal of World History*, 15(2), 155–89.

McMichael, P. (1984) *Settlers and the Agrarian Question: Capitalism in Colonial Australia*. Cambridge: Cambridge University Press.

Mann, Michael (1986) *The Sources of Social Power, Vol. I: A History of Power from the Beginning to 1760 AD*. Cambridge: Cambridge University Press.

Moch, L. P. (2007) 'Connecting Migration and World History: Demographic Patterns, Family Systems, and Gender'. *International Review of Social History*, 52(1), 97.

Northrup, David (1995) *Indentured Labor in the Age of Imperialism, 1834–1922*. New York: Cambridge University Press.

Park, Hyun Ok (2000) 'Korean Manchuria: The Racial Politics of Territorial Osmosis'. *The South Atlantic Quarterly*, 99(1), 193–215.

Pearson, M. N. (1991) 'Merchants and States'. In James D. Tracy (ed.) *The Political Economy of Merchant Empires*. Cambridge: Cambridge University Press, 41–116.

Perdue, P. C. (1987) *Exhausting the Earth: State and Peasant in Hunan, 1500–1850*. Cambridge, MA: Harvard University Asia Center.

van der Pijl, Kees (2007) *Nomads, Empires, States*. London: Pluto Press.

Reid, Anthony (1992) 'Economic and Social Change, c. 1400–1800'. In Nicholas Tarling (ed.) *The Cambridge History of Southeast Asia*, Vol. I, Part 2. Cambridge: Cambridge University Press, 116–63.

——— (2004) 'Chinese Trade and Southeast Asian Economic Expansion in the Later Eighteenth and Early Nineteenth Centuries: An Overview'. In Nola Cooke and Tana Li (eds.) *Water Frontier: Commerce and the Chinese in the Lower Mekong Region, 1750–1880*. Lanham: Rowman & Littlefield, 21–34.

Rudner, D. W. (1994) *Caste and Capitalism in Colonial India: The Nattukottai Chettiars*. Berkeley: University of California Press.

Schwartz, H. (2010) *States vs. Markets*. Basingstoke: Palgrave.

——— (2012) 'Anglo-America as Global Suburbia: The Political Economy of Land and Endogenous Multiculturalism'. In P. J. Katzenstein (ed.) *Anglo-America and Its Discontents: Civilizational Identities beyond West and East*. London: Routledge, 56–78.

Simmel, Georg (1971) *Essays on Individuality and Social Forms*, ed. Donald Levine. Chicago: University of Chicago Press.

Sylla, Richard (1972) 'American Banking and Growth in the Nineteenth Century: A Partial View of the Terrain'. *Explorations in Economic History*, 9, 197–227.

Taylor, A. (2002) *American Colonies*. New York: Penguin.

——— (2010) *The Civil War of 1812: American Citizens, British Subjects, Irish Rebels, and Indian Allies*. New York: Vintage Books.

De Tocqueville, Alexis (1945)[1831] *Democracy in America*. New York: Vintage.

Trocki, Carl A. (2004) 'The Internationalisation of Chinese Revenue Farming Networks'. In Nola Cooke and Tana Li (eds.) *Water Frontier: Commerce and the Chinese in the Lower Mekong Region, 1750–1880*. Lanham: Rowman & Littlefield, 159–74.

Weaver, J. C. (2003) *The Great Land Rush and the Making of the Modern World, 1650–1900*. Montreal: McGill-Queen's University Press.

Zolberg, A. R. (2008) *A Nation by Design: Immigration Policy in the Fashioning of America*. Cambridge, MA: Harvard University Press.

10 The assemblage of American imperium

Hybrid power, world war and world government(ality) in the twenty-first century

RONNIE D. LIPSCHUTZ

[T]he nature of war consisteth not in actual fighting, but in the known disposition thereto during all the time there is no assurance to the contrary.

Thomas Hobbes, Leviathan, *ch. 13*

Laissez-faire was planned; planning was not.

Polanyi 2001, 147

Introduction

What might be the legacies of American imperium,[1] now said to be in serious decline and, if some pundits are to be believed, soon to be flung into the dustbin of history? How will these legacies mark the world(s) to come and how long might they last? Will they resemble those left behind by previous empires, in the form of infrastructures, practices, borders, legal systems and class systems? Or will their mark come through the Anglo-American capitalism that has permeated every nook and cranny of twenty-first century life? As Sandra Halperin and Ronen Palan have suggested in their introduction to this volume, empires in the dustbin do not simply go away, even when their capitals and armies vanish, leaving behind only ruins and recollections. In their dimly-remembered glory, empires are endlessly recreated in all sorts of places and forms, if only in the hope that some of that glory might rub off on their successors.

---

[1] I use the term 'imperium' here and elsewhere (Lipschutz, 2009) to distinguish between imperial rule and empire by military conquest.

In this chapter, I argue that the primary legacy of American empire to those future world(s) is an 'assemblage of imperium'. An 'assemblage' is an arrangement constituted by a 'multiplicity of heterogeneous objects, whose unity comes solely from the fact that these items function together, that they "work" together as a functional entity' (Haggerty and Ericson 2000: 608, citing Patton 1994: 158).[2] In this instance, the assemblage of imperium consists of a decentralized system of worldwide power, articulated through the electronic capillaries of the global capitalist political economy and underpinned by similar vessels supporting the 'technical apparatuses of security' that sustain a condition of permanent and omnipresent warfare (see, e.g. Roth 2013; DOJ 2012). Together, political economy and security (re)mix public and private authority and action in a new, hybridized framework of governmentality (Foucault 1980) that may be described in ideological terms as 'marketism'. The empires of the past left their marks on monetary systems, languages, administration and geopolitical epistemes, but none of these seem to have been as expansive, intensive and interventionist as what will be left behind by imperium. Recognizing that legacies of Greece and Rome continue to operate even today, more than 1,500 years after the collapse of the Western Empire, we might expect at least some features of the American imperium to linger for some time as well.

How are these legacies manifested? First, the contemporary global political economy, which ties together almost all of the national economies of the world to varying degrees through a web of institutions, rules, practices and electrons, has been shaped by a range of US-directed and inspired institutional strategies and instrumental tactics quite distinct from those envisioned in the original Bretton Woods agreements of 1945. Second, the deployment of the US military across the world has not only shaped the militaries and military practices almost everywhere but also played a central role in supporting the global political economy through a constant state of war. This has been complemented, in more recent decades, by a system of surveillant security whose targets of observation are, ultimately, the world's people. Third, the various and many regulatory institutions created through the offices of the United States since 1945 (e.g. domestic agencies with global reach and so-called international regimes) reflect,

---

[2] The term comes from Deleuze and Guattari (1987).

to a significant degree, American techniques, ideologies, materiality and practices projected into the world. Finally, the global electronic networks growing out of telecommunications systems based largely in the USA serve not only to rapidly move money and information around the world, they also operate as potent technologies of surveillance, discipline and punishment. Taken together, this assemblage of imperium has reshaped global social life in ways that will continue to have significant impacts and implications for many decades to come.

This chapter proceeds in four steps. I begin with a short discussion of the method of genealogy and the concepts of marketism and hybrid power. I then offer a crude history of how implementation of the Bretton Woods system has led to a global political economy that is quite distinct from what was anticipated 'at the creation'.[3] In the third part of the chapter, I take up the concept of 'perpetual' warfare, its transformation from a multinational to an inter-governmental system under the aegis of the USA and its increasingly deep penetration into everyday social being. Finally, I examine the ways in which these elements have led to the assemblage of imperium, its forms of global rule and the legacies of empire that it will mark upon the world of the future.

Matters of method and mechanism

Genealogy as method

To fully unearth the archaeology of the assemblage of imperium, we turn to Michel Foucault's method of genealogy, whose central principle is that:

The forces operating in history do not obey destiny or regulative mechanisms, but the destiny of the battle. They do not manifest the successive forms of a primordial intention and their attention is not that of a conclusion, for they always appear through the singular randomness of events ... The world such as we are acquainted with it is not this ultimately simple configuration where events are reduced to accentuate their essential traits, their final meaning, or their initial and final value. On the contrary, it is a profusion of entangled events. (2003a: 361)

---

[3] Acheson 1969. Acheson's title for his memoir came from: 'Had I been present at the creation, I would have given some useful hints for the better ordering of the universe' (Alfonso the Wise, King of Castile, León and Galicia, r. 1252–84).

In more comprehensible terms, I take this to mean that the causal relations and effects we attribute to agency, structure, causality and history, human decisions, behaviours, actions and outcomes rarely, if ever, follow each another in an orderly, logical or rational fashion, even though, in hindsight, we see actions and events succeeding one another in that fashion. Long-term strategic plans (e.g. Bretton Woods), as carefully made and laid as they might appear in retrospect, almost always fall victim to short-term contingencies and displacements that result from the strategic intentions and instrumental responses of others with their own long-term plans and visions.[4] Projects are constantly being diverted from the official programme and to get them back 'on track', people (i.e. planners, decision makers, etc.) must constantly formulate and deploy *ad hoc* tactics. These actors hew to broader principles but inevitably change both methods and goals. Agents make deliberate choices thinking to control the behaviour of their subjects who are, in fact, also agents making constrained decisions, and who may or may not act as desired or imagined. New tactical responses require the (re)allocation of real resources, the rearrangement of real material goods and the enactment of real policies with real consequences that are prone to generate further reactions and resistance from the objects of action, leading to even greater deviation from the original, desired trajectory and objective. Ultimately, notwithstanding intentional agential decisions and actions, the results may be quite distinct from what anyone would have imagined or desired.

We can see how this process operates by considering 'histories' of US foreign policies since 1945. Conventional historiography tends to argue that the Cold War began around 1946 and ended in 1989 or thereabouts, constituting what John Lewis Gaddis has called 'the Long Peace' (1987). The interregnum of the 1990s has not been named – except, perhaps, as 'The End of History' – while the decade plus since September 11, 2001 has been subsumed under various terms, with the view that, notwithstanding a growing chorus of warnings about China rising, the threat of terrorism is unlikely to end anytime soon. From a crude (neo)-liberal perspective, the seven post-war decades were characterized by an effective balance of power between two primary competitors followed by the now-declining global dominance of the United

---

[4] 'Victory has a hundred fathers but defeat is an orphan' [La Vittoria trova cento padri, e nessuno vuole riconoscere l'insuccesso] (Ciano 1947, 521).

States. A 'hot' World War Three never broke out; there were only a number of close calls in which deterrence and cooler heads prevailed, plus a rash of peripheral struggles that, from the neo-realist standpoint, were largely irrelevant to the central balance. US leadership and perspicacity fostered Western prosperity and power and, following the crises of the 1970s and a healing dose of high interest rates, market-driven neo-liberalism took hold, illuminating the growth potential of privatization and propelling the world into a new, frictionless economic era. Even with the trials, travails and bubbles of the last decade, those 70 years stand as a relatively peaceful and prosperous run. That story remains largely the consensus narrative.

This admittedly crude and Whiggish view elides one significant constant under American domination: perpetual war. Even as the 'nuclear peace' was lauded as a major accomplishment of US policy, since 1950 world war has been a perpetual feature of global politics, playing a central role in shaping today's world and the assemblage of imperium.[5] War is always a revolutionary and revolutionizing process and, in this respect, during the Long Peace it has functioned as a much more immanent and formative force than is generally recognized.[6] Most framings of US policy and empire rest on the synergies between the institutions and practices of American capitalism as distinct from the worldwide reach of its security strategies. In such framings, US foreign policy is said to be driven by an ongoing search for comparative advantage, on the one hand, and fear of unseen, omnipotent enemies, on the other. This view pays homage to Friedrich List (1983) and his many neo-mercantilist successors (e.g. Gilpin 1981), who argue that a strong economy feeds a strong military even as military deployments safeguard inputs into the economy (Lipschutz 1989) but maintain the separation between politics (or states) and markets. This simplistic model fails to articulate fully the dynamic and necessary relationship between capitalism and security, or the ways in which the two have

---

[5] Apparently, the USA has been in a more-or-less constant 'State of National Emergency' since 1933. The State of National Emergency declared by Harry S. Truman in December 1950 has not been cancelled but has been 'rendered . . . ineffective by returning to dormancy the statutory authorities they [SOEs] had activated, thereby necessitating a new declaration to activate standby statutory emergency authorities' (Relyea 2007: 12).

[6] This might be characterized as a permanent Schmittian 'state of exception', decreed by the sovereign. Such a description elides the political struggle required to sustain a permanent war (govern)mentality.

become, to paraphrase Harry S. Truman, a single, global-scale walnut.[7] These arguments are elaborated in the second and third sections of this chapter.

Hybrid power as mechanism

The particular shape of the *assemblage* of imperium has been strongly inflected by the emergence and consolidation of 'hybrid power', which denotes here a particular mixing of public and private resources and practices that facilitate pursuit of the functions and goals of governing. Today, most public policy and politics are articulated through the global political economy and its expression through markets. Hybrid power has become a means of extending and expanding rules and practices through the various mechanisms, arms and institutions of the global political economy, incorporating not only markets and civil society into its operation but also international regimes, national governments and their like. This is a consequence of regulation through the global political economy and reliance on market mechanisms to achieve ostensibly political goals (Hurt and Lipschutz forthcoming, 2016). In this instance, the result is the fusion of techniques of security (largely public) with the surveillance capabilities of the market (largely private), and related changes in institutions, beliefs and practices. I call this phenomenon 'Marketism': a discourse (beliefs, practices, material outcomes) through which all can be addressed and solved through the market.[8]

Hybrid power is not being exercised when private entities act as agents in the name of, or on behalf of, states and governments (as, for example, privateers or royal corporations of yore). Throughout the long and multifarious history of the modern state, there have been many instances of corporate and private agents taking on notionally regulatory and governmental roles at the behest of sovereign states and other territorialized entities. Private industries have frequently produced military and other products under contracts to states and, during

---

[7] While this metaphor is attributed to Truman, it first appeared in Walter LeFeber's work on the Cold War and has become generalized throughout the literature. I have not been able to find any primary attribution to Truman.

[8] For a rather grim and thought-provoking vision of consumption as a form of consumer fascism, see Ballard 2006.

times of war, have often been nationalized. But this is simply 'contracting out'. The 'private sector' has often exercised undue influence over, or even control of states and governments, in pursuit of specific sectoral interests. This more closely resembles Marx's notion of the state as the committee serving the interests of the bourgeoisie. However we understand and describe these activities, and whosoever interests they have served, they have been undertaken in the name of state (i.e. public) power.

Hybrid power differs from these because it is executed through markets in the name of global security and well-being. It is a form of governing (along the lines of regulation theory) that comprises something vaguely resembling a 'world leviathan', rather than, as is often claimed, the 'privatization of public authority'. More to the point, economy has become, in Foucault's words, 'the principle form of knowledge' even as 'apparatuses of security' have become the 'essential technical means' of government (2003b: 244). Indeed, economy and security have become co-constitutive: knowledge of the economy is an essential technical means through which the apparatuses of security operate (and vice versa). The result is the assemblage of imperium, which operates not only on categories of populations but also on individuals operating in their own spheres of 'consumer sovereignty' (Schwarzkopf 2011).

First legacy: present at the creation

I now turn to a rough and incomplete genealogy of the global political economy and its development into today's assemblage of imperium. The shaping of economic policy and planning began in 1945 with Bretton Woods and is manifest (so far) in what some wags have recently dubbed 'A G-Zero World' (Bremmer and Roubini, 2011).[9] Notwithstanding the heroic version of Bretton Woods told to all American political science undergraduates, the programme never worked as originally imagined or designed (Block 1977). The initial arrangements did not even see the end of 1946 before Britain required a loan to keep sterling afloat, and only repeated and timely interventions ('planning', as Karl Polanyi put it) by the United States allowed the

---

[9] John G. Ruggie (1983, 1991, 2008) has called this 'embedded liberalism', reflecting the central role of planning in creating the Bretton Woods institutions.

Bretton Woods institutions to function in ways that resembled planners' original intentions. Neither the Truman Doctrine nor the Marshall Plan were part of a foreign policy strategy even though dressed up in security clothes; rather, they were tactics meant to address the international liquidity shortage that seemed to threaten a return to Great Depression conditions.

Whether or not Congress was scared of communism, military expenditures and transfers became a dominant means of financing the West's international economy. NSC-68, the National Security Council report written by Paul Nitze and his colleagues, went so far as to urge the Truman Administration to ramp up defence spending for this purpose, in quantities that even the Marshall Plan was unable to fully match (NSC 1950). With the outbreak of the Korean War, the US defence expenditures grew almost overnight from $12 billion to $50 billion, with most of that going to allied rearmament rather than the war in Asia. Deployment of US troops and weapons abroad facilitated international trade and recycling of dollars.

During the decades that followed, the USA was able to take advantage of the dollar's status as an international reserve currency to finance war and security through deficit spending and rising debt, via Mutual Security Aid in the 1950s, the Vietnam War in the 1960s, the petrodollar economy of the 1970s, Reagan's budget deficits during the 1980s and US trade deficits throughout the 1990s (even though the Clinton Administration ran budget surpluses through much of the 1990s).[10] The Bush tax cuts of 2002 deprived the US government of some $2 trillion in revenues over the following decade, with massive and ever-growing war-related spending and deficits financed through domestic and international borrowing (see, e.g. Lipschutz 2009; Lewis 2009, 2011). This level of defence expenditures has not declined during the Obama Administration. Not all of the capital collected, foregone, borrowed and spent during the post-war era went abroad, of course, but it seems safe to say that the export of dollars has played an outsize role in global economic growth – but almost certainly not in a way anticipated in 1945.

---

[10] If anything, the impacts of budget reductions and base closures on the presidential election of 1992 alerted everyone to the political reality that the important percentages were not how much of GDP was allocated to the military but rather, in which electorally important states the funds were being spent.

Can we estimate how important US military spending has been in the global political economy over the past six decades? Between 1947 and 1951, something like $25 billion ($250 billion in 2011$) was exported to its allies by the United States. Roughly speaking, over the period from 1951–59, something like $650 billion (2011$) in assistance flowed out to US allies (relative to a total allied GDP over the same period of $16–18 trillion in 2011$), although a significant fraction was returned in the form of military purchases by allies. From 1960 to 1970, almost $5 trillion (2011$) was injected by the USA into the national and global economy for defence alone (NATO 1980, 2001, 2011). It does not seem entirely amiss to suggest that these sums played a critical role in the Western *Wirtschaftwunder* during the golden age of capitalism. Indeed, average annual US defence expenditures have not fallen below $400 billion (2005$) in real terms since the early 1950s (NATO 1980, 2001, 2011), for a total of more than $25 trillion spent over that period. While this has amounted to only about 20 per cent of total US budget outlays in a typical year and represents a relatively small fraction of national GDP (around 3–4 per cent), such numbers do not take account of the full impact of security-related spending on either sectors or the broader economy. They also exclude intelligence budgets and, more recently, homeland security and off-budget wars, which are considerable. Nor do they include multiplier effects (on which there is disagreement; see, e.g. Hosek *et al.* 2011; Pollin and Garrett-Peltier 2011; Barro and Redlick 2009).

Moreover, a focus on the direct and measurable impact of war and security expenditures on the global political economy elides the seminal role played by military research and development in launching major civilian sectors, such as computing, electronics, biology, agriculture and manufacturing (Ruttan 2006). Whether the eventual civilianization of these sectors should be attributed to their military origins is open to debate, and whether these sectors would have emerged and expanded as they did in the absence of military stimulus, is a counterfactual difficult to work out (Ruttan 2006: 110). There was, however, a 'really-existing' experiment conducted between 1945 and 1991: in the old Soviet Bloc, military production was firewalled from the civilian sector, and military technologies were rarely, if ever, spun-off into the civilian economy. As a result, the Bloc's member states remained considerably poorer than their Western European counterparts (O'Hearn 1980; Łoś 1987).

In its initial phase, financing of the US military acted as a source of Keynesian military stimulus to the free world. As the American fiscal position moved from global creditor to debtor, financing the US military increasingly relied on the willingness of other countries to put their dollar surpluses into US Treasury Bonds and other American investments. Again, even though military expenditures represented a small fraction of the aggregate GDP and national budgets of NATO countries, they undoubtedly played an important stimulus role after 2001. Between 2001 and 2007, the $3–4 trillion spent by the USA and its allies on defence, intelligence, homeland security and the three ongoing wars was almost certainly a critical if unintentional prop to the wan economic growth during that period.[11] Now that US defence cuts are looming – although few think they will amount to much in the long-run – this particular source of fiscal stimulus could disappear.

The argument that military spending is 'good for the economy' is something of a hoary cliché, with its origins in the experience of World War II, when UK, Allied and US military expenditures pulled the country out of the Great Depression (Ruttan 2006; Harrison 2011). There is, as well, a longstanding tradition that links capitalist growth to perpetual war, whether in the form of imperialism (Hobson 1902) or the 'permanent war economy' (Melman 1985). Whether this relationship continues to obtain remains a matter of some dispute; relative to national and global GDPs, the magnitude of US federal security spending – currently in the order of one trillion dollars if all security-related expenditures are taken into account – is too small to have much of an effect on growth, according to most economists (see, e.g. Aizenman and Glick 2003; Auerbach and Gorodnichenko 2010; Harrison 2011; CBO 2002). But such calculations tend to elide broader 'spin-off' effects from military-related research, development and deployment and the regional and sectoral impacts in places such as California.

There is another way to think of such security spending: not as the largest item in the US budget covered by taxpayers but, rather, as a globalized levy on US debtors, who have little choice but to park their excess foreign exchange in US Treasury bonds. In essence, global security and economic stability have become hybridized public goods

---

[11] The linkage between the housing bubble and financing of the three wars is discussed in Lipschutz 2009.

financed substantially by American borrowing; indeed, even so-called rising powers are financing American military and security policies and practices. Because no one expects the principal on these bonds to ever be redeemed, and no one dares to sell off their holdings for fear of creating a global currency panic, the Treasury securities ought to be regarded as taxes on debtors rather than investments by them. This particular feature of government also acts, we might say, as a constraint of sorts on military adventurism in some parts of the world, and suggests a little-noted legacy of the assemblage of imperium.[12]

My point here is that massive infusions of US military dollars into the global economy since the 1950s have had unintended impacts on the structure of and relationships among the national economies comprising the 'Free World' and, more recently, much of the rest of the world as a whole. Not only did those monies cement Western alliances, they also fostered shared industrial and intellectual interests and commitments to continual prosperity and security, far beyond their absolute magnitude. As growth rates in the 'material' economy began to decline, the search for high returns to capital in the face of both low inflation and interest rates led banks, stock markets, hedge and pension funds, sovereign wealth funds and other pools of capital into constructing a complex web of opaque monetary relationships and flows across national borders, with securitization of all kinds of mutually held, supposedly low-risk investments. When these bubbles burst, new forms, flows and relationships only made the web ever more tangled, such that, short of an economic collapse that would make the Great Depression look like child's play, they can never be unwound. This, then, is the first legacy of American empire: a global financial system in which a broad-range of cross-cutting economic commitments expose some societies to the foibles, activities and appetites of others, with little or no recourse except to bail out those 'too big to fail'. The architects of Bretton Woods envisioned a world of discrete nation states managing their own economic affairs and regulating trade, interest rates and capital flows in order to control and moderate domestic business cycles, deal with monetary imbalances and sustain high levels of employment; there was no evident intention among those planners

[12] In place of Thomas Friedman's 'hamburger theory of capitalist peace' (1996), does it make sense to point out that countries to which the United States is in hock appear to be relatively stable, even if not violence-free?

to create the global political economy in which we live today, and it almost certainly would horrify them were they to see it in action.

I do not want to claim that this first element of the assemblage of imperium was in any way determined or inevitable, or that other types of relations and interventions might not have resulted in substantially different arrangements. Empire, as many have noted, is a costly proposition, and its returns over time do not always result in net benefits. Genealogy warns us to pay attention to the political and social struggles that lie beneath broad historical trajectories and apparently coherent policies. The successes of tactical interventions obscure the internal political processes that make them possible. But, the language and technologies of security play a role in facilitating policies and practices with economic implications and consequences, rendering opaque what 'really happens' in terms of shaping systems and structures in the longer term.

Second legacy: war is peace!

Perpetual war as an essential consequence of 'technologies of security' began with the outbreak of the Korean War, albeit as an expedient tactic rather than application of the strategy laid out in NSC-68 (Gaddis 2005). The ever-present threat of 'hot' war, sustained by a myriad of large and small crises, provided the institutional organization within which a near-permanent state of emergency could be sustained (Relyea 2007). Not only did fear of nuclear war between the USA and the USSR facilitate constant (re)placement and (re)armament, it also permitted both superpowers to consolidate their positions of imperium vis-à-vis erstwhile allies. As suggested above, this took the form of growing integration within the respective economic systems of East and West, the free world and the Soviet Bloc and, in the West, the fusion of security and economy.

But the end of the Cold War left behind a material substructure not so easily dismantled or converted to other purposes. The dissolution of the Warsaw Pact failed to vaporize the sizable military forces of the ex-Soviet Bloc states or shut down their metal-bashing industries and closed cities so dependent on weapons production. In the West, attempts to downsize the military met with some initial success but arguably with electoral consequences that neither political party has since wished to repeat on any scale. At any rate, during the 1990s, and notwithstanding periodic adventures such as Somalia, Kuwait and Kosovo, the US military-strategy-production complex struggled to define new threats and missions that could rationalize massive forces and rising expenditures (Lipschutz 1999). Long before 9/11, the founders of the Project for the New American Century, among others, called for an invasion of Iraq in order to erase doubts about American supremacy and the willingness to ramp up military spending. From the perspective of these neo-conservative internationalists, the attacks on New York and Washington were a godsend. Not only did they render material a globally pervasive security problem whose previous existence had been doubted, they also offered an opportunity to revive the state of perpetual war, especially in the Global War on Terror. Elsewhere, I have argued that terrorism represents more than just aggrieved, anti-Western salafist jihadis striking out at American Empire; it is a manifestation of a much deeper structural problem of government that cannot be addressed by military force alone (Lipschutz 2008). This problem arises from the unregulated capacity of the 'sovereign consumer' to wreak havoc in and on the global political economy. That is, the disintegration of prior forms of social discipline and constraint, under the pressures of the 'high individualism' so essential to the neo-liberal project, has led to a world of unruly bodies whose behaviours are increasingly difficult to anticipate, let alone govern.

During the Cold War, nationalism and the national welfare-security state as well as the peer pressures endemic in conservative societies operated to rein in the anarchic tendencies of markets and behaviours in civil society. Where threats might arise from unregulated pursuit of self-interest, there existed domestic legal and institutional mechanisms for preventing and penalizing economic activities that might impinge on national security and order (a theme evident in the film *Invasion of the Body Snatchers*). By the end of the Cold War, however, such forms of social discipline had been weakened by the rampant individualism that regarded unlimited accumulation and consumption as social goods. A short decade later, the premium put on 'freedom in the economy' for capital, technology and even labour pointed increasingly towards a market-based anarchy, undisciplined by the constraints of security and only weakly governed by 'laws, institutions, social mores, customs and hegemonies that collectively create the institutional conditions for long-run profit-making' (Peet, Robbins and Watts 2011:

19). More to the point, as Karl Polanyi (2001) argued, markets cannot self-regulate and agents in the market, given the opportunity, can endanger both economy and society. Global securitization (in both senses) was deployed as a tactic to regulate market behaviour even as a pervasive fear of terrorism became the rationale for expanding and enmeshing the world in the growing 'steel web' of security. Whatever it is called, we now exist in a constant and pervasive state of globalized war, one that is used to justify an expansive system of surveillance and containment of individuals and which extends the reach of the assemblage of imperium into the everyday lives of billions.

This war does not resemble our experience or understandings of world war, or even civil or social warfare. It is does not involve evidently hostile forces arrayed against each other, across battlefronts around the world, seeking to kill and destroy as many of the enemy as possible.[13] Rather, it is a war in which the world's people are segmented into friends and foes, and in which the order of battle has come to rely heavily on market-based surveillance and securitization on top of the global reach of military and police forces (Lipschutz 2008). That the market comes to play a central role in securitization should come as no surprise; after all, the market has played a central role in fostering 'terrorism' through metastasis of means of destruction, diffusion of the technologies of war-making (e.g. in the form of AK-47s and Toyota trucks) and the spread of 'dual-use' knowledge and practices (e.g. apps and coding). Cars, trucks and aircraft are no longer simply means of transport; they are now also delivery systems for high explosives and social disruption. Communication technologies serve not only to foster commerce and 'friending'; they also allow for cyber-hacking, disruptive mobilizations and even the planning of organized violence. Activities as banal and mundane as cooking, cleaning and farming apparently lend themselves to the possibilities of threatening behaviour, through the mixing together of household chemicals, agricultural fertilizers and nuts and bolts.

---

[13] Witness the recent flurry of articles and pronouncements in *The New York Times* about cyberwarfare, apparently triggered by American cyberattacks on Iran (Sanger 2012a, 2012b; Kramer and Perlroth 2012; Bharara 2012), as well as debates over the status of civilian casualties as a result of US drone attacks. The outing of the NSA's myriad activities only reinforces the condition of perpetual war.

In the absence of hot war and civil mobilization, fear and compulsion are much more powerful mobilizers than peace or opportunity (Malešvić 2010). Fear of the mundane and banal can be heightened and communicated constantly, especially through the myriad communication channels and transaction practices of modern electronic society. Workplaces, whether academic, non-governmental or charitable must be certified as 'terrorism free', which in the USA now extends even to provision of legal advice to individuals and charities that might have remote associations with groups certified as 'terrorists'. Michael Bloomberg, as the Mayor of New York City, could claim 'I have my own army in the NYPD, which is the seventh biggest army in the world. I have my own State Department, much to Foggy Bottom's annoyance' (Walker 2011), while the US Department of Homeland Security has a 'Social Networking/Media Capability' branch that hires contractors to monitor 'public reaction to major governmental proposals with homeland security implications' (Savage 2012).

Algorithms developed in the commercial sector are almost certainly available to intelligence agencies and, while the data collected from instore and online commerce may be compiled in proprietary databases (Duhigg 2011), these are probably available to intelligence agencies, such as the NSA. It is highly likely, moreover, that much of the research into the refining of data-mining techniques has been funded by security agencies, such as DARPA and the DIA. Ultimately, we are enjoined to accept near-constant surveillance as the price of safety and we are self-disciplined into ensuring that our economic behaviours and practices comport with the security requirements of global war.[14] A steel web of surveillance and discipline contains and makes us 'secure' even as it also enchains each of us (Landau 2010). We become the obedient subjects of a regulatory system that must be obeyed, lest we be identified, isolated, interrogated and imprisoned as potential combatants in a perpetual war. This is the second legacy of the American assemblage of imperium.

Third legacy: government through hybrid power

Government(ality) is not like Topsy; it does not simply 'happen' but is a result of many small decisions and actions, as suggested by the earlier

---

[14] 'Paranoia is the logical endpoint of obsession with security. There is a cruel irony in that meaning of secure which is "unable to escape"' (Buzan 1990: 37).

discussion of genealogy.[15] To chart the genealogy of hybridized government would be a near-impossible undertaking, if only because its
primary channel of articulation, through securitization of economy and
economization of security, is only beginning to be widely acknowledged. What is required to see this hybridization is reconciliation of the
apparently 'liberal' aspects of a global market economy and the 'disciplinary' features of the global security network or, as the matter is
sometimes framed, the tensions between liberty and security (Kiersey
2008). Hybridized government is especially puzzling in the notional
face of neo-liberalism, privatization and campaigns to 'shrink the state'
and liberate the individual from its shackles. Like skimmed milk masquerading as cream however, privatization has been much less widespread or effective than is often assumed. It has not worked well where
instituted nor resulted in the spin-off of public goods and services into
the market sector and it does not necessarily lead to more efficient
delivery of services (Hibou 2004; Hurt and Lipschutz forthcoming,
2016). Nonetheless, these policies have had transformative effects in
shifting modes of international government from diplomacy to economy. To be sure, economic considerations have long been important to
interstate relations but, as Paul Kennedy (1976) pointed out during his
pre-pundit academic career as a British naval historian, in an article
entitled 'The Tradition of Appeasement in British Foreign Policy 1865–
1939', economy was not always the primary driver of international
relations. While the historical practices of diplomacy were in decline
long before the 1970s, their basis was nonetheless political, rooted in the
mutual recognition of and respect for the dignity and desires of states
(mostly Great Powers). The unique legacy of the American assemblage of
imperium has been to transform the dances of diplomats into the
exchanges of economists, to turn summits into salesrooms. Bargaining
has replaced conferences and Edgeworth boxes have replaced boundary
commissions. I call this 'marketism', to connote both the ideology and
practices of seeking policy solutions through market economy.

How might we explain the rise of marketism (aka, hybrid government)? As societies become more complex, they also require greater
management and managers with appropriate competencies. As societies

---

[15] Topsy was, of course, the young slave girl in Harriet Beecher Stowe's novel
Uncle Tom's Cabin, who, when asked if she knew who made her, replied
'I s'pect I grow'd. Don't think nobody never made me.'

face complicated problems, they rely more and more on experts and specialists to tell them what to do and how to do it; and as societies engage in growing numbers of cross-border transactions, they more and more need agents with the skills and knowledge appropriate to navigating other bureaucracies, languages and cultures (Burnham 1941). This sounds much like technocracy, but whereas technocracy rests on specialized organizational and bureaucratic skills, marketism relies on notionally apolitical and naturalized logics of market exchange. Consequently, government through markets has come to be utilized for political actions and ends, both domestic and international (Lipschutz with Rowe 2005). Rather than engagement in political struggle over ethical values and goals, a rationalistic, utilitarian logic comes to define normative ends and naturalized means.

Marketism, as a form of global rule, has also been the mechanism whereby elements of civil society have been enrolled in the exercise of hybrid power, thereby extending government into the private sector. Private and civil society actors contracted by various agents and agencies to deliver 'public goods' also find themselves subject to considerable government oversight and come to be treated as extensions of state authority rather than independent operators. Thus, private security contractors in Iraq have discovered that their supposed freedom in battle zones does not mean they are free to do whatever they wish; private water providers in Bolivia have found that local governments are not about to give them a free hand in setting rates; non-governmental organizations delivering medical, education, development and other services to rural and urban people find themselves enmeshed by state and international strings and interference. Delivering services privately does not mean that the services are private goods and of no interest to the state (Leander 2006).

The United States has, not surprisingly, played a central role in the emergence and spread of hybrid government. In the past, holding an empire together required a great deal of coercion and the ability to deploy military force where needed. Most empires relied on the permanent garrisoning of troops, often composed of local draftees, in colonial territories or along the imperial marches. As Tarak Barkawi (this volume) reminds us, the USA has more than 700 military bases around the world, divided into zones of military 'command', and has trained, funded and armed friends and allies around the world ('rule'). The framing and shaping of the global political economy ('rules') has been equally important in managing and governmentalizing the assemblage of imperium (Onuf 1989). Indeed, even the Pentagon has come to play a significant role in hybridized global government, as much through its economic heft as its military prowess, drawing in the military forces of many countries. This has been supplemented by intelligence coopera-tion among national agencies as well as the establishment of FBI offices in numerous capital cities around the world. While we cannot predict with any certainty how long this assemblage of security and economy will be sustained, it will almost certainly exist as a legacy of imperium for many decades to come.

Conclusion, but not an ending

In this chapter, I have argued that the American assemblage of imper-ium has bequeathed to the world three enduring legacies: a global economy in which national ones are deeply enmeshed, a perpetual state of war married to markets and global government through hybrid power. This assemblage is a result of the expansion and diffusion throughout the world of American modes of management, forms and practices in markets and technologies of surveillance. Through modes of economy and means of security, operationalized and articulated in order to regulate and stabilize tendencies towards disorder and disrup-tion in the global political economy, the beliefs, policies and practices of what I have called 'marketism' are deeply imprinted on and in world affairs. Hybrid government bears more than a passing resem-blance to world government, although it lacks the notional concen-trations of political authority that would characterize such global rule. Nevertheless, by marshalling the levers and channels of global capitalism, the pursuit of political objectives is carried on with more or less coherence, albeit not always or often with the desired outcome. How long might the legacies of this assemblage of imperium continue to influence the international-cum-world relations of the future? In Zhou Enlai's apocryphal but famous paraphrasing of the effects of the French Revolution (whether 1789 or 1968), it is too soon to tell.

References

Acheson, Dean (1969) *Present at the Creation: My Years in the State Department*. New York: Norton.

Aizenman, Joshua and Reuven Glick (2003) 'Military Expenditure, Threats and Growth'. NBER Working Paper 9618, April. Available at: www. nber.org/papers/w9618

Auerbach, Alan J. and Yuriy Gorodnichenko (2010) 'Measuring the Output Responses to Fiscal Policy'. NBER Working Paper 16311, August. Available at: www.nber.org/papers/w16311

Ballard, J. G. (2006) *Kingdom Come*. London: Fourth Estate.

Barro, Robert J. and Charles J. Redlick (2009) 'Macroeconomic Effects from Government Purchases and Taxes'. NBER Working Paper 15369, September. Available at: www.nber.org/papers/w15369

Bharara, Preet (2012) 'Asleep at the Laptop'. *The New York Times*, 3 June. Available at: www.nytimes.com/2012/06/04/opinion/preventing-a-cyb ercrime-wave.html

Block, Fred L. (1977) *The Origins of International Economic Disorder*. Berkeley: University of California Press.

Bremmer, Ian and Nouriel Roubini (2011) 'A G-Zero World'. *Foreign Affairs*, March/April, 2–7.

Burnham, James (1941) *The Managerial Revolution*. New York: John Day.

Buzan, Barry (1990) *People, States & Fear*. Boulder: Lynne Rienner.

CBO (Congressional Budget Office) (1992) *The Economic Effects of Reduced Defense Spending*. Washington, DC: Government Printing Office.

Ciano, Galeazzo (1947) *The Ciano Diaries*, ed. Hugh Gibson. Garden City: Garden City Publishing.

Deleuze, Gilles and Felix Guattari (1987) *A Thousand Plateaus*. Minneapolis: University of Minnesota Press.

DOJ (US Department of Justice) (2012). 'White Paper: Lawfulness of a Lethal Operation Directed against a US Citizen Who is a Senior Operational Leader of Al-Qa'ida or an Associated Force'. Washington, DC. Available at: http://msnbcmedia.msn.com/i/msnbc/se ctions/news/020413_DOJ_White_Paper.pdf

Duhigg, Charles (2012) *The Power of Habit*. New York: Random House.

Foucault, Michel (1980) 'The Confession of the Flesh'. In Colin Gordon (ed.) *Power/Knowledge: Selected Interviews and Other Writings 1972–1977*. New York: Pantheon, 194–228.

    (2003a) 'Nietzsche, Genealogy, History'. In Paul Rabinow and Nikolas Rose (eds.) *The Essential Foucault*. New York: The New Press, 351–69.

    (2003b) 'Governmentality'. In Paul Rabinow and Nikolas Rose (eds.) *The Essential Foucault*. New York: The New Press, 229–45.

Friedman, Thomas L. (1996) 'Foreign Affairs Big Mac I'. *New York Times*, 8 December. Available at: www.nytimes.com/1996/12/08/opinion/ foreign-affairs-big-mac-i.html

Gaddis, John Lewis (2005) *Strategies of Containment: A Critical Appraisal of American National Security Policy during the Cold War*, rev. and expanded edn. New York: Oxford University Press.

(1987) *The Long Peace: Inquiries into the History of the Cold War*. New York: Oxford University Press.

Gilpin, Robert (1981) *War and Change in World Politics*. Cambridge: Cambridge University Press.

Haggerty, K. D. and Ericson, R. V. (2000) 'The Surveillant Assemblage'. *British Journal of Sociology*, 51(4), 605–22.

Harrison, Mark (2011) 'Capitalism at War'. Prepared for 'Ten Lectures about the War', German Historical Institute, Moscow, 17 and 18 June. Available at: www2.warwick.ac.uk/fac/soc/economics/staff/academic/harrison/papers/capitalism_ver_1.pdf

Hibou, Beatrice (2004) *Privatizing the State*. New York: Columbia University Press.

Hobson, John A. (1902) *Imperialism – A Study*. London: Nisbet & Co.

Hosek, James, Aviva Litowitz and Adam C. Resnick (2011) 'How Much Does Military Spending add to Hawaii's Economy'. RAND National Defense Research Institute. Available at: www.dtic.mil/cgi-bin/GetTRDoc?AD=ADA545969&Location=U2&doc=GetTRDoc.pdf

Hurt, Shelley and Ronnie D. Lipschutz (forthcoming, 2016) 'Bringing Politics Back In'. In Shelley Hurt and Ronnie Lipschutz (eds.) *The Public–Private Hybridization of the 21st Century State*.

Kennedy, Paul (1976) 'The Tradition of Appeasement in British Foreign Policy, 1865–1939'. *British Journal of International Studies*, 2, 195–15.

Kiersey, Nicholas J. (2008) 'World State or Global Governmentality? Constitutive Power and Resistance in a Post-Imperial World'. *Global Change, Peace & Security*, 20(3), 357–74.

Kramer, Andrew and Nicole Perlroth (2012) 'Expert Issues a Cyberwar Warning'. *The New York Times*, 3 June. Available at: www.nytimes.com/2012/06/04/technology/cyberweapon-warning-from-kaspersky-a-computer-security-expert.html

Landau, Susan (2010) *Surveillance or Security – The Risks Posed by New Wiretapping Technologies*. Cambridge, MA: MIT Press.

Leander, Anna (2006) *Eroding State Authority? Private Military Companies and the Legitimate Use of Force*. Rome: Rubbettino.

Lewis, Michael (2009) *The Big Short: Inside the Doomsday Machine*. New York: Norton.

(2011) *Boomerang: Travels in the New Third World*. New York: Norton.

Lipschutz, Ronnie D. (1989) *When Nations Clash: Raw Materials, Ideology and Foreign Policy*. New York: Ballinger/Harper & Row.

(1999) 'Terror in the Suites: Narratives of Fear and the Political Economy of Danger'. *Global Society*, 13(4), 411–39.

(2008) 'Imperial Warfare in the Naked City: Sociality as Critical Infrastructure'. *International Political Sociology*, 3(3), 204–18.

(2009) *The Constitution of Imperium*. Boulder: Paradigm.

Lipschutz, Ronnie D. with James K. Rowe (2005) *Globalization, Governmentality and Global Politics: Regulation for the Rest of Us?* London: Routledge.

List, Freidrich (1983) *The National System of Political Economy 1837*. Trans. W. O. Henderson. London: Frank Cass.

Łoś, Maria (1987) 'The Double Economic Structure of Communist Societies'. *Contemporary Crises*, 11, 25–58.

Malešvić, Siniša (2010) *The Sociology of War and Violence*. Cambridge: Cambridge University Press.

Melman, Seymour (1985) *The Permanent War Economy: American Capitalism in Decline*. New York: Simon & Schuster.

NATO (1980) 'Defence Expenditures of NATO Countries, 1949–1980'. NATO Press Service, Brussels, 9 December, M-DPC-2(80)26. Available at: www.nato.int/nato_static/assets/pdf/pdf_1980_12/20100830_1980-026.pdf

(2001) 'Table 1: Defence Expenditures of NATO Countries'. NATO Press Office, Brussels, 5 December, PR/M-DPC-2(2000)107. Available at: www.nato.int/nato_static/assets/pdf/pdf_2000_12/20100614_p00-107e.pdf

(2011) 'Defence Expenditures of NATO Countries (1990–2010)'. NATO Public Diplomacy Division, Brussels, 10 March, PR/CP(2011)027. Available at: www.nato.int/nato_static/assets/pdf/pdf_2011_03/20110 309_PR_CP_2011_027.pdf

NSC (1950) 'United States Objectives and Programs for National Security (NSC 68)'. Washington, DC: Policy Planning Staff, US Department of State, 7 April.

O'Hearn, Dennis (1980) 'The Consumer Second Economy: Size and Effects'. *Soviet Studies*, 32(2), 218–43.

Onuf, Nicholas (1989) *World of Our Making: Rules and Rule in Social Theory and International Relations*. Columbia: University of South Carolina Press.

Patton, P. (1994) 'Metamorpho-Logic: Bodies and Powers in *A Thousand Plateaus*'. *Journal of the British Society for Phenomenology*, 25(2), 157–69.

Peet, Richard, Paul Robbins and Michael J. Watts (2011) 'Global Nature'. In Richard Peet, Paul Robbins and Michael J. Watts (eds.) *Global Political Ecology*. London: Routledge, 1–47.

Polanyi, Karl (2001) *The Great Transformation*, 2nd edn. Boston: Beacon.

Pollin, Robert and Heidi Garrett-Peltier (2011) 'The US Employment Effects of Military and Domestic Spending Priorities: 2011 Update'. Political Economy Research Institute, University of Massachusetts, Amherst. Available at: www.peri.umass.edu/fileadmin/pdf/published_study/PER I_military_spending_2011.pdf

Relyea, Harold C. (2007) 'National Emergency Powers'. Congressional Research Service, updated 30 August. Available at: www.fas.org/sgp/c rs/natsec/98-505.pdf.

Roth, Kenneth (2013) 'What Rules Should Govern US Drone Attacks?' *New York Review of Books*, 60(6), 16, 18.

Ruggie, John G. (1983) 'International Regimes, Transactions, and Change: Embedded Liberalism in the Postwar Economic Order'. In Stephen D. Krasner (ed.) *International Regimes*. Ithaca: Cornell University Press, 195–232.

        (1991) 'Taking Embedded Liberalism Global: The Corporate Connection'. In David Held and Mathias Keonig-Archibugi (eds.) *Taming Globalization: Frontiers of Governance*. Oxford: Policy, 93–129.

        (ed.) (2008) *Embedding Global Markets: An Enduring Challenge*. Aldershot: Ashgate.

Ruttan, Vernon W. (2006) *Is War Necessary for Economic Growth?* Oxford: Oxford University Press.

Sanger, David E. (2012a) 'Obama Order Sped Up Wave of Cyberattacks against Iran'. *The New York Times*, 1 June. Available at: www. nytimes.com/2012/06/01/world/middleeast/obama-ordered-wave-of-cyberattacks-against-iran.html

        (2012b) 'Mutually Assured Cyberdestruction?' *The New York Times*, 2 June. Available at: www.nytimes.com/2012/06/03/sunday-review/ mutually-assured-cyberdestruction.html

Savage, Charlie (2012) 'Federal Security Program Monitored Public Opinion'. *The New York Times*, 13 January. Available at: www.nytimes.com/2012/ 01/14/us/federal-security-program-monitored-public-opinion.html

Schwarzkopf, Stefan (2011) 'The Political Theology of Consumer Sovereignty: Towards an Ontology of Consumer Society'. *Theory, Culture & Society*, 28(3), 106–29.

Walker, Hunter (2011) 'Mayor Bloomberg: "I Have My Own Army"'. *New York Observer*, 11 November. Available at: www.politickerny.com/2011/ 11/30/mayor-bloomberg-i-have-my-own-army-11-30-11/

11 | *Conclusions*

SANDRA HALPERIN AND RONEN PALAN

One of the core assumptions spanning the disciplinary fields of international law, political science and international studies is the idea that a new political order, known as the Westphalian system, emerged in Europe in the seventeenth century and then colonized the entire world. According to this assumption, this new order was based on the principles of state sovereignty and national self-determination. Along its historical journey, it gathered additional attributes, among them perhaps the most important being nationalism, capitalism, industrialization and liberal internationalism. Historians debate, of course, whether the series of treaties signed in Augsburg and Nuremberg in 1648 were of such world-shattering importance, or whether the new order emerged in an evolutionary rather than revolutionary manner over two, three perhaps even four centuries.[1] Less debated, however, is the core conceptual paradigm associated with the Westphalian thesis: a paradigm that treats the world as essentially divided among same-like political communities, each distinct in having their own separate political processes.[2] The problem is that analysis tends to begin by envisioning a world separated into bounded national units.

This conceptual paradigm, which may be described as the 'nationalist paradigm', is what the contributors to this volume have sought to challenge. They advance a common claim: that the nation state model that is, at most, about two hundred years old, emerged in and out of conditions of imperial political organizations that have controlled large swathes of the earth for at least four millennia. Does this historical fact have relevance for the contemporary world? All of the contributors to

[1] See, for instance, De Carvalho *et al.* 2011; and Osiander 2001.
[2] Despite their claims and aspirations, critical perspectives on the origins and nature of our contemporary world have been, by and large, unable to escape from methodological nationalism. They have been unable to escape the snares of national historiography and avoid being subverted or assimilated by it.

this volume argue that it does. The chapters in this volume begin to inventory imperial legacies, both within the same broad time periods, as well as cross-historically. Many of the contributions are based on empirical case studies, both historical and contemporary, and these focus on a number of different issues. To develop what we have begun here will require a much broader, wide-ranging inventory of imperial legacies (e.g. Hapsburg, Ottoman, French, Dutch, Soviet, Japanese, Byzantine, Ottoman and Muhgal) and consideration of their role in shaping contemporary regional and global structures and processes. It will also require a broader range of case studies, not only of empires but of spheres and institutions. The re-surfacing of pre-existing systemic or institutional logics can be discerned in the break-up of Yugoslavia and re-establishment of linkages reminiscent of the Austro-Hungarian Empire, and the Black Sea Pact and the resurfacing of the domain of Ottoman political economy. The Soviet legacy is seen in the trajectories of state building and the international relations of the post-Soviet space. The legacies of empire in South Asia, though much explored, have not considered post-independence elites and the foundation of South Asian economies as legacies of empire.

We would like to stress, however, that the value of the imperial lens used in this book is not only in telling some fascinating stories about the historical origins of some of the most 'modern' aspects of modernity: the armies, finance, multicultural societies, even the United Nations. The imperial perspective lends support to broader challenges and debates that are taking place in the social sciences, by homing in specifically on the notion of methodological nationalism. The volume demonstrates that the modern world is not only based on previous eras of world history; in important ways it is also defined more by institutional continuity than by any radical disjuncture or discontinuity. This is not simply a historical point, but a theoretical proposition. The nationalist paradigm is predicated on the idea either that new political formats emerged in the past two centuries and have now colonized the world, or that more authentic formats emerged around that time that geographically correspond more fully to historical cultural groups. Either way, and although accepting of some degree of differentiation among nation states, such as the differences between advanced and developing, democratic or despotic states, nationalist ideology has tended to stress the underlying similarities among the units. A competitive international environment would encourage a certain degree of differentiation and niche-seeking strategies, no doubt, and the field of comparative studies has encouraged research into differentiation as a theme, but differentiation is limited.

The contributors to this volume argue each in their own way that nationalist debate is not a contained and esoteric discussion about the history of state formation; the nationalist paradigm is an important if somewhat less acknowledged component of the rise of modern 'scientific' political science that has tended to operate on the basis of what Charles Ragin calls, 'homogenising assumptions'. Ragin believes that conventional Political Science is predicated on an epistemological pre-ordering of the world. Social scientists have tended to 'homogenise' their objects of inquiry in order to apply variable-oriented methods of analysis. Such assumptions, he notes, 'structure how social scientists view populations, cases, and causes and thus constrain the dialogue between ideas and evidence in ways that limit discovery' (2000: 5). Of course, there is great value is such methodology. But it comes into constant conflict with historical studies.

Variable-oriented techniques, writes Ola Agevall, 'and their tendency to dissolve cases into single variables, block their ability to test the kind of configurational ideas which are part and parcel of sociological theory' (2005: 9). An historical approach is configurational; it is attentive to differentiations among political formations. As the contributors to this book demonstrate, variations and differentiations among states are partially explained by the lingering impact on the modern world of empires thought long gone. Different areas and regions of the world are still deeply affected by these imperial formations. They are still with us, so to speak. This perspective lends support to the view that variable-oriented political science is predicated on a mythology of disjuncture and difference, propagated by those with a stake in promoting ideologies of the nation state and of nationalism. It underlines the extent to which what is characterized as the 'scientific' tradition or approach in Political Science is highly ideological.

A configurational approach suggests that nation states and empires are not opposing, mutually exclusive, forms of state: imperial structures continue to shape today's states and state system. From the imperial perspective, the distinction conventionally defined between 'nations' and empires appears to be neither empirically valid nor analytically productive. This binary opposition of old and modern leads to profoundly erroneous conclusions about the past and the present. The coexistence of empires and nation states in the past and present, and the interaction between persistent imperial structures and practices, on the one hand, and the state system, on the other, is a theme that runs through many of the chapters in this volume. What these chapters reveal is the existence of important continuities and overlaps between empires and modern national states, rather than the decisive break that Francis Fukuyama and countless others have defined.

Our conclusions, however, are not meant to deny or understate the novelty of the nation state, but to contextualize it. The 'imperial perspective' that emerges from this volume highlights the well-known observation that the nation state is the product of a broad-based social engineering project that crucially depends for its success on concerted and considerable denial and forgetting.[3] The nationalist trick is to assume the prior existence of just that national entity (the nation) whose creation the nationalist project is actively working to bring about. It assumes the existence of a 'people' sharing a common language and history and connected by a deep, spiritual unity, while at the same time, the state is working to create this 'people' through enforcing a national dialect, inventing a shared history and actively constructing the semblance of a 'national' economy. Ernest Gellner argued that it is the mobilization of large 'free' workforces for industrial production that, for the first time in history, makes it desirable to create a culturally homogeneous mass connected by culture to the elite. This 'nation-building' project costs enormous amounts of money and effort in story-telling and narrative construction, making nation states energy-hungry enterprises.

Empires are characterized by more varied political formats. They often have more limited logistical capabilities-limited, of necessity, by the technical and technological capabilities of their time. Some have occupied vast lands, but their mode of political control had to be more flexible, tolerant of diversity and more energy efficient. Others, as for instance, the Venetian Empire, some African Empires and the Japanese Empire, were no larger than some of today's nation states. But as Gellner and others have described in detail, they have tended to

---

[3]   As Benedict Anderson compelling by described a chapter on 'Memory and Forgetting' (Anderson 1991).

reinforce a sharp cultural divide rather than a cultural unity between elites and masses.

As many contributors to this volume have noted, empires were politically, logistically and ideationally flexible in their quest to shift resources from their peripheries to their centre, and from the majority, consisting typically of peasants, to a militarized aristocratic ruling minority – and they did this largely without finding it necessary or desirable to engineer a unity of identity and purpose between themselves and the mass of the populations over which they ruled. They relied on local emissaries, a class of administrative functionaries, chiefs and militarized nobilities to form a chain of control and command that ensured a regular shifting of resources from masses and peripheries to minorities and centres. These emissaries performed a well-defined role in a vast enterprise of material concentration and worked essentially on commission.

The shallow organization and minimal effort devoted to ideational story-telling that characterizes empires in relation to nation states, obscures the durability and continuing power of their legacies in the modern world. Because of their existence throughout so much of human history and throughout the world, their techniques of power and control are woven into the very fabric of the contemporary state, and their shadows are made material in the shaping of regional geographies and political boundaries. From the 'corrupt' political practices of the Mongol empires, to the service-led, financially oriented economy of the 'second' British Empire, to the continuing function of rather successful 'city-states' in a world in which they appeared anachronistic, empires have always – and continue to do so – shaped the political processes and institutional propensities both of contemporary states and of the state system.

Their strategic control of trade routes and 'foreign' bases is still with us; and the modern army, a sophisticated machine equipped with the latest technology of war, remains, at bottom, intrinsically connected to an imperial enterprise. The multiculturalism of the modern world emerged from patterns laid down in the old agrarian empires, reinforced by market dynamics that the more successful modern empires unleashed. Even that symbol of modernity, an innovative product of the modern nation state system, the United Nations, is shown to be, at its roots, an imperial organisation!

If so much remains of previous empires, then something will likely remain of the American Empire as well, and possibly for a very long time. Ronnie Lipschutz argues that the legacy of American empire will be an 'assemblage' of practices of 'imperium' that will sustain a condition of permanent and omnipresent warfare.

The concept of assemblage is critical here. Conventional Political Science and IR theory favour homogenising assumptions about the nature of the state, power and the international system. However, historical and institutional methodologies favour assumptions that lead to a view of the social field as profoundly heterogeneous. Appearances notwithstanding, a given institutional configuration consists of a patchwork of institutional logics and rationalities. In the words of Karen Orren and Stephen Skowronek, 'Institutions, both individually and collectively, juxtapose different logics of political order, each with their own temporal underpinnings.' Consequently, it is 'less meaningful', they argue, 'to talk about a political universe that is ordered than about the multiple orders that compose it and their relations with one another' (1994: 320).

The editors and contributors are keenly aware that the study of imperial legacies – based on the assumption that the existence for four millennia of the imperial political form has left its legacy on the modern world – is still in its infancy. So this volume is only a 'taster', a sample of what might be the sort of findings and implications of systematic investigation of a far larger terrain. There is clearly scope for empirical exploration of a far greater variety of imperial legacies and their impacts, which in turn will allow for much deeper reflection on the nature of the current order and enable scholars to produce a historically grounded consideration of future transitions.

We have used the word 'legacies' to suggest that past empires reach into present times. But this term is a somewhat ambiguous one: it doesn't convey anything about the mechanisms through which structures and processes are neither displaced nor destroyed, but transformed by and intertwined with (seemingly) new ones, and how, in this way, they have had an important impact in the construction and operation of the contemporary order. Are there any generalizable observations about the way imperial legacies intertwine with contemporary states? Is there a logic, a dynamic or rhythm that captures the reasons why and ways in which prior forms become elaborated and transformed by those which appear to replace them? Have we done nothing more, and mean nothing more by the term 'legacies of empires', than confirm that to empires are historical formations that are finished but remain somehow in bits and pieces? Discussion of these issues among the contributors to this volume was carried out over the course of two workshops, but we have left them unresolved. What we resolved to do was to offer a 'taster' that would generate interest and, by so doing, encourage research on empires and their legacies. It is only this that would make possible the broad comparative analyses from which generalizable patterns might emerge.

We are also aware that we use the term 'empire' somewhat ambiguously. What constitutes an empire? What are the essential features of imperialism? In what ways does imperialism differ from hegemony? The volume shows that systematic comparison of different settings may either (1) illustrate that there are common processes or structures at work, or (2) lead us to conclude that the legacies of empire are highly distinctive in different historical settings or across contemporaneous spatial domains.

These are questions that this volume does not answer. But we hope our work will encourage others to join our search for them.

References

Agevall, Ola (2005) 'Thinking about Configurations: Max Weber and Modern Social Science'. *Ethics & Politics*, 2, 1–20.

Anderson, Benedict (1991) *Imagined Communities: Reflections on the Origin and Spread of Nationalism*. London: Verso.

De Carvalho, Benjamin, Halvard Leira and John M. Hobson (2011) 'The Big Bangs of IR: The Myth that your Teachers Still Tell You About 1648 and 1919'. *Millennium: Journal of International Studies*, 39(3), 735–58.

Orren, K. and Skowronek, S. (1994) 'Beyond the Iconography of Order: Notes for a New Institutionalism'. In L. C. Dodd and C. C. Jilson (eds.) *The Dynamics of American Politics, Approaches and Interpretations*. Boulder: Westview Press, 311–30.

Osiander, Andreas (2001) 'International Relations and the Westphalian Myth'. *International Organization*, 55(2), 251–87.

Ragin, Charles (2000) *Fuzzy-Set Social Science*. Chicago: Chicago University Press.

Index